ALFRED PUBLISHING CO., INC., NEW YORK

PUBLIC POLICY

for the

Black

community

STRATEGIES & PERSPECTIVES

PUBLIC POLICY

for the

Black

community

STRATEGIES & PERSPECTIVES

Marguerite Ross Barnett
Howard University

and

James A. Hefner
Morehouse College

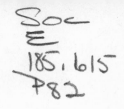
Published by Alfred Publishing Co., Inc.
75 Channel Drive, Port Washington, N.Y. 11050

Copyright © 1976 by Alfred Publishing Co., Inc.
All rights reserved.

Printed in the United States of America

Library of Congress Cataloging in Publication Data
Main entry under title:

Public policy for the Black community.

    1. Afro-Americans—Politics and suffrage—Addresses,
essays, lectures. 2. Afro-Americans—Economic condi-
tions—Addresses, essays, lectures. 3. Afro-Americans
—Legal status, laws, etc.—Addresses, essays, lectures.
I. Barnett, Marguerite Ross. II. Hefner, James.
E185.615.P82   301.45'19'6073   76-24466
ISBN 0-88284-039-8
ISBN 0-88284-038-X pbk.

In memory of Fred Eubanks

and

In appreciation of Edwina Hefner

CONTENTS

PREFACE:

THE CONTINUING DILEMMA

The bicentennial decade is a particularly appropriate time to reassess the position of Black Americans. In 1776 most American Blacks were the victims of an economic system of brutal servitude, legally excluded from even minimal participation in the political arena, and relegated to the very margins of a society that believed Africans savage, barbaric, and semi-human. One hundred years later, by 1876, slavery had been abolished and Blacks had gained constitutional recognition of their citizenship and definition of their political rights. However, it was not until the 1960s that the promises of the 1860s became reality when legal segregation was dismantled as a result of the civil rights movement—one of the greatest social movements in American history—judicial decisions and congressional action. It was the Voting Rights Act of 1965 that finally enabled large numbers of southern Blacks to register and vote.

If we view 1976 in comparison with 1776, the progress of Black Americans seems dramatic. Black elites can be found, albeit in small numbers, spread throughout American society; Black physicists, engineers, doctors, lawyers, judges, professors, mayors, businessmen, diplomats, and other professionals fill the ranks of the tiny, but growing, Black middle class. No longer "firsts," the presence of these Blacks has lulled many into complacency but the painful disjunction between upper-middle-class Black progress and continued lower-class Black impoverishment has led some thoughtful Black intellectuals to cynically characterize the progress since the 1950s as more chimerical than real. It is too easy to become trapped between those who effusively tout the progress of race relations in the last twenty years and those who challenge the very term *progress.*

The first step in evaluating where Blacks are now (and thus laying the groundwork for the development of strategies for the future) is to ask what constitutes progress for Blacks in the American racial context. In chapter 1, I develop a theoretical framework for analyzing the structural position of Blacks and for developing criteria for evaluating the effectiveness of racial public policy. Racial public policy strategies, to be effective, must attack structural constraints. I argue that "hierarchy" and "collectivism" constitute the unique factors that hamper Black movement into the American mainstream. The fundamental argument of chapter 1 is that the position of Blacks is qualitatively different from that of white ethnic groups and therefore public policies must reflect that difference. Starting with an awareness of the unique problems faced by Blacks, the authors of this volume assumed a two-fold task: analysis of the major problems Blacks will face in the next decade and development of viable strategies for achieving public policy solutions.

In chapters 2 and 3 respectively, economist James Hefner and political scientist Hanes Walton examine two geographical areas of particular Black concern, the urban ghetto and the South. Urban rebellions of the 1960s highlighted depressed ghetto conditions. Ghetto deterioration has been accelerated by the current recession/depression. As the soaring rates of Black unemployment and underemployment indicate, affirmative action programs and the romantic egalitarian rhetoric of the 1960s did little to move lower-class Blacks from the American economic underclass—the last hired and the first fired—an exploited, reserve labor supply. Hefner examines the current ghetto situation and concludes that massive, even revolutionary change is needed to halt the deteriorating urban Black condition.

Turning to the South, Hanes Walton critically reviews the two main political strategies utilized by southern Blacks and the counter strategies of white resistance. Finding both coalition and separatist strategies only partially adequate. Walton notes that the mere election of Blacks to political office should not be confused with Black power. He concludes by outlining methods for operationalizing Black power in the South.

Chapters 4 and 5 move from a locational context to focus on a problem area. Political scientist and legal authority Lois Moreland and legal scholar Henry Richardson III examine legal questions that will affect Blacks in the future. Building on "settled" legal doctrine, Lois Moreland develops a legal theory for the 1970s and 1980s that would challenge our most fundamental notions of what is public and what is private. While Moreland meticulously builds a specific theory, Richardson concerns himself with the impact of technological change on Blacks. In this post-Watergate era, his thoughts on political surveillance are singularly provoking. In broader terms he is concerned with the possibility of developing diverse legal strategies to insure Blacks "a piece of the pie" in the coming technological age of rapid change.

In chapters 6 and 7 we move from legal to economic issues. In chapter 6 Marcus Alexis reports on the dramatic differences in Black and white wealth accumulation and concludes that Blacks are far from achieving "anything approaching economic parity." Taking a broad overview, Thaddeus Spratlen in chapter 7 puts the problem of disparities in wealth accumulation in context in his survey of Blacks and the American economy. He points out areas of weakness and outlines broad strategies for positive change.

Chapter 8, authored by Charles V. Hamilton, examines the political impact of some of the federal "Great Society" programs undertaken during the 1960s. The authors in this volume advocate strategies grounded in an understanding of the structural barriers that thwart Black advancement. As ill-conceived as many of the Great Society programs were, they still deserve careful analysis because of the substantial political impact they had on Black communities. It is this political impact that concerns Professor Hamilton. Going beyond an analysis and critique of the Great Society programs, he argues for a Black political strategy based on a precise organizational orientation toward electoral politics.

The conclusion, by James Hefner, underscores a consistent [theme of all the authors by cautioning against confusion of symbolic and real power.] He sharply punctures the myth of Black inclusion in the mainstream of American life. Blacks, he argues, must confront the "illusion of inclusion."

As America turns inward during this bicentennial period to ponder the meaning and contemporary relevance of its past, it is crucial that the plight of Blacks be closely examined. As in the past, the Black struggle for justice will be the key to continued democratization of American society in the future. The Black "quiet crisis" of the 1970s results from fundamental problems, contradictions, and disjunctions in American life. In that sense the public policy strategies that are suggested for Blacks may also constitute the central strategies for American survival as well.

Marguerite Ross Barnett

PUBLIC POLICY
for the
Black
community
STRATEGIES & PERSPECTIVES

1

A THEORETICAL PERSPECTIVE ON AMERICAN RACIAL PUBLIC POLICY

Marguerite Ross Barnett

Marguerite Ross Barnett is Professor of Political Science at Howard University. She is the author of *The Politics of Cultural Nationalism in South India* and numerous articles on Indian and American politics. She is currently completing a study of the Congressional Black Caucus, begun while she was a guest scholar at the Brookings Institution. Professor Barnett has taught at the University of Chicago and Princeton University where she was James Madison Bicentennial Preceptor. She has served as a consultant for many national organizations concerned with urban problems and American racial public policy issues.

"The American Negro is a unique creation; he has no counterpart anywhere and no predecessors."

James Baldwin, *The Fire Next Time*

THE QUIET CRISIS IN PUBLIC POLICY

The problems of Black Americans have once again gone out of fashion. Public justification of "benign neglect" rests on two contradictory assumptions: (1) prior programs have been unsuccessful and therefore public attention and funds were "wasted," and (2) the problems of Blacks, both political and economic, have been alleviated. In its most hopeful form benign neglect expresses an assumption that left alone Blacks will progress as "other ethnic groups" have. An impression has already developed, at least among many nonacademics, that economic progress is being made, racism is on the wane, and Black power has become a reality. A common variation of this argument uses the 1970 U.S. census as a source of optimism. Daniel Moynihan, for example, states:

Simply put, during the 1960s young black husband-wife families (families with or without children in which both spouses are living together) began to

3

approach—and in a number of important categories to reach—income parity with whites. Everywhere these younger blacks are closing the gaps. This is the hardest to do in the South, where gaps were and are wider than elsewhere; but outside the South, it is practically a *fait accompli.* Thus in the noncommittal prose of the Bureau of the Census: "There was no apparent difference in 1970 between the incomes of white and Negro husband-wife families outside the South where the head was under 35 years old."[1]

Moynihan goes on to claim this as an event: "young couples from an oppressed minority starting their lives as full equals, in income terms at least, of their contemporaries in the 'majority group.' "[2]

However, a more comprehensive recent study conducted by the Black Economic Research Center presented a less rosy picture. Summarizing their findings for 1947 to 1971, David H. Swinton and Julian Ellison write:

There has been absolute real improvement in the income of non-whites.

On a national basis this income has grown faster than white income, and, thus, there has been modest relative improvement.

Much of the observed rise in relative income between 1960 and 1970 was due to cyclical factors.

The remaining improvement in the relative income of non-whites has been brought about by structural changes and internal migration of laborers.

Structural changes have had an unfavorable or limited impact on the relative income of black males in all regions and a favorable impact on the relative income of black females over the 20 years from 1950-1970.

Most of the non-cyclical improvement in the relative income of non-whites was due to inter-regional shifts of the non-white population.

> The relative income of the non-white population has deteriorated since 1953 in the North East and North Central regions, has deteriorated since 1960 in the West, and has improved since 1960 in the South.[3] (emphasis added)

Thus, according to this study the Black economic position has deteriorated in many crucial ways in recent years and is likely to deteriorate even more if the present course of benign neglect continues.

The common impression that Blacks are making great economic strides is matched by an impression of enormously enhanced political power; and in fact, migration of Blacks from the rural South to the urban South and to the urban North has produced dramatic Black mayoralty victories in Detroit, Cleveland, Los Angeles, Atlanta, Newark and Gary, Indiana. An upsurge in Black voting in the South has led to election of Black public officials in areas where Blacks had been disenfranchised since Reconstruction. Yet many Black politicians, activists, and scholars interested in Black politics express the view that these political "gains" are more chimerical than real—the trappings of power rather than "real" power.[4] Agreeing with that stance, Edward Greenberg concluded, "conventional forms of political participation, as commonly defined, have little potential payoff for Black people."[5]

As difficult as it is to extract progressive public policy payoffs for Black political participation, it is more difficult to force positive implementation of the favorable racial public policies that do exist. As recently as the 1960s a plethora of Great Society programs, long on promise and short on fulfillment, failed to produce qualitative change, thus leaving impoverished target groups with little other than truncated hopes.[6] Leaving the Great Society programs aside, we now have anti-discrimination policies in many areas including education, housing, and employment. Yet these are exactly the crucial areas where massive discrimination continues. A recent study found: Blacks would reach 1968 white levels in percent of men completing high school in 1973; percent completing 4 years of college in 1987; percent unemployed in 1982; percent teenagers

5

unemployed in 1989; percent persons below the poverty level in 1992; infant mortality in 1994; and life expectancy at 35 years in 2019.[7]

We must ask several crucial questions: why have recent progressive public policies failed to effect a perceived qualitative change in the lives of Black people, including the large Black lower class, and, more importantly, what constitutes qualitative change? What is "real" power? What criteria should be used to gauge public policy success or failure? The very nature of the questions suggests the necessity of a theoretical framework that would elucidate the dynamics of American racial public policy. At present no such comprehensive theory exists.[8]

There are two racial public policy models (institutional racism and the ethnic group analogy) that are often implicitly or explicitly used in much racial public policy analysis, but neither framework provides answers to the above questions. While the institutional racism framework captures the importance of the past in shaping the present, it fails to articulate, explain, and analyze the complex linkages between historical patterns of racism and discrimination and present public policies. In contrast, the ethnic group analogy (as applied to American Blacks) leads to superficial diachronic and synchronic analyses. Defining Blacks as "just another ethnic group" elides crucial distinctions, flattens our view of the past and the present, and obscures the social and political relations among white ethnic groups. Furthermore, most ethnic group models cannot explain the persistence of ethnicity nor can they account for the ethnic resurgence of the 1960s and 1970s.

What I shall suggest below is that the starting point for racial public policy analysis is delineation of the structural position of Blacks, definition of what would constitute structural transformation of that position, and description of the ideology that justifies (or obscures) that structural position. Discussion of the ideology of American racial policy will shed light on Black politics and the capacity of Blacks to transform the character of racial public policy. First, I shall examine the institutional racism and ethnic group models in greater detail and then proceed to build on these models to develop a framework for analyzing the structural position of Blacks.

CURRENT PERSPECTIVES ON
RACIAL PUBLIC POLICY

Institutional Racism Model

The theory of institutional racism presents the most popular analysis of racial public policy failure and the low political payoffs received by Blacks for political participation. Greenberg defines institutional racism as:

> ... those practices built into the ongoing process of institutions that, perhaps through no intent of the people involved, serve to exclude or to disadvantage members of minority racial or cultural groups.

He elaborates on the operation of institutional racism:

> Thus, members of building trade craft unions wishing to have sons and nephews follow in the family tradition design apprenticeship programs in such a way as to accomplish that goal. Yet by their very nature, such programs exclude Blacks. Universities, insisting on certain admission standards, bypass most Black students who have been burdened by inferior elementary-school and high-school educations. Ordinary citizens and homeowners, wishing to maintain the integrity of an ethnic neighborhood, reduce the supply of housing available to ghetto residents. The list of examples could easily be expanded because most elements of American society are institutionally racist. Racism is built into the very structure and process of most operating institutions. The political system, with its apparent inability to alter the fundamental relationship of Black and White, its contribution to the racial status quo, is institutionally racist.[9]

As used in the current literature, the theory of institutional racism contributes little, beyond description, to understanding racial public policy. Answers to a number of important questions are left ambiguous by those using an institutional racism framework: How does institutional racism operate in

7

different contexts? Are there important institutional differences (e.g., universities versus labor unions)? Has institutional racism varied over time? What causes either synchronic or diachronic variation? These rather obvious questions pose a problem for the institutional racism framework because they focus on the dynamics of social change, and institutional racism is fundamentally static and descriptive. What is missing from the theory of institutional racism is a theory of racism. Without a theory of racism, the notion of institutional racism tells us little about what variables induce or constrain change.

The idea of historical racist carryovers into the present is an important notion but to be useful it must illuminate the complex, diverse, multifaceted, and dynamically changing racial public policy process. Although the institutional racism framework may have the potential for accounting for the lack of qualitative change, it has often been used in theoretically effete, substantively bare, and overly simplistic terms. Even when the institutional racism framework has been used most effectively in the literature, it has not been useful in elucidating the questions with which we are herein concerned. Inherent in an elaborated theory of institutional racism—one capable of linking past patterns to the dynamics of differentiated contemporary change—would be an analysis of the structural position of Blacks. Thus in certain crucial ways a structural analysis of American racial public policy builds onto the notion of institutional racism.

The Ethnic Model

More common than the institutional racism framework is the application of an ethnic group model to Blacks. In its pristine and simplistic form the ethnic group model likens recent developments in Black history to the processes of ethnic group integration into the political system and socioeconomic assimilation into American life.[10] It is in this context that Blacks are compared to the progression of white ethnic groups that controlled major northeastern cities. One obvious problem with this analogy is that ethnic group political victories and economic assimilation often proceeded apace. The ethnically balanced ticket was not only a reflection of ethnic majorities in urban areas but it also reflected economic clout. The vast immigrant migrations occurred at a point in American history when the country was experiencing tremendous economic growth. The need for unskilled labor was great enough to absorb vast numbers of uneducated European peasants. White ethnic groups, therefore, were not seeking to use urban or national politics to improve their economic position. Rather, having achieved economic gains, they could enter the political system and accept its noninvolvement in the economic questions of the time.

Another important problem with the ethnic group analogy is that white ethnic groups took control of American cities at a time when the cities were still the major centers of commerce and industry. Most manufacturing jobs were concentrated in the cities by the mid eighteenth century; and by the early decades of the twentieth century, banking, real estate, and service functions became located in the central cities. Control of these economically important and viable cities (particularly in the era of the machine, when power was concentrated, and before civil service reforms were fully institutionalized) meant urban politicians had substantial power. But while these issues are important, there are other more serious theoretical problems with the model. Analyzing Blacks as an ethnic group ignores structural differences between Blacks and white ethnic groups.

There are two characteristics central to white ethnicity in the American context: (1) Ethnic *groups* are politically integrated in the American system. The relationship of the Irish, Italians, Armenians, etc., to the American political community is a settled issue. (2) Ethnic group political integration reflects the fact that individuals from these ethnic groups find a congruence (at the structural level) between American political ideology (the "American creed") and their day-to-day existence.[11] These two characteristics define the structural "internality" of white ethnicity, which will be explored in greater detail below.

Individualism, Egalitarianism, and Ethnicity

To argue that white ethnic groups are internal to the American ideological system implies a concept of what the core values of that system are. Although the nature of American ideology and political culture is complex, at the heart of the American political value system are the twin notions of individualism and egalitarianism. It is at once easy and difficult to point out that individualism and egalitarianism are central to American ideology—the American creed. The Declaration of Independence states the position with respect to equality: "We hold these truths to be self-evident, that all men are created equal, that they are endowed by their Creator with certain unalienable Rights, that among these are Life, Liberty and the pursuit of Happiness." Who shall pursue life, liberty and happiness? Individuals. It is individuals who theoretically enter into a social contract in western political theory. In fact, individualism is a core concept not only in the American creed but in western philosophy. To paraphrase Louis Dumont, in western society ultimate value is found in the concrete human indivisible element taken as an end in itself.[12]

Individualism and egalitarianism are themselves linked and are structurally opposed to hierarchical and collectivist ideological conceptions of society. Individualism is not "natural" or innate as we so often think; rather individualism developed with the growth of industrialization. As C. B. MacPherson states:

> Previously, people had been, and had thought of themselves as, not individuals but members of ranks or orders or communities. Their fairly fixed place in a customary society had given them some security but little freedom. Now, people began, with delight or with fear, to think of themselves as individuals free to choose.[13]

MacPherson makes clear what individuals could choose:

> Individuals were free to choose their religion, their pattern of life, their marriage partners, their occupations. They were free to make the best arrangements, the best bargain they could, in everything that affected their living.[14]

MacPherson also makes it clear that this choice was further rooted in the market economy.

> They [individuals] offered their services, their products, their savings, or their labor, on the market and got the market price, which was itself determined by all their independent decisions. With the income they got they made more choices—how much to spend, how much to save, what to spend on, and what to invest in. They made these decisions in the light of the going prices, and their decisions in turn made the prices, and so determined what could be produced, that is, determined how the whole energies and accumulated capital of the society would be allotted between different possible uses.[15]

Thus not only are individualism and egalitarianism interrelated but they are both linked, furthermore, to capitalist notions of freedom. Freedom, as MacPherson points out, came to be understood as the ability to choose in the context of a capitalist, market economy. When white ethnic groups were integrated into the developing American industrial society during the nineteenth century as wage laborers, it set the stage for their subsequent political integration and empowerment.

The nonranked (in contrast to hierarchical) differentiation among white ethnic groups creates at least proximate congruence between the individualism and egalitarianism of the American creed and the social realities of individual white ethnic experience. This nonranked differentiation stems from at least three factors: First is psychological empathy based on the acceptance of all white ethnic groups as composed of persons who are not qualitatively different in kind. Although intolerance and discrimination marred the first encounter of many different ethnic groups with American society, that intolerance never included questioning the fundamental humanness (for a prolonged time period) of any white ethnic group. Symbolically, the psychological empathy of all white ethnic groups is expressed in kinship perceptions. For example, offspring of ethnic group unions are defined by a hyphenated linkage between the two ethnic identities. For example,

French-Italian, Polish-Irish, German-Armenian are all possible ways of describing the offspring of unions between these *equal* ethnic groups.

Second, the kinship example highlights the fact that capacity for white ethnic individualism is rooted in ideological equality among white ethnic groups. Although white ethnic groups differ in economic resources, education, political power, etc., *there is no nationwide ideology or principle that consistently ranks any white ethnic group above the others.* In one city French, Irish, Italian, Polish, or WASP groups may be at the top of the ethnic hierarchy but in another city the ranking may be quite different.[16] One region of the country may be consistently more congenial to one ethnic group but in another region that same group might have low status. One group may claim superiority but that claim might have little support among competing groups. In short, the "pecking order" among white groups is unclear. Since there is no built-in hierarchy in white ethnicity, individual interaction among representatives of various white ethnic groups can occur, in at least some contexts, on a basis of equality.

Finally, ethnic individualism stems from the existence of large secular, "ethnicity-free" arenas in American life. These are arenas in which white ethnicity is irrelevant because treatment is according to achieved, not ascribed, criteria.

Thus, even a brief discussion of white ethnicity in the American context shows that the existence of named groups has only limited behavioral implications for individual whites.

Ethnic Politics

Having stated that white ethnic groups are internal to American political ideology, integrated in the political system, and assimilated into the economic system, what are the resulting political and public policy implications? Since white ethnicity does not imply a direct confrontation with core American political-cultural values, ethnic group politics typically have not revolved around systemic issues (e.g., who is part of the political community, what shall be the nature of the regime, should capitalism be destroyed, etc.) but around the distribution or redistribution of goods, services, and values in an agreed-upon system according to agreed-upon processes.

Ethnic group political behavior is heavily oriented toward participation in political parties, voting, involvement in interest groups, petitioning governmental bureaucracies, etc. In short, white ethnic groups have used traditional political methods with perceived success. In the absence of a national ranking of white ethnic groups and therefore creation of nationwide ethnic problems, ethnic group political organization is largely local or, at best, regional in character. White ethnic political participation on overtly ethnic grounds finds its most pronounced expression in urban politics as the ethnically balanced ticket.

Power, in white ethnic group political culture (as in American political culture generally) is understood to be specific, divisible, and best exercised through electoral politics for limited ends. Incremental change, issue-oriented politics, and the give-and-take of political bargaining among competing interests is, as mentioned previously, the accepted mode of political participation.

Blacks: An Ethnic Group?

In comparing Blacks to white ethnic groups, we must decide in what ways these groups are similar and in what ways they are dissimilar, and the political significance of these similarities and differences. I shall argue that in contrast to white ethnic groups, Blacks are external to the American ideological system and not effectively integrated into the political system. In structural terms, Blacks are qualitatively different from white ethnic groups. For white ethnic groups there is no nationwide ideology that ranks specific groups. In contrast, racism is a pervasive ideology that ranks Blacks as a group below all others because it assumes the inherent genetic inferiority of Blacks. The stress on phenotypic differences (in this case skin color) and its expression in racist ideology determines the character of white-Black interaction in every part of the country. From the earliest days, definitions of humanness were crucial to decisions about the composition of the political community. Racism, therefore, is a fundamental factor that makes the Black situation distinctly different from that of all white ethnic groups. That raises the key theoretical issue: What are the structural implications of racism? We now turn to that issue.

Racism as a Structural Phenomenon

The emergence of racism is a long, complex process and one that I cannot begin to adequately discuss here except to point out the etiological link to slavery. Put bluntly, racism emerged as a rationalization for African slavery.[17] For our purpose, however, the intriguing issue is why there was a need for a rationalization. Louis Dumont and others have suggested that the need grew out of western philosophy's emphasis on human rights, human equality, and human freedom as natural rights.[18] African slavery, therefore, either had to be rationalized and the natural rights of Africans modified, or it had to be abolished as a contradiction of nature and nature's law. After the Revolutionary War, this became an acute dilemma when more of the masses became politicized by the egalitarian war ideology.

Thomas Jefferson typifies the intellectual confusion engendered by the confrontation of the lofty egalitarian ideology with sordid, oppressive slave reality. As the major drafter of the Declaration of Independence, Jefferson declared all men to be created equal. Yet Jefferson, in fact, was firmly convinced that Blacks would never be incorporated into white society on equal terms.

> Deep rooted prejudice entertained by the whites; ten thousand recollections, by the Blacks, of the injuries they have sustained; new provocations; *the real distinction which nature has made* [emphasis added]; and many more circumstances, will divide us into parties, and produce convulsions which will probably never end but in the extermination of the one or the other race.—To these objections, which are political, may be added others, which are physical and moral.[19]

14

Elsewhere Jefferson was even more explicit about the innate differences between whites and Blacks:

> Comparing them by their faculties of memory, reason, and imagination, it appears to me, that in memory they are equal to the whites; in reason much inferior, as I think one could scarcely be found capable of tracing and comprehending the investigations of Euclid; and that in imagination they are dull, tasteless, and anomalous.[20]

Thomas Jefferson, a slaveholder, was a verbal opponent of slavery[21] and did not argue that the intellectual inferiority he attributed to Africans was a justification of their slavery. However, Jefferson was unconcerned about the sufferings of Blacks under slavery, reserving his sympathy for the master who, Jefferson felt, suffered deleterious moral effects from having to administer the slave system.[22] Jefferson established the idea that there are two types of men—full men with developed intellectual powers and Blacks, whom he believed lacked the capacity for creative, imaginative, and abstract reasoning.[23]

In his passage specifying the constraints on Black participation in American society on equal terms, Jefferson makes it clear that this dichotomy, this Black-white hierarchy, has political consequences. As early as Jefferson's day, America had become a self-declared white man's country. Racism was a political statement about the place of Blacks in white America. Arbitrary political inequality would have contradicted the fundamental creed that established white rights, hence the political statement of Black inequality is couched in a "scientific" justification of Black political inequality based on their "natural" inferiority. Racist ideology asserts that whites have not debased Blacks, Blacks have been debased by nature. Blacks emerged as mediators between nature and culture as manifested by the conceptualization of Africans as the "missing link" between apes and man in the hypothetical chain of being.[24] Being debased by nature, then, Blacks are less human and do not possess inalienable political rights. They are not and cannot become full members of the political community.

15

After emancipation settled the issue of Blacks as property, racism continued to flourish and the white-Black hierarchy became a deep-rooted feature of American culture. A virulent and militant racist ideology continued after emancipation. Blacks were widely depicted as animal-like, potentially violent, and lustful. Scientific racism was used to argue the inferiority of Blacks and to "substantiate" the perceived vast gap between "civilized" whites and "savage" Blacks. Arguments in the tract "The Negro a Beast," (1900) are typical of this literature:

> All scientific investigation . . . proves the Negro to be an ape, . . . stand[ing] at the head of the ape family, as the lion stands at the head of the cat family. When God's plan of creation [is] properly understood, it will be found that the teachings of scripture upon this, as upon every other subject, harmonize with those of science. . . . [I]t follows that the Negro is the only anthropoid, or man-like ape; and that the gibbon, orangutan, chimpanzee and gorilla are merely negro-like apes. Hence, to recognize the Negro as a "man and a brother," they were compelled to declare man an ape. Thus, the modern Christian, like the atheist, takes man, whom God created "in his own image," and takes the Negro, whom God made "after his kind"—the ape kind—and places them in the same family, as different "races" of one "species" of animal. . . .
>
> The Bible plainly teaches that man was created a single pair, "in the image of God." And we feel assured that a careful consideration of this subject must lead any rational mind to decide that the white, with his exalted physical and mental characters, and the Negro with his ape-like physical and mental characters, are not the progeny of one primitive pair. . . . [I]f the white was created "in the image of God," then the Negro was made after some other model. And a glance at the Negro indicates the model; his very appearance suggests the ape.[25]

Here Blacks are no longer perceived as mediators between nature and culture but are considered savage products of

16

nature. In contrast, whites were perceived as civilized. This civilization meant that culture controls nature—a capacity to control violent "natural" urges. Since these postslavery perceptions of Blacks dramatically polarized nature and culture and emphasized the animal character of Blacks, the argument that Blacks had uncontrollable lusts and savage urges became plausible. Violence against Blacks was justified as a method of controlling Black bestiality. The Ku Klux Klan, American Gentile Army, United Sons of Dixie, and White Citizens Council were a few of the white "protective" associations that emerged. Justifications of violence against Blacks flowed easily from the tongues of flowery southern orators. For example, the Reverend Harrison said at a Klan meeting in Atlanta, Georgia, on November 1, 1948: "In God's sight it is no sin to kill a n—r, for a n—r is no more than a dog."[26] At the same meeting, "Itchy Trigger-Finger Nash," an Atlanta policeman who was given a Klan citation for having killed so many Blacks, expressed the hope that he would "not have to kill all the n——s in the South, but would get some help from his brother Klansmen."[27]

More "moderate" voices advocated stringent social control, reinforced by moderate use of violence. For example, William Gregg Blanchard, leader of the White Front Organization in Miami, Florida, wrote in the official organization organ, *Nation and Race:*

> When the Federal Government recognizes biological values and proceeds systematically to solve the South's problem by expatriation, birth control, and rigid segregation, the long race vigil will be over. . . . That dusky race which enslaved was happy and lovable must today be recognized for the sullen revolutionary mass it is and be disciplined accordingly. . . . Racial nationalism demands that the Negro be made a ward of the nation and governed by special codes befitting the dignity of a white state.[28]

As in the pre-Civil War South, the perception of Blacks and the character of racism had political implications. Among others, Hiram W. Evans, Imperial Wizard of the Ku Klux Klan,

17

made these implications clear in his tract, *Negro Suffrage—Its False Theory*:

> The first essential to the success of any nation, and particularly of any democracy, is a national unity of mind. Its citizens must be One People. They must have common instincts and racial and national purpose. . . . It follows that any class, race or group of people which is permanently unassimilable to the spirit and purpose of the nation has no place in a democracy. The negro race is certainly unassimilable; no one can claim that more than a few blacks are fit. We should see in the negro a race even more diverse from ourselves than are the Chinese, with inferior honesty, and greatly inferior industry.[29]

While we might be tempted to characterize the connection made by Evans between race and American nationality as simply the ramblings of an extremist, the U.S. Supreme Court decision in *Hirabayashi* v. *United States,* 320 U.S. 81 (1943) is more difficult to dismiss so lightly. The case involved the program undertaken by the U.S. government during World War II to exclude Japanese-Americans from the West Coast in spite of their American citizenship. There were many aspects of the program, ranging from curfew regulations to prison camp detention. *Hirabayashi* v. *United States* upheld the curfew features of the program. In upholding a curfew for West Coast Japanese Americans, the Court stated:

> There is support for the view that social, economic and political conditions which have prevailed since the close of the last century, when the Japanese began to come to this country in substantial numbers, have intensified the solidarity and *have in large measure prevented their assimilation as an integral part of the white population.* (emphasis added)

> Whatever views we may entertain regarding the loyalty to this country of the citizens of Japanese ancestry, we cannot reject as unfounded the judgment of the military authorities and of Congress

that there were disloyal members of that population, whose number and strength could not be precisely and quickly ascertained.[30]

Notions of individual, personal guilt before the law and civil citizenship ties rather than blood ties as the basis of national unity are directly challenged by the Japanese-exclusion cases. Although these cases do not represent the Court's final or only view on these matters, the easy identification of the American nation with the white population and the blithe equation of loyalty with white blood cannot be overlooked. Related to the tension between the ideal of individualism and egalitarianism and the reality of racial hierarchy and collectivism is the unresolved conundrum of American national identity. While the ideal is equal citizens born or naturalized into one ethnically and racially heterogeneous political community, the equation of the nation with the white population has persisted since the eighteenth-century declaration of America as a white man's country.

Even with the abolition of Jim Crow laws as a result of the civil rights movement, racism has not abated as the underpinning of white-Black hierarchy. Joel Kovel has argued that racism is deeply imbedded in the white psyche and is part and parcel of white American culture. In an analysis of contemporary racism Kovel observes: "Racism is ultimately indivisible from the rest of American life, a fact few of us wish to face."[31] He also stated:

> A really deep survey of white Americans would doubtlessly reveal a great mixture of racial patterns in everyone, but it might be predicted that the substantial majority continue to reserve their most intense feelings for the hallowed racial patterns of yore; that is, they hold to a mixture of dominative and aversive racist beliefs, according, one would expect, to their authoritarianism and the degree to which their superego has internalized aggression. Certain other Americans—a minority, perhaps—would be revealed as free from racist tinge; not entirely, *for no one can escape his culture to that extent.* (emphasis added)[32]

19

Kovel argues there has been a transformation in expression of racism from the dominative variety typified by Hiram Evans to the aversive type. The aversive racist still believes in white racial superiority. However, in the aversive racist "an intra-psychic battle goes on between these sentiments and a conscience which seeks to repudiate them."[33] Both dominative and aversive racists share the same racial fantasies according to Kovel. In spite of this slow transformation from dominative to aversive racism and the appearance of a very small nonracist minority, the main strands of racism against Blacks have not changed essentially over the generations;[34] and racism, whether dominative or aversive, remains at the root of American hierarchy, collectivism, and Black structural externality.

To recapitulate, hierarchy specifically means the existence of a principle (racism) that ranks groups consistently and pervasively, *and is enforceable through social control.* Collectivism means that each individual member of a group is treated according to some principle that defines the whole. Ultimate meaning resides in the definition of the whole—the characteristics ascribed to the group as a whole.[35] Hierarchy and collectivism define the Black structural position in the United States.

Quite obviously, the above characterization of Black American existence as hierarchical and collectivist is meant to be ideal-typical. These features define the structure of the overall system and provide the encompassing model for inter-group social behavior. The point is not that there are no exceptions. Rather, exceptions underscore the structure from which they diverge. For Blacks there are no large, secular arenas in which race is irrelevant—although it may be more or less salient. Income, geographical mobility, and lifestyle can exacerbate or mitigate but not fundamentally change the encompassing relevance of hierarchy and collectivism for Blacks. Blacks are not seen as persons in an egalitarian system but are individually subject to "rules" of interaction consistent with collectivist stereotypes.

While egalitarianism is an obvious distortion of the reality of Black existence in the United States, individualism is a more subtle illusion. Blacks are socialized, to some extent, by an

American culture rooted in the white experience. To the extent that general cultural models are internalized, a tension is created between the ideal of America as a social arena characterized by free, individual choice, on the one hand, and the realities of Black existence, on the other. This tension is crucial because it helps situate the Black middle class.[36]

It is among members of the Black middle class that the tension between individualism and collectivism is most keenly felt. In a structurally hierarchical system, middle-class Blacks often have to confront the meaning of individual Black achievement. Often stunned and alarmed by strident lower-class Black assertiveness, many middle-class Blacks seek a retreat into individualism.

However, given the structural context, individualism becomes a form of cooptation (as symbolized by the pejorative term "tokenism") when conclusions about group social and political status are drawn from equations of individual Black achievement with individual white achievement.[37] The equation of Blacks to white ethnic groups masks the primacy of racism and the constraints imposed on Blacks by racial hierarchy and collectivism. Individualism, therefore, is a form of cooptation when the structural barriers faced by Blacks are obscured by it. However, despite the tensions within the structural position outlined above, in general the pervasiveness of hierarchy and collectivism places the Black experience in direct confrontation with, makes it a challenge to, and exposes the contradictions in the American creed.

BLACK POLITICS AND RACIAL PUBLIC POLICY

I have argued that institutional racism is too narrow and static to serve as a framework for elucidating the racial public policy process. As we have seen, the ethnic model has logical difficulties as applied to Blacks because it assumes structural similarities where in fact there are structural differences. In the broadest terms, the ethnic group model is a surrogate for other frameworks[38] that fail to capture the structural separation of Blacks; the contradictions between creed and reality as a crucial

21

contextual factor; and the tension between an individualistic structure that leads to an ethnic group-like approach to politics and a collectivist structure which generates different forms of political expression. Since the Black structural position raises questions of American political identity and political integration, analysis of Black politics is central to elucidation of the racial public policy process.

Black politics and the racial policy-making process reflect the fundamental externality of Blacks in the United States. It is not only externality but also the hierarchical and collectivist underpinnings of that externality that have shaped the dynamics of Black politics. In illustration four distinctive characteristics of Black politics will be discussed: the perception of power; definition of issues and public policy priorities; orientation toward processes of social change; and the articulation of ideology.

Four Central Characteristics of Black Politics

Power

Although many Blacks view power as divisible, specific, and best exercised through electoral processes for limited ends, this is by no means the only or the dominant meaning of power in Black political culture. The exercise of power is also seen by many Blacks as a zero-sum game in which power is an indivisible quantity. In this conception of power, one either wins or one loses; one either has power or one is powerless. Since it is clear that Blacks do not have absolute control, this view manifests itself in perceived Black powerlessness. While there is no view that all whites are powerful, there is a perception of all Blacks as powerless. Two consequences of this view of power are crucial. One is the creation of a political climate of Black dependency, which is congruent with the climate of economic dependency present in many Black urban areas with substantial welfare populations.

Another consequence is a deep and serious concern with

22

fundamental social change. It is not that a majority of Blacks evince this concern, but in comparison with other groups in American society, Black communities produce an inordinately large number of talented individuals and organized groups concerned with fundamental systemic change. Because of competing notions of power in the Black community (i.e., power as indivisible and absolute versus power as divisible and limited), political dialogue in the Black community has a sharper tone, more militant posture, greater intensity, and a much broader spectrum of legitimate opinions and opinion makers than elsewhere. Perceptions of power, how it is organized, exercised, and what you have to do to get it and use it effectively go right to the heart of politics and therefore influence issues, ideology and process. The competing models of power, in turn, reflect the individualist-collectivist tension explored above. The zero-sum game view of power is directly rooted in the collectivist character of Black-white relations. Power is seen as group power and possibilities for maximizing individual Black choice are linked to the capacity for the group to restructure Black-white relations.

Issues

One manifestation of the view of the political process as a zero-sum game and power as having an absolute, all-or-nothing quality, is a stress on systemic issues.[39] Given that Blacks are external to the American creed, much of Black politics has involved challenging constitutional issues in an effort to bridge the gap between the Black experience and the American creed. Black concern with structural change has led to the development of a considerable body of intellectual opinion that criticizes such fundamental aspects of the American system as capitalism, federalism, and states' rights. Frequent Black articulation of powerlessness in the context of movements for social change has constituted a challenge to the legitimacy of the political system. (Although forms of Black protest have been imitated by white radical groups, what these radical groups do not realize is that given the Black structural position—that is,

23

given the peculiarities of racial hierarchy and collectivism as applied to Blacks—the Black model is not appropriable by other groups.) The central question that has concerned numerous Black politicians, intellectuals, and activists has been the relationship of Blacks to American society, or, what shall be the political community.

Whereas the spectrum of American politics in general and white ethnic politics in particular is limited to use of pluralistic modes of political participation for specific, issue-oriented ends, the spectrum of Black politics is heavily weighted toward attempts to change the fundamental character of the political system. Changing political authorities would do little to assuage the basic concerns of Blacks about the nature of the economic system and its ability to "work" for Blacks, the legitimacy of the political system, and the nature of the political community. Hence, because of this broader and more penetrating concern with systemic issues, electoral politics is viewed ambivalently in Black political culture.

Process

Such methods of influencing public policy as formation of movements, violence, reliance on a single charismatic leader, and articulation of political utopias, which are characteristic only of extraordinary circumstances for non-Blacks, are used more routinely in Black political life. Political processes that work routinely for whites fail Blacks and necessitate the search for other, more effective methods. Furthermore, Black political organizations have not been oriented toward any one set of goals such as monitoring, implementing or even blocking racial public policies but instead are involved in a variety of issues, utilizing a rich array of techniques to influence the political process.

Ideology

Finally, in contrast to any ethnic group in the American context, there is a strong expression of nationalist thinking in

Black political culture. In recent years there has been white ethnic imitation of Black nationalism. For ethnics it has been a way to create group concern; for Blacks, nationalism grows out of the exigencies of everyday life, and thus has a long history reaching back into the slavery period [Since Blacks have been excluded from becoming internal to the American system, their ideological options are fundamentally different from those of whites.]In this context, a combination of imposed collectivism, qualitative separation of Blacks from all others, and the desire on the part of Black politicians to destroy the hierarchy between whites and Blacks has led to the articulartion of Black nationalism. Black nationalism retains a form of Black collectivism by differentiating between internally generated, culturally rooted (positive) collectivism and externally generated stereotypically based (negative) collectivism. It defines the United States as consisting of two nations, both equal, one white, one Black. Self-determination (the recognition of nationalism) would also be a way of redressing Black powerlessness in that it would create a new legitimate arena of power that would exist by virtue of Black nationhood.

Toward New Perspectives on Racial Public Policy

[Power, issue priorities, process and ideology are often perceived differently by Blacks, and this divergence along racial lines reflects the unique structural position of Blacks in American society.]Specifically, the unique dynamics of Black politics often revolve around structurally created problems. For example: (1) the tension among Blacks between participation in politics *as if* Blacks were an ethnic group (i.e., as if the structural contradictions were mediated) and rejection of traditional forms of political participation as irrelevant, and (2) attempts to remove hierarchy from white-Black relations but retain positive collectivism (nationalism) versus attempts to remove both collectivism and hierarchy from white-Black relations (integrationism). Both of these problems reflect the more fundamental tensions and contradictions between the

25

individualistic, egalitarian American ideological model and the collectivist, hierarchical Black reality as they come into conflict in different guises.

⌊Public policy problems, perceptions, and experiences are similarly different for Blacks, and the difference reflects the dynamics of Black politics and the structural position of Blacks in the United States.⌉Hence, not only do Black public policy concerns, as a matter of course, involve broader questions of systemic change and structural transformation but the very question of public policy raises historical, built-in dilemmas. Two public policy dilemmas are of particular significance: recurrent, but unresolved, issues; and persistent public policy failure.

In a New York speech, Julian Bond recently stated:

> The central debate in the American Black community in the 70s as it was in the 1960s and as it was in the 1860s—is what form, and under what terms our relationship with majority America will be defined.... You know that America's white problem continues despite the New Deal, the New Frontier, the Great Society and the New Federalism. ... In an earlier period of American History, Black Americans had their political rights guaranteed by the federal government at gunpoint. That period—Reconstruction, the only 10 years in our history in which democracy for Blacks in Mississippi began to mean what it has always meant for whites in Maine—ended with a deal ... [which] consigned the destiny of Black Americans to a century of political and economic limbo.[40]

At the heart of this political and economic "limbo" is the unresolved question of Black identity—are blacks an ethnic group, "minority" group, race, or nation? These identity issues cannot be solely resolved within the Black community because some options (for example, the ethnic group option) require a level of integration and assimilation into American society that Blacks cannot control. The identity problem, however, is fundamental and intimately related to questions of strategy and issue priorities.

26

Another crucial unresolved issue concerns the best way to strengthen the Black economic position. This issue has also taken a separationist versus integrationist form.[41] Again and again the question has been posed: Should Blacks build their own economic institutions or try to democratize and gain economic power through white institutions? This issue is linked to the conflict made popular by the famous Booker T. Washington-W. E. B. Du Bois debates: Should Blacks focus on internal community economic development as a route to power or on acquisition of political power through protest politics? Related questions include: Can economic development occur without protective political power and/or can political power exist without economic underpinnings? This recurring debate has been the source of periodic emotional and vitriolic intellectual conflict throughout Black political history. Because of the scarcity of resources in the Black community, it has never been possible for Blacks to bridge these dichotomies and pursue diverse strategies simultaneously and effectively.

Other specific issues have been recurrent. To mention the issue of school integration is to cite an issue going back to the Reconstruction period. Payment of reparations, an item on the platform of the 1972 Black political convention,[42] is a modern restatement of the Reconstruction Black slogan of "40 acres and a mule."

The list of recurring issues is too long to cite completely. We must ask what the consequences are of recurring issues, and why they do recur and are not resolved. Two obvious reasons are the lack of sufficient autonomy and resources within the Black community to force a resolution of these issues for itself and on the entire society. Lack of autonomy has led to an oscillation between two models: an ethnic model which achieves a certain legitimacy through the illusion of individual achievement, and a nationalism model which conforms to structural imperatives but runs counter to (and in fact challenges) important aspects of the encompassing American ideology. All these recurring issues are themselves vital or linked to crucial principles held by society at large; therefore, society-wide social control mechanisms play an important role in determining the way issues are posed, the legitimacy and credence given to various policy proposals, and the weight of countervailing economic and political forces in the policy process.

In a context in which fundamental issues are left unresolved, it is not surprising that specific racial public policies are often disjointed, naive, misconveived, irrelevant and/or dated, and exploitative rather than regenerative. Added to the dilemma of recurrent issues, therefore, has been the problem of persistent public policy failure.

Types of Racial Public Policy

In looking at public policy failure it is necessary to define what the different kinds of racial public policy are and to specify what is meant by "failure." Richard Burkey has defined four types of racial public policy:

> The first type is concerned with guaranteeing the civil rights of minority groups by eliminating the restrictions that have historically been placed as barriers to the freedom of action of these groups. What is generally assumed in this traditional civil rights policy is that elimination of illegitimate discrimination will have an effect upon the inequality of the subordinate racial group.

> The second type of policy may be termed "affirmative action" or "preferential treatment." This type of policy goes further than the first in that pressure is put upon the targets of the policy to take some form of positive action other than just eliminating the barriers to hire minorities, to integrate schools or neighborhoods, to promote minority business, to increase the level of education of minority races, etc.

> The third type of policy, not yet (if ever) an aspect of American governmental action, may be called "discrimination-in-reverse." Discrimination in reverse is a policy whereby the allocation of resources, services, and opportunities is primarily based on

28

group affiliation to the exclusion of or subordination of technically relevant criteria for determining such allocations.

The last type of policy does not *directly* focus on racial issues or racial discrimination. This type is concerned with programs designed to reduce inequality generally, primarily focusing on the lowest socio-economic strata.[43]

A fifth type of public policy would redefine and restructure fundamental constitutional relationships between racial groups. This type of policy differs from Burkey's type 1 in that type 1 merely extends existing rights of the majority community to minorities. Type 5 public policy would restructure the political system and create new rights for both racial groups.

A sixth type of public policy, revolutionary public policy, would involve the restructuring of the entire society, including the political, economic, and social systems, in ways that would improve the quality of life of the lowest socioeconomic strata. Although we have not seen a type 5 policy since abolition of slavery and passage of the thirteenth, fourteenth and fifteenth Amendments,[44] and we have not seen the sixth type of public policy at all, it is necessary to add them because, as is emphasized below, they are included in the spectrum of public policy debate in the Black community, and therefore they compete with other incremental public policies for attention and Black political action.

Public policy types 5 and 6 reflect the necessity for Blacks to eventually confront and define their unique position in American society. If, at some future time, Blacks decide collectivism is by itself not harmful but in fact desirable as long as it does not carry hierarchical implications, one demand might be for constitutional recognition of the unique Black position in American society. In that case we might see the development of Black collectivity rights that would be constitutionally defined and protected. This is one example of a type 5 policy.

Type 6 public policy raises special questions. If Blacks define their ultimate goal as transformation to ethnic group status with maximized individual free choice, it may be that that goal is not possible without a total restructuring of society. For example, one might ask whether Blacks, whose labor has been traditionally exploited and who are still disproportionately concentrated on the exploited end of the economic scale, can attain the economic ascendancy that buttresses western notions of freedom.[45]

Burkey's typology provides one way of categorizing racial public policies, but it provides only limited insight into criteria for judging the success or failure of these policies. Given the structural analysis developed above, racial policies might be further divided into ethnic policies, collective policies, and structural policies. Central to this categorization are the concepts of divisible and indivisible benefits developed by Robert Dahl:

> Certain benefits are divisible in such a way that they can be allocated to specific individuals; jobs, contracts, and welfare payments are examples of divisible benefits. Other benefits are more nearly *indivisible;* parks, playgrounds, schools, national defense and foreign policies, for example, either cannot be or ordinarily are not allocated by dividing the benefits piecemeal and allocating various pieces to specific individuals.[46]

Ethnic policies would be those which provide divisible benefits; collective policies those which provide indivisible benefits (i.e., benefits which accrue to the entire racial group *qua* group); and structural policies those which would attack the structural basis of racial inequality. Specifically, structural policies would attack hierarchy and the (negative) stereotypical aspects of collectivism. As previously noted, Black collectivism may be both internally and externally generated. Internally, it may be rooted in the existence of a uniquely Black symbol system; that is, in a Black culture that creates particular commonality among Blacks and that provides Blacks with a shared sense of intense affinity. This internal collectivism might persist—and could provide the basis for a positive Black nationalism—even if the external racist roots of collectivism were destroyed.) Since racism undergirds hierarchy and (externally generated) collectivism and since (as the institutional racism theory rightly suggests) racism has become an intrinsic part of seemingly non-racist practices, structural policies would require far-reaching societal changes.

It is unlikely that ethnic style politics would produce either collective or structural racial policies. As Charles V. Hamilton has observed, ethnic politics have traditionally produced divisible benefits:

> The traditional rewards of ethnic politics have been divisible benefits. It has been enough to distribute goods and services to deserving individuals of a particular group, and in the process, this has enabled party leaders to approach the group on terms of ethnic identification, avoiding the issue of making more substantive changes in both the political *process* and the political *product*.
>
> This kind of traditional ethnic group approach has enabled the political system to focus only on an equitable distribution of goods and services and not on the fundamental question of a redistribution of decision-making power.[47]

[The Great Society programs of the 1960s were mainly ethnic policies. They were incremental, nonsystem-challenging attempts to make minor alterations in what was assumed to be a basically egalitarian society. To the extent these policies succeeded, they helped individuals who, often because of serendipitous circumstances, were in the right place at the right time. They did not alter the life chances of Blacks as a collectivity.] They were distributive policies involving resource allocation to individuals and nonascriptive groups. Thus, whites and non-Black minorities also benefited substantially from Great Society programs. In contrast, the court cases and congressional legislation which led to the dismantling of legal segregation were collective policies with indivisible benefits; but all of those benefits have not been forthcoming. Indeed white opposition to collective racial policies for Blacks has increased. Collective

31

policies have redistributive potential. Fears that redistribution of resources, political access, benefits and political legitimacy could lead to Black group equivalence (i.e., Black ethnic group status) with whites stimulated the vehement, and sometimes violent, white reactions which shaped the politics of the late 1960s and early 1970s.[48]

Black perceptions of public policy failure reflect expectations of structural change. Bitter condemnations of ethnic policies and the racial public policy process arise because Black demands for structural change cannot be assuaged by the trappings of equality for a limited number of Black individuals.

Racial public policy failure, therefore, is a complex phenomenon. Structural barriers must be removed before there is an institutionalized potential for generalized replication of individual success. Until that time ethnic policies may succeed as particular programs but fail according to collective or structural criteria; and collective policies may exist but fail to realize their full potential unless reinforced by structural policies which change the "rules of the games" and institutionalize new racially equivalent and racially just redistributive processes. This is not to argue that ethnic or collective policies are totally worthless without structural change. Rather, it is to underscore the structural limitations of these types of racial policies. And indeed, misperceptions of structural barriers can lead to dangerous consequences.

The Dangers of Misperception

Perspectives on racial public policy differ. Certainly many analysts would argue racial discrimination is no longer the main deterrent to Black advancement. Prominent urbanologist Edward Banfield states:

> Discrimination was not the *main* obstacle in the way of the Irish, the Italians, the Jews, and other minorities that have "made it" [notice the use of the ethnic group model]. Nor is it the *main* one of the Negro— not to mention the Puerto Rican and the Mexican— today.[49]

32

Banfield believes that what appears to be racial prejudice is actually class prejudice. Banfield has equated the elimination of legally sanctioned segregation with the elimination of racial discrimination. Thus he totally ignores or rejects the ideas of covert racism and institutional racism. But he goes further. Banfield believes that even if there were racism against Blacks it should *not* be emphasized as a factor inhibiting Black upward mobility.

> Even if nonracial factors had not in recent years superseded the racial ones as the Negro's main handicap, it would be well to pretend that they had, for a self-fulfilling prophecy of the unimportance of racial factors would be as great a blessing as its opposite would be a curse.[50]

Unfortunately, cold hard facts cannot be so easily obscured through benevolent pretense. As the Urban Insitute study cited above indicates, it will take years before Blacks reach white 1968 levels in housing, health care, employment, etc. For Banfield the crucial governmental action in racial public policy has been taken. Yet he does not ignore the continued existence of high levels of deprivation among many Blacks. Rather he attributes urban Black slum conditions to the pathology of Black lower class culture. Since Banfield's views are widely held they are worth some detailed attention.

Blacks, Banfield tells us, have a very large lower class, and lower class culture contributes to turning lower income areas into slums (defined as an area in which ". . . a squalid and wretched style of life is widespread.")[51] Banfield's theory of class should not be confused with the common view that class is defined by objective criteria such as income, wealth accumulation, or relation to the dominant mode of production—owners of the means of production versus wage laborers. Banfield's definition of class is psychological: the upper class is future-oriented; the lower class present-oriented. Thus an upper class individual, Banfield tells us:

> . . . places great value on independence, creativity, happiness, "developing one's potentialities to the full," and consideration for others.

33

> Future-oriented culture teaches the individual that he would be cheating himself if he allowed gratification of his impulses (for example, for sex or violence) to interfere with his provision for the future.[52]

In contrast to the provident, prudent upper class is the lower class:

> ... the lower-class individual lives from moment to moment. If he has any awareness of a future, it is of something fixed, fated, beyond his control: things happen *to* him, he does not *make* them happen. Impulse governs his behavior, either because he cannot discipline himself to sacrifice a present for a future satisfaction or because he has no sense of the future. He is therefore radically improvident. ... His bodily needs (especially for sex) and his taste for "action" take precedence over everything else—and certainly over any work routine.[53]

Lower class culture is pathological, Banfield asserts:

> The implication that lower-class culture is pathological seems fully warranted both because of the relatively high incidence of mental illness in the lower class and *also because human nature seems loath to accept a style of life that is so radically present-oriented.* (emphasis added)[54]

Banfield does not state that the present-orientation of the lower class is genetic but he subtly plants the suggestion: "Ability (or willingness) to take account of the future does not appear to have much relation to intelligence or IQ; however, it is not implausible to conjecture that some genetic factor may influence it."[55]

Despite the strident, self-confident tone of his writings, Banfield is not basing his detailed descriptions of class culture and his assertion that it is the cause of urban slums on empirical research. It is not from empirical research that we "know" (1) lower class individuals create slums; (2) individuals can be distinguished by their orientation to the future. (One might hypothesize there is no basis for an ideal-typical characterization of orientation to the future because it is an insignificant part of individual psychological make-up; or it may be humans tend to be both present and future oriented in ways which are impossible to neatly separate.); (3) orientation to the future is correlated with independence, creativity, etc., and orientation to the present is correlated with improvidence, violence, high and uncontrollable bodily needs for sex. (Suppose for a moment that psychological orientation to time is important. The person oriented to the present, living day by day, might still be highly organized, provident, non-violent and even asexual. Why would a present oriented person necessarily abjure a work routine? Indeed a narrowly focused, limited person of few interests and truncated perspective might feel most comfortable in a highly structured work setting.); or (4) that it is in any way plausible to believe ability or willingness to take account of the future is influenced by some genetic factor.[56] Banfield's elaborate argument and his highly authoritarian policy suggestions are at bottom unsupported and non-empirical.[57]

Though Banfield emphasizes that not all present-oriented (lower class) people are Black,[58] he stresses (again without evidence) that Blacks have a very large lower class[59] (that is, in his terms a large number of people with a pathological culture) and that ". . . most lower-class people in the large cities are black."[60] By the concluding chapters it is clear that his main concern is the Black "lower class." What makes this unsubstantiated study so convincing that it is one of the best-selling books on urban problems?[61] It is a reassertion of an old idea: whites have not debased Blacks, Blacks have debased themselves or perhaps Blacks have been debased by nature. Indeed Banfield candidly restates traditional racial themes: the bestial character of Blacks; the superiority of whites (most of whom have what Banfield terms "normal" culture); and the inferiority of Blacks. He manipulates and rationalizes deeply held racial fantasies.

Banfield advocates public policies that make southern segregation seem tame and unsophisticated by comparison. A sample of his recommendations are reproduced below:

1. Avoid rhetoric tending to raise expectations to unreasonable and unrealizable levels, to encourage the individual to think that "society" (e.g., "white racism"), not he, is responsible for his ills, and to exaggerate both the seriousness of social problems and the possibility of finding solutions.

2. If it is feasible to do so (the disagreement among economists has been noted earlier), use fiscal policy to keep the general unemployment level below 3 percent. In any case, remove impediments to the employment of the unskilled, the unschooled, the young, Negroes, women, and others by (a) *repealing the minimum-wage and occupational licensure laws* and laws that enable labor unions to exercise monopolistic powers, (b) *ceasing to overpay for low-skilled public employment,* (c) ceasing to harass private employers who offer low wages and unattractive (but not unsafe) working conditions to workers whose alternative is unemployment, and (d) offer wage supplements in the form of scholarships to enable boys and girls who have received little schooling to get jobs with employers who offer valuable on-the-job training. (emphasis added)

3. Revise elementary and secondary school curricula so as to cover in nine grades what is now covered in twelve. Reduce the school-leaving age to fourteen (grade 9), and *encourage (or perhaps even require) boys and girls who are unable or unwilling to go to college to take a full-time job or else enter military service* or a civilian youth corps. Guarantee loans for higher education to all who require them. Assure the availability of serious on-the-job training for all boys and girls who choose to go to work rather than to go to college. (emphasis added)

4. Define poverty in terms of the nearly fixed standard of "hardship," rather than in terms of the elastic one of "relative deprivation," and bring all incomes above the poverty line. Distinguish categorically between those of the poor who are competent to manage their affairs and those of them who are not, the latter category consisting of the insane, the severely retarded, the senile, the lower

class (inveterate problem families), and unprotected children. Make cash income transfers to the first category by means of a negative income tax, the rate structure of which gives the recipient a strong incentive to work. Whenever possible, assist the incompetent poor with goods and services rather than with cash; depending upon the degree of their incompetence, *encourage (or require) them to reside in an institution or semi-institution (for example, a closely supervised public housing project).* (emphasis added)

5. *Give intensive birth-control guidance to the incompetent poor.* [emphasis added]

6. Pay problem families to send infants and children to day nurseries and preschools, the programs of which are designed to bring the children into *normal culture.* (emphasis added)

7. Intensify police patrol in high-crime areas; *permit the police to "stop and frisk" and to make misdemeanor arrests on probable cause;* institute a system of negative bail—that is, an arrangement whereby a suspect who is held in jail and is later found innocent is paid compensation for each day of confinement. [emphasis added]

8. *Abridge to an appropriate degree the freedom of those who in the opinion of a court are extremely likely to commit violent crimes.*[62] Confine and treat drug addicts. (emphasis added)

Banfield tells us that these policies are feasible but not generally acceptable measures because many politicans would object to them. Banfield makes clear that he would go as far as encouraging or requiring what he terms "the incompetent poor" to reside in an institution or "semi-institution." Recall, the lower class is by Banfield's own definition, "radically improvident" and an affront to human nature ("... human nature is loath to accept a style of life that is so radically present-oriented.") Negroes, Banfield further asserts, have a very large lower class and it is lower class culture which has contributed in a major way to the creation of urban slums. Furthermore, Banfield believes most lower class people in large cities are Negro. Who, therefore, would be institutionalized in large measure? Urban Blacks!

Thus we see the repressive potential of a shift from overt to covert racism accompanied by a failure to understand the structural features of Black existence in the United States. The old form of overt, ascriptively based discrimination can be replaced by a new form: covertly ascriptive; justified by supposedly objective criteria; just as pernicious; differing from legal segregation only in the ideological rationalization given to racial hierarchy and collectivism.

DISCUSSION

In recent years, economists and political scientists have become increasingly interested in the analysis of public policy. This enhanced interest has produced a literature that ranges in character from highly abstract econometric models of public service delivery systems to impassioned pleas on behalf of various public policy panaceas. Typically, this public policy literature accepts certain economic, political, or other constraints as givens and proceeds from these to detailed discussion of methods to make public service delivery systems more efficient, and to rationalize public policy implementation and make it more effective. For those interested in progressive racial public policy the consequences of accepting certain constraints must be examined and analyzed. Efficient embellishments of the status quo must be recognized as such and their relationship (or lack of relationship) to qualitative change made clear. Proponents of progressive racial public policy must expand the normal boundaries of public policy analysis if their goal is qualitative, that is, structural change. Racism is not a mere blemish on American society, but intrinsic to it. In both overt and covert form it maintains Black externality.

To answer the key question—what would constitute qualitative change in the position of American Blacks—and to gain some insight into racial public policy failures to date, it has been necessary to explore the structural position of Blacks in the American context. It was found that hierarchy (the existence of a principle [racism] that ranks groups consistently and pervasively and is enforceable through social control) and collectivism (treatment of individual group members according to a standard stereotype, or principle that supposedly defines the whole group) defined the structural position of American Blacks. These structural features differentiate Blacks from white ethnic groups and hence render ethnic group theoretical models misleading for analysis of Black politics and racial public policy.

The above analysis revealed the dimension and character of Black externality in the American context. Fundamental social change would require the destruction of hierarchy. Abolition of legal segregation was an initial step in this direction. However, as was noted above, hierarchy is rooted in racism which in turn has deep roots in American culture. Thus, complete destruction of racial hierarchy would entail a tranformation of American culture so thorough as to alter the subconscious racism of the aversive racist and eradicate even the most subtle rationalization available to the dominative racist.

It should not be assumed that termination of legal segregation and the transformation from dominative to aversive racism will mean an evolutionary end to racial hierarchy. Rather racial hierarchy can take a new form in which the structural position of Blacks is masked by the dominant American ideology of individualism and egalitarianism and by the lack of overt markers such as existed with legal segregation. If both hierarchy and collectivism were destroyed Blacks would be transformed into an ethnic group. Individual Blacks would then have the same access, alternatives, freedom, as white Americans. (Recall that the essence of American white ethnicity is that group membership carries no behavioral implications for individual members. White ethnicity is neither collectivist nor hierarchical in the American context.) Black integration, therefore, would be wholly consistent with the maintenance of a Black ethnic group, given the elimination of hierarchy and collectivism. Ironically, those who call for Black ethnic group unity and those who seek Black integration are pursuing interrelated goals in spite of the bitter rhetoric which is often exchanged on this subject.[63]

Some form of two-nation (and by implication, Black

39

nationalist) solution could result from maintenance of internally based collectivism and simultaneous destruction of hierarchy and externally generated collectivism. This might entail constitutional recognition of both individual and group rights. In India efforts to uplift scheduled (ex-untouchable) tribes and castes and backward classes led to the reservation of seats in universities and legislatures and of jobs in the administrative service for depressed groups.[64] Recognition of group rights to representation in certain areas is constitutionally recognized in India. In the U.S., we could envision a similar innovation which would give Blacks group rights to a percentage of all university admissions, jobs, cabinet posts, etc.[65]

Either form of structural change would entail far-reaching transformations in American society as a whole. One crucial issue which would have to be faced would be the capacity of capitalism to accommodate Black aspirations. Blacks have traditionally been economically exploited. Any change which destroyed racial hierarchy would, in time, entail some form of economic redistribution. Thus opposition to structural change would not be solely racially motivated. In a country characterized by high levels of concentrated wealth,[66] the very suggestion of economic redistribution is anathema to vastly powerful, vested interests. Even among white workers, class interests are often muted and encompassed by racial concerns.[67]

The purpose of this discussion has been clarification of theoretical issues and illumination of certain aspects of Black politics which are central to racial analysis, rather than the proposal of specific racial policy alternatives. Nevertheless, with that caveat clearly in mind, certain general conclusions can be drawn. If we are to avoid the false and dangerous practice of blaming the victim for societally caused, structurally rooted deprivations, structural constraints must be squarely faced and challenged. The limitations of ethnic policies and ethnic-style politics are crucial problems, particularly given the current emphasis on electoral politics by many Black leaders. These same leaders are often perplexed and angered by low levels of Black voting and political participation. It is ironic and sad that comfortably situated Black middle class elites criticize the Black masses for their low levels of political participation without

40

realizing ethnic politics produces ethnic policies; and the divisible (individualistic) benefits of ethnic policies are more likely to go to middle class individuals who possess those qualities which make them acceptable to dominant political authorities. Thus it is not surprising that Black political participation, as measured by registration and voting, is lower than white political participation.[68] Ethnic politics often provides no more than symbolic benefits for poor, urban Black masses.

Unfortunately, the particularistic, incrementalist, narrow potential of ethnic public policies has not prevented cynical politicians from selling them as revolutionary panaceas. Thus the very real benefits which a few individuals gained, over a short time span, from the "War on Poverty" were obscured by the claim that the hodge-podge of well-meaning but limited social programs would actually end poverty. Even the nomenclature subtly suggests the possibility of a victory over poverty. At best the Great Society programs were vehicles for economic and/or political mobility for a very few people and sources of temporary increments in resources for a larger number of individuals and families. While it is not incorrect to criticize ethnic policies, on their own terms, as incremental, particularistic, and limited, it is conceptually misleading and unhelpful to criticize ethnic and collective racial policies for not producing structural results.

Ambivalence toward ethnic politics is a rational response of lower class Blacks given the limited policy potential of ethnic politics. Yet a viable ideology of collectivism and new forms of Black collectivist politics have not replaced ethnic political styles in the Black community. Thus the limbo created by the ethnic-collective oscillation in Black politics continues and becomes a contributing factor to political malaise and recurrent issues. A latent result of recurring, unresolved policy issues and perceived racial policy failure is the high levels of conflict and fragmentation within the Black community. Lacking the power to impose policy solutions and therefore to test various ideological positions, ideological positions crystallize, become reified and recur again and again—each time generating intense, debilitating, and ultimately unenlightening conflict.

Indeed, not only is there an unsettling character to intra-

Black community political debate, but the present period has a disturbing similarity to the Reconstruction era. Immediately after slavery was ended, Blacks made dramatic political gains, only to see them eroded year by year until the compromise of 1877 finally reconciled southern whites and northern whites at the expense of southern Blacks.[69] The compromise of 1877 set the stage for the onset of legal segregation. Legal segregation, "Jim Crow," then became the object of much Black political effort. Yet, as we now know, "Jim Crow" was only a manifestation of hierarchy and collectivism, not the total phenomenon. Thus the paradox of *Brown* v. *Board of Education,* 347 U.S. 483 (1954). As Robert Carter has noted:

> Brown's indirect consequences, therefore, have been awesome. It has completely altered the style, the spirit, and the stance of race relations. Yet the pre-existing pattern of white superiority and Black subordination remains unchanged; indeed, it is now revealed as a national rather than a regional phenomenon. . . . Few in the country, Black or white, understood in 1954 that racial segregation was merely a symptom not the disease; that the real sickness is that our society in all its manifestations is geared to the maintenance of white superiority. . . .[70]

Black politics and racial policy must change to reflect the new nuances and subtle conundrums of the post-Brown era. James Baldwin has called the American Negro "a unique creation." The dimensions of that uniqueness are just beginning to become clear. That uniqueness disqualifies much of white ethnic group experience as a predictive guide for Blacks and makes development of progressive racial public policy a challenge to academics, politicians and policy-makers alike.

NOTES

I would like to thank Steve Barnett, Duane Lockard, and Thaddeus Spratlen for their thoughtful comments on a previous version of this article.

42

1. Daniel P. Moynihan, "The Schism in Black America," *The Public Interest,* no. 27, (spring 1972): 9. D. P. Moynihan was an architect of the Nixon administration's benign neglect policy. Ben J. Wattenberg and Richard Scammon are two other academic proponents of the Moynihan position. In an article in the April 1973 issue of *Commentary* magazine, they asserted that 52 percent of Black Americans can be classified as middle class today; that a substantial number of Black husband-wife families outside the South and under age 35 have achieved income parity with whites similarly situated; and that in those families where the wife also works, parity has been achieved and even surpassed. Thus Wattenberg and Scammon suggest that Black leaders and white liberals realize and acknowledge that the liberal legislation of the 1960s did work. In the February 1974 *Black Scholar,* Harrington Bryce answered the Moynihan and Wattenberg and Scammon arguments. He showed that the under 35, husband-wife, Black family outside the South accounts for only 10 percent of all Black families. Bryce states: "The other 90% of Black families continues to be unequal! As a matter of fact, Black families as a rule found that the absolute gap between their incomes and white family incomes *increased* from roughly $2,500 in 1947 to just over $4,000 in 1971." (Harrington Bryce, "Are Most Blacks Middle Class?" *The Black Scholar* 5, no. 5 [February 1974] : 33.)

2. Moynihan, "The Schism in Black America," 10.

3. David H. Swinton and Julian Ellison, "Aggregate Personal Income of the Black Population in the U.S.A., 1947-1980," Monograph no. 3 (New York: Black Economic Research Center, 1973), pp. 55-56.

4. For example, Mack Jones, "Black Politics: Symbolism and Reality," Paper delivered at Second Annual Political Science Seminar at South Carolina State College, March 15, 1972.

5. Edward S. Greenberg, Neal Milner, David J. Olson, *Black Politics* (New York: Holt, Rinehart & Winston, 1971), p. 14.

6. A number of books have appeared analyzing various programs of the 1960s, their limited successes and often more dramatic failures. See for example Kenneth Clark and Jeannette Hopkins, *A Relevant War on Poverty* (New York: Harper & Row, 1970); Theodore J. Lowi, *The End of Liberalism* (New York: Norton, 1969) (although Lowi's principal target is the liberal state itself, he focuses on the 1960s); Sar Levitan, *The Great Society's Poor Law: A New Approach to Poverty* (Baltimore: Johns Hopkins Press, 1969); and *Programs in Aid of the Poor for the 1970s* (Baltimore: Johns Hopkins Press, 1969). David M. Gordon's *Problems in Political Economy: An Urban Prospective* (Lexington, Mass.: Heath, 1971) looks at a wide variety of 1960s public policies, documenting the inadequate results, and probing the underlying reasons for failure in each policy area. Also informative are Charles Sackrey, *The Political Economy of Urban Poverty* (New York: Norton, 1973); Daniel P. Moynihan, *Maximum Feasible Misunderstanding* (New York: Free Press, 1969); Samuel F.

Yette, *The Choice* (New York: Putnam, 1971); and J. David Greenstone and Paul E. Peterson, *Race and Authority in Urban Politics* (New York: Russell Sage Foundation, 1973).

7. Michael J. Flax, *Blacks and Whites* (Washington, D.C.: The Urban Institute, 1971). Quotation based on data from pages 68-77.

8. This lack of theory in the area of Black politics has been occasionally noted. For example, John H. Strange ("The Negro in Philadelphia Politics, 1963-1965," unpublished Ph.D. dissertation, Princeton University, 1966) notes, "Most of those doing research concerning the Negro and politics make no explicit attempt whatever to delimit or even identify the phenomena they are investigating other than state they are studying 'Negro politicians,' 'Negro voters or registrants,' 'Negro protest,' or 'Negro politics'" (p. 5). While the general state of theory on Black politics and racial public policy is disappointing, there are some notable exceptions. Hanes Walton, *Black Politics* (Philadelphia: Lippincott, 1972) argues that "black politics is a function of the particular brand of segregation found in different environments in which Black people find themselves." His subsequent pathbreaking analysis shows how Black pressure group, party, bureaucratic, urban, etc. political activity is structured by contextual variables. Professor Walton's work focuses on input processes. The seminal work by Stokely Carmichael and Charles Hamilton (*Black Power* [New York: Random House, 1967]) also presents a modernization theory, which focuses on input rather than public policy processes. In his recent two-volume study, Matthew Holden offers a theory of input processes and proposals for future racial public policy but does not offer a theory of the racial public policy process. See Matthew Holden, *The Politics of the Black 'Nation'* and *The White Man's Burden* (New York: Chandler, 1973). Harold Cruse, *The Crisis of the Negro Intellectual* (New York: Morrow, 1967) contains a theory of Black politics and American ethnic and racial public policy that focuses on cultural pluralism. Cruse's main concern, however, is to focus attention on the need for Black intellectuals to squarely confront the nationalism issue.

9. Greenberg, et al., *Black Politics*, pp. 14, 15.

10. Many authors define ethnicity as a form of primordial group cohesion and then apply this understanding to Blacks and various white ethnic groups with little or no attempt at analytical differentiation. Even within white ethnic groups one might want to think about differentiating Jews from other white ethnic groups. Other ethnic groups not discussed here include Puerto Ricans, Chicanos, American Indians, Chinese-Americans, etc. The paradigm sketched in this paper with respect to Blacks could be developed for analysis of these groups and for a finer breakdown of white ethnic groups. However, that endeavor is beyond the scope of this article. Numerous studies discuss ethnic politics but fail to adequately distinguish between Blacks and white ethnic groups and therefore fall into the "trap," seeing experiences of Black and white ethnic

groups that descriptively resemble each other as in fact the same. The thrust of my argument is that appearances are deceptive. Seeming similarities in ethnic group and racial behavior and experience actually stem from radically different structural positions. Thus what seems to be the same may actually be very different. Edgar Litt, *Ethnic Politics in America* (Glenview, Ill.: Scott, Foresman, 1970); Nathan Glazer and Daniel P. Moynihan, *Beyond the Melting Pot* (Cambridge, Mass.: M.I.T. Press, 1963); Milton Gordon, *Assimilation in American Life,* (New York: Oxford University Press, 1964) are among the standard works on ethnicity that fail to adequately analyze Blacks.

11. In recent years there has been an explosion of interest, research, and written work on ethnicity. It would be impossible to list all of the books and articles that shaped my thinking about white ethnic groups and that therefore laid the foundation for the discussion in this section. Among the books with a general perspective have been: Milton H. Gordon, *Assimilation in American Life* (New York: Oxford University Press, 1964); Andrew M. Greeley, *Why Can't They Be Like Us?* (New York: Institute of Human Relations Press, 1969); Oscar Handlin, ed., *Children of the Uprooted* (New York: Braziller, 1966); Stanley Lieberson, *Ethnic Patterns in American Cities* (Glencoe, Ill.: Free Press, 1963); R. A. Schermerhorn, *Comparative Ethnic Relations* (New York: Random House, 1970); Tamotsu Shibutani and Kran M. Kwan, *Ethnic Stratification* (New York: Macmillan, 1965); and William W. Warner and Leo Srole, *The Social Systems of American Ethnic Groups* (New Haven, Conn.: Yale University Press, 1945). Works on specific groups included Edward M. Levine, *The Irish and Irish Politicians* (Notre Dame, Ind.: University of Notre Dame Press, 1966); William V. Shannon, *The American Irish* (New York: Macmillan, 1966); Marshall Sklare, ed., *The Jews* (New York: Free Press, 1958); Gerald Suttles, *The Social Order of the Slum: Ethnicity and Territory in the Inner City* (Chicago: University of Chicago Press, 1968); and Arthur E. Wood, *Hamtramck: A Sociological Study of a Polish-American Community* (New Haven, Conn.: College and University Press, 1955).

12. Louis Dumont, *Homo Hierarchicus: An Essay on the Caste System* (Chicago: University of Chicago Press, 1970), p. 253. Dumont was the first sociologist to see the Black position in America as a hierarchical residue in a society in which the cultural ideal is egalitarianism. Dumont is arguing against the theory that Blacks are a caste in the United States and therefore does not develop the theory and its implications. Gunnar Myrdal, *An American Dilemma: The Negro Problem and Modern Democracy,* 2 vols. (New York: Harper & Row, 1944) also recognized the link between egalitarian ideology and the rise of racism, but misunderstood Blacks as a caste in American society—as merely an extreme form of class. The classic sociological analysis of the sociology of race is that of Oliver C. Cox, *Caste, Class and Race* (New York: Monthly Review Press,

1948). Cox, like Dumont, argues against the view that Blacks constitute a caste. In doing so Cox recognizes also that there are similarities (e.g., hierarchy and collectivism in my terms) between Indian caste and American racism. More importantly, Cox recognizes that one cannot speak of one caste but of the caste system and *caste ideology*. Louis Dumont, "Caste, Race and Stratification: Reflections of a Social Anthropologist," Appendix A in Dumont, *Homo Hierarchicus* makes the same point: "the Indian system is a coherent social system based on the principle of inequality, while the American 'color bar' contradicts the equalitarian system within which it occurs and of which it is a kind of disease" (p. 30). Thus while there are similarities, American racism is *not* the same as caste.

13. C. B. MacPherson, *The Real World of Democracy* (Oxford: Claredon Press, 1965), p. 7.

14. Ibid.

15. Ibid., p. 6.

16. WASPs present the most difficult case because in the past becoming Americanized was sometimes equated with becoming Anglicized, which was again equated with becoming more like WASPs. Thus, Anglicizing activities such as changes in name sometimes characterized immigrant assimilation. However, it is too easy to misread these actions. An immigrant who changed his name to Smith might do so simply as a pragmatic step to facilitate settling in a new culture. It might *not* involve belief that his Protestant neighbors were superior to his Catholic neighbors; Catholics might say Catholics were superior. Protestants might say Protestants were superior. In contrast after a short time off the boat he would know that whites believed themselves superior to Blacks. Our mythical immigrant might be confused about white ethnic ranking if he were in an area where, say, Irish Catholics were wealthy and politically powerful and white English Protestants were poor. In contrast, there would be no confusion about the Black-white hierarchy. Persistence of white ethnicity and the resurgence of ethnicity as an important focal point for political mobilization during the 1960s should suggest earlier notions of the assimilation of ethnic immigrants into an Anglicized WASP society were simplistic and need radical revision.

17. For further analysis, see Dumont, "Caste, Race and Stratification," pp. 36-38; and Cox, *Caste, Class and Race.*

18. Gunnar Myrdal states the issue succinctly: "race prejudice is, in a sense, a function of equalitarianism. A nation less fervently committed to Democracy [as ideology] could probably live happily in a caste system" (*An American Dilemma*, p. 89).

19. Thomas Jefferson, *Notes on Virginia.* Quoted in Winthrop D. Jordan, *White Over Black* (Chapel Hill: University of North Carolina Press, 1968), p. 436.

20. Ibid.

21. Ibid., p. 432.

22. Winthrop Jordan concludes: "Jefferson went to his grave convinced that slavery was a blight on the white community. With slavery's effect on Black men he simply was not overly concerned" (ibid., p. 433).

23. Others used Black inferiority to justify slavery. See Eric L. McKitrick, *Slavery Defended: The Views of the Old South* (Englewood Cliffs, N.J.: Prentice-Hall, 1963). The issue is best stated by James Henry Hammond, a proslavery intellectual (1807-1864). He states: "Our slaves are Black, of another and inferior race. The *status* in which we have placed them is an elevation. *They are elevated from the condition in which God first created them, by being made our slaves"* (p. 123). [emphasis added]

24. For discussion of the hypothetical chain of being see Jordan, *White Over Black,* pp. 216-264 and particularly pp. 493 and 494.

25. Charles Carroll, "The Negro A Beast, or In the Image of God; The Reasoner of the Age, The Revelation of the Century! The Bible as It is, the Negro and His Relations to the Human Family! . . . The Negro Not the Son of Ham" (St. Louis, 1900) quoted in Richard Bardolph, ed., *The Civil Rights Record: Black Americans and the Law, 1949-1970* (New York: T. Y. Crowell, 1970), p. 102.

26. William Patterson, *We Charge Genocide: The Crime of Government Against the Negro People—A Petition to the United Nations* (New York: Civil Rights Congress, 1951), p. 191.

27. Ibid.

28. Ibid.

29. Ibid., p. 190.

30. *Hirabayashi* v. *United States,* 320 U.S. 81 (1943).

31. Joel Kovel, *White Racism: A Psychohistory* (New York: Vintage Books, 1971), p. 177.

32. Ibid., p. 212.

33. Ibid., p. 54.

34. Kovel states: "Nor has the main strand of Black symbolism changed essentially over the generations: after all, the bigot knows even today that *blacks are wild, impulsive, hypersexual, violent, potential insurrectionaries"* (ibid., pp. 185-186). [emphasis added]. There have been numerous surveys of white attitudes toward Blacks and Black attitudes toward whites. Survey questionnaires, however, are a dubious source of information. Certainly the deep-rooted psychological basis of racism discussed by Kovel would not be articulated on a survey questionnaire. Despite the problems with using survey data, it is still the case that evidence from survey research supports the general view outlined above. Respected opinion researcher Angus Campbell states:

> White Americans are racist in degree. Some would like to keep
> the Black man in his place, send him back to Africa if neces-

sary. Most would not go that far but many would oppose legislation that would bring Negroes closer, especially into their neighborhoods. Some white people give verbal approval to equalitarian principles as they apply to race but they are disturbed by the pace of change in race relations which they see going on around them. Finally there is a minority of the white population who seem to have no apparent racist orientation, who are sympathetic to the various aspects of Black protest, and in some cases contribute to it. [Angus Campbell, *White Attitudes Toward Black People* (Ann Arbor: Institute for Social Research, 1971) p. 156.]

Similarly, survey data on Black attitudes is also of dubious value. Yet much of the data which does exist would support the view, developed below, that Black political culture differs in important ways from that of the larger society. One attitudinal study finds:

Thus, it is important to recognize that Black alienation, as represented by high scores on this index, occurs at both the personal level of primary group relationships and at the level of citizen-to-society connections. It involves distrust of the possibilities of friendship across racial lines in daily life, and of the possibilities of fair treatment for Blacks in the larger occupational, political, and other major structures of the total society. [Howard Schuman and Shirley Hatchett, *Black Racial Attitudes* (Ann Arbor: Institute for Social Research, 1974) p. 114.]

35. Louis Dumont, *Homo Hierarchicus,* is a study of hierarchy and collectivism as they form the underpinnings of the Indian caste system. In the traditional Indian setting, as Dumont points out, there was congruence between Hindu theology and ideology (culture) and the behavior transactions of caste. Dumont's analysis and theory of the structure of the Indian caste system has been instrumental in shaping my own approach to U.S. racial politics and public policy. While agreeing with Dumont, Cox, and others that Blacks *do not* constitute a caste in American society and that the nature of the ideological context is crucial in distinguishing the Indian and American situations, I have found the application of Dumont's theories helpful in understanding race and ethnicity in the American context.

36. On the Black middle class see E. Franklin Frazier, *Black Bourgeoisie* (New York: Free Press, 1957); and Nathan Hare, *The Black Anglo-Saxons* (London: Collier-Macmillan, 1965). Of particular interest is the introduction by Oliver C. Cox.

37. This likening of Blacks to white ethnic groups becomes a form of substitution. Henri LeFebvre, *Everyday Life in the Modern World* (New York: Harper & Row, 1971) develops the general theory of substitution, which, he argues, characterizes modern capitalist society. "A system of

substitutions emerges, where every compendium of meanings—apparently independent and self-sufficient—re-echoes another in endless rotation" (p. 51). S. A. Barnett first applied this theory to the analysis of class in the American context and I would like to thank him for bringing LeFebvre's analysis to my attention.

38. None of the major theoretical interpretations of American politics adequately analyzes the Black political experience. Pluralist, elitist, and class interpretations of American politics focus on whites, and if any reference is made to Blacks, it is usually in the form of a gratuitous generalization about Blacks being like lower-class whites. Analytically, however, the often unexamined assumption is that the same generalizations apply to Blacks and whites. The notion of "nondecisions" comes closest to providing a relevant framework for analyzing Black politics. See Peter Bachrach and Morton S. Baratz, *Power and Poverty* (London, Toronto: Oxford University Press, 1970); and "Two Faces of Power," *The American Political Science Review* 56 (1962): 947-952. However, although Bachrach and Baratz use a case study involving Blacks in their study of Baltimore poverty program politics, they still consider their findings as relevant to a large class of people, including Blacks and whites. The question "What persons or groups in the community are especially disfavored under the existing distribution of benefits and privileges?" is a good one. Their answer, however, fails to deal with crucial racial differences. Perhaps the most important issue is class consciousness. Black oppression is more obvious to Blacks than white oppression is to whites and therefore there is a more developed radical "consciousness" among Blacks. Lower-class whites have the "luxury" of believing in the individualistic (Horatio Alger) illusion. Thus there is a subtle systemic threat posed by Blacks: Making the individualistic, egalitarian illusion obvious in the case of Blacks might reveal the limited, illusory character of individualism, egalitarianism, and free choice as it exists for everyone. Free choice, as was pointed out earlier, is defined by the existence of a market economy. The individualism that is perceived in the West as "natural" is a historical development rooted in a rather recent economic development.

39. "System" is used here in the sense developed by David Easton. See David Easton, *A Systems Analysis of Political Life* (Chicago: University of Chicago Press, 1965).

40. Julian Bond, "People, Policy Politics Administration," speech delivered in New York City; text in *A.S.P.A. News,* March 24, 1972.

41. See Cruse, *The Crisis of the Negro Intellectual;* and *Rebellion or Revolution* (New York: Morrow, 1969).

42. *Black Political Agenda.* Presented to the National Black Political Convention, Gary, Indiana, March 11, 1972.

43. Richard Burkey, *Racial Discrimination and Public Policy in the United States* (Lexington, Mass.: Heath, 1971), pp. 38-39.

44. For example, the Fourteenth Amendment to the Constitution, although passed in the context of slavery abolition and with the overt purpose of protecting the newly freed slaves, created new rights for all Americans and became the basis for far-reaching constitutional change.

45. For additional perspective on this issue see David Gordon, *Theories of Poverty and Unemployment* (Lexington, Mass.: Heath, 1972); Sidney Willhelm, *Who Needs the Negro?* (New York: Doubleday, 1971); Paul A. Baran and Paul M. Sweezy, *Monopoly Capitalism* (New York: Monthly Review Press, 1966); Richard C. Edwards, Michael Reich, Thomas E. Weisskopf, *The Capitalist System* (Englewood Cliffs, N.J.: Prentice-Hall, 1972); C. L. R. James, "The Revolutionary Answer to the Negro Problem in the U.S. (1947)," *Radical America* 4, no. 4, (May 1970): 12-19 (special issue); Donald J. Harris, "The Black Ghetto as 'Internal Colony': A Theoretical Critique and Alternative Formulation," *The Review of Black Political Economy* 2, no. 4 (Summer 1974): 3-33.

46. Robert A. Dahl, *Who Governs?* (New Haven: Yale University Press, 1961) p. 52.

47. Charles V. Hamilton, "Racial, Ethnic, and Social Class Politics and Administration," *Public Administration Review* 32 (October 1972): 638.

48. It is in this context that the late 1960s resurgence in white ethnically based political activity can best be understood. The white ethnic resurgence grew out of the politicization of ascriptive identities which occurred during the civil rights movement. The civil rights movement created an identity crisis because it seemed to threaten the ethnic status quo. When it became clear that Blacks would not gain ethnic equivalence, white ethnic mobilization declined—unless stimulated by the "threat" of busing.

49. Edward Banfield, *The Unheavenly City Revisited* (Boston: Little, Brown and Co., 1968, 1970, 1974), p. 78.

50. Ibid., p. 284.

51. Ibid., p. 52.

52. Ibid., p. 57.

53. Ibid., p. 61.

54. Ibid., p. 63.

55. Ibid., p. 57.

56. There are so many faulty aspects of Banfield's argument, it is not possible to begin to cover them all. The reader interested in pursuing these issues should see the many reviews of *The Unheavenly City*. Though somewhat more cautious *The Unheavenly City Revisited* is thus far less well reviewed, but every bit as opinionated and unsubstantiated as his first effort.

57. Banfield admits his theory of present and future orientation cannot be called a fact (p. 54) but nowhere does he suggest authoritarian

measures such as institutionalization of what he terms the incompetent lower class should await verification. One would have thought someone who characterizes himself as well-meaning (p. xi) would have called for extensive, prolonged testing lest innocent people suffer because of his incorrect "heuristic hypothesis."

58. Ibid, p. 56. ". . . members of a class as the word is used here are people who share 'a distinct patterning of attitudes, values, and modes of behavior,' not people of like income occupation, schooling, or status." Thus in the earlier sections of the book the lower class seems multi-racial and could be located in all income groups. But by the concluding chapters the lower class gets blacker and poorer. Though he states he is not talking about only Blacks (p. 235) the statement is contradicted by his own choice of references and the pattern and priorities of his own analysis.

59. Ibid., p. 87, "The lower class is relatively large among Negroes. . ."

60. Ibid., p. 259.

61. *The Unheavenly City* went through twenty-two printings and is characterized by the publisher's note in *The Unheavenly City Revisited* as one of the most widely read of all books on American urban problems.

62. Ibid., pp. 269-270.

63. Thus, the ethnic-collective oscillation developed in this analysis differs from the idea of an integrationist-separationist conflict. Insofar as many "separationists" are referring to a form of Black ethnic group status, they are theoretically demanding the same structural change as integrationists. Ethnic and collective concepts can further be broken down into "left" and "right" ideological views as differentiated by views on preferred mode of economic organization. Thus:

	Marxist/Socialist Ideology	Capitalist Ideology
Ethnic Political Orientation	Ben Davis	Most Black Political Leaders
Collective Political Orientation	Angela Davis Imamu Baraka	Marcus Garvey

64. See Marguerite Ross Barnett and Steve Barnett, "Contemporary Peasant and Post-Peasant Alternatives in South India: The Ideas of a Militant Untouchable," Annals of the New York Academy of Sciences, 1974, vol. 220, article 6, pp. 385-410, for an analysis of how ex-untouchables have fared as a result of constitutional innovations such as reservation of seats and political attempts to include ex-untouchables in leadership positions in political parties. While nationally ex-untouchables

51

have unquestionably benefited from the Indian government policy, ex-untouchables remain oppressed and exploited in many parts of India. It should be mentioned that the major drafter of the Indian constitution was an untouchable, Dr. B. R. Ambedkar, who was a very active organizer of untouchables and very aware of their problems. In assessing the value of the Indian experiment of reservation of seats, etc., it is important to realize that fifty years ago untouchables were, as the name implies, literally not to be touched and in some places they could not be seen or heard. Untouchability has been legally abolished. The fact that ex-untouchables now occupy important positions in many walks of Indian life has to be seen against that background. However, as the article cited above indicates, changes affecting ex-untouchables must also be seen in light of their structural position.

65. I do not suggest this change would be easy. As stalwart a supporter of civil rights as Justice Douglas made it quite clear in his dissenting opinion in *DeFunis* v. *Odegaard*, 416 U.S. 312 (1974) that racial criteria are forbidden even when used for "benign purposes."

> There is no constitutional right for any race to be preferred. The years of slavery did more than retard the progress of Blacks. Even a greater wrong was done the whites by creating arrogance instead of humility and by encouraging the growth of the fiction of a superior race. There is no superior person by constitutional standards. As DeFunis who is white is entitled to no advantage by reason of that fact, nor is he subject to any durability, no matter his race or color. Whatever his race, he had a constitutional right to have his application considered on its *individual merits* in a racially neutral matter. (emphasis added) [Quoted in Derrick A. Bell, Jr. (1975 Supplement) (Boston: Little, Brown and Co., 1975) p. 85.]

However, in *Gomperts* v. *Chase,* 329 F. Supp. 1142 (N.D. Col.), injunction denied pending Appeal 404 U.S. 1237 (1971) Justice Douglas suggested *Plessy* v. *Ferguson* 163 U.S. 537 (1896) "had not been overruled on its mandate that separate facilities be equal." (Bell, p. 547) *Plessy* v. *Ferguson* embodied a notion of racial collectivism. Put together with *Brown* v. *Board of Education* (in which the court said: "To separate them [Blacks] from others of similar age and qualifications solely because of their race generates a feeling of inferiority as to their status in the community. . . .") (Bell, p. 436). There may be a hint of a possibility of benign collectivism being given constitutional sanction. If facilities and opportunities are genuinely equal and if the separation is benign and does not generate inferiority, is it constitutional?

66. See Ferdinand Lundberg, *The Rich and the Super-Rich* (New York: Bantam Books, 1968).

67. A poignant example appeared in a 1972 *New York Times* article on busing:

> One day during the [1972] campaign Michigan's Democratic candidate for Senator, Frank Kelle, saw a line of people waiting for unemployment compensation. He went up and asked a man what was on his mind in this election. The man answered: "Busing." [Quoted in Bell, *Race, Racism and American Law*, p. 515.]

White opposition to busing grew and intensified during each year of the 1970s making Reverend Jesse Jackson's early observation that "Its not the bus, its us," seem prophetic. In a country in which long distance busing of school children was historically common for a number of purposes, including maintaining racial segregation, busing for desegregation was not objectionable because it was busing but because it was for the purpose of desegregation.

68. For tables showing voter participation in Standard Metropolitan Statistical Areas by size, race and region for November 1968 and November 1970 see, "Abridging the Right To Vote" (New York: National Urban Leage, Inc., 1972) pp. 48-49.

69. Rutherford B. Hayes, the Republican presidential candidate in 1876, offered to withdraw federal troops from the region and allow the south to have a free hand (a "let alone" policy) with respect to Blacks in exchange for electoral votes in the disputed election. Hayes was elected. Rayford W. Logan, *The Betrayal of the Negro* (New York: Collier Books, 1965) p. 26.

70. Robert Carter "The Warren Court and Desegregation" in R. Sayler, B. Boyer, R Gooding, eds. *The Warren Court: A Critical Analysis* (1969) quoted in Bell, *Race, Racism and American Law*, p. 461.

2

THE GHETTO

James A. Hefner

James A. Hefner is the Charles E. Merrill Professor of Economics at Morehouse College. He has taught at Princeton University, lectured in many Black institutions, and published numerous articles and one book in his special field of manpower and urban economics. Dr. Hefner has been a research consultant to the Congressional Black Caucus and the National Advisory Council on Minority Business Enterprise.

INTRODUCTION

Since the publication of the Kerner Commission Report in 1968,[1] the ghetto has come to be seen as an inner-city area "characterized by poverty and acute social disorganization."[2] The words *acute social disorganization* may not be entirely accurate, for as Lee Rainwater has carefully observed, ghetto residents "creatively adapt to the larger system and develop their own solution to recurrent issues"[3] in that system that victimizes them. In this chapter, we endorse an even broader view of the ghetto and its residents:

> In its *racial* sense, a ghetto is an area to which members of an ethnic minority, particularly Negroes, are residentially restricted by social, economic, and physical pressures from the rest of society. In this meaning, a ghetto can contain wealthy and middle-income residents as well as poor ones. In its *economic* sense, a ghetto is an area in which poor people are compelled to live because they cannot afford better accommodations. In this meaning, a ghetto contains mainly poor people, regardless of race or color.[4]

To understand clearly the racial and economic nature of the ghetto, we will examine (1) some specific problems of the ghetto; and (2) micro- and macrostrategies for dealing with these problems. The chapter concludes with a statement concerning the future of Blacks in American ghettos.

 ## SPECIFIC PROBLEMS OF THE GHETTO

Population

In 1970, the majority of Blacks in America resided in metropolitan areas; most of them—approximately 60 percent—within central cities.[5] There were 14.7 million nonwhites in all U.S. central cities, with 90 percent of the population being Black. In 1971, of those individuals residing in central cities (primarily in ghettos), 30 percent had incomes below the poverty level. This level was equal to an income of $4137 annually for a family of four.[6]

The Black ghetto represents only 7.6 percent of the total population of the United States.[7] Yet this percentage is important because the population growth of Blacks in the ghetto has increased by 3.3 million each decade since 1950, with growth rates of 50 and 30 percent for the 1950s and 1960s, respectively. However, the population growth rate of areas outside the ghetto has been larger: 43.3 and 44.1 percent for the decades of the 1950s and 1960s, respectively. The overriding reason for the larger population growth rate in areas outside the ghetto is the out-migration of whites from the central cities to the suburbs. Between 1950 and 1970, the white population in the central cities increased only 7.1 percent.[8] The number of Blacks outside the central cities has declined by .3 million since 1960, while the population of these non-urban areas has *increased* by .8 million.[9]

Poverty

Since 1965, the median income of Blacks as a percentage of white income has increased by only 6 percentage points, from 54 percent to 60 percent in 1971.[10] The median family income

58

was $6400 for Black families and about $10,670 for white families. Although the gain in the median family income for Blacks may be impressive to those who remember it as 40 percent of the median family income for whites in the 1940s, its significance is offset by the fact that Black women had to participate more in the labor market than white women. Nationally, about 68 percent of Black wives as compared to 56 percent of white wives worked to contribute to family income. This excludes families headed by women.

Black and white income differentials have traditionally been used to measure the progress of Blacks moving out of poverty. Some analysts have suggested this measure will have to be eliminated or modified in light of the dubious contention in 1973 by Ben J. Wattenberg and Richard Scammon that "a majority of Black Americans have reached middle class status."[11] Taking into consideration the measure of income differentials and the Scammon-Wattenberg thesis, it can be noted that although the proportion of Blacks and whites below the poverty level decreased between 1959 and 1971, the decline was greater for whites. In 1971, about 10 percent of whites and 32 percent of Blacks were below the poverty level, while in 1959, there were 18 percent of whites and 55 percent of Blacks below the level. The level of poverty dropped over a 12-year period by 44 percent for whites, as compared to 24 percent for Blacks.

The composition of Black poverty makes the situation even more acute. About 50 percent of all Blacks in 1971 were under 18 years of age. They represented about 37 percent of all persons in poverty. Put differently, Blacks who represented 11 percent of the total American population accounted for 37 percent of the persons in poverty under 18 years of age.

Unemployment

Since World War II, Black unemployment has typically been twice that of white unemployment. (Data for 1972 bear this out: The white unemployment rate was 5 percent, contrasted with a Black unemployment rate of 10 percent.)[12] In

Black ghettos, the unemployment rate is often as large as three times the Black unemployment rate in general. This represents a continuing chronic state of crisis. Moreover, Blacks in these low-income areas suffer from a high proportion of under-employment, which is believed to be two and a half times the unemployment rate.[13]

It has been estimated that the subemployment rate (under-employment plus unemployment) in Black ghettos is about 8.8 times greater than the unemployment rate for all workers in the United States.[14] Such deleterious circumstances have negative effects on the extent of labor market participation, and are functionally related to the fact that the largest per-centage of Blacks are employed in "maintenance" occupa-tions,[15] which limit their housing choices.

Housing

Housing for Blacks in the ghetto has alway been poor, from the first migration into urban settings. Drake and Cayton[16] and Osofsky[17] describe the unscrupulous ways of landlords in renting dilapidated dwellings to Blacks at exorbitant prices, causing many tenants to give "rent parties" and to seek roomers to share their expenses.[18]

In 1972, housing expenses absorbed an extremely high portion (25 percent) of the family income of more than a third of the Black families in the United States, as against 13 percent of the income of white families. Yet, 22 percent of the Black familes lived in crowded housing, as compared to 10 percent of the white families.[19]

Residential segregation is a primary determinant of this situation. In a study based solely on the patterns of segregation observable over time, Karl and Alma Taeuber discovered that "residential segregation prevails regardless of the relative economic status of white and Negro residents. It occurs regard-less of the extent of other forms of segregation."[20] In that study, the Taeubers discovered that residential segregation was so pervasive that an average of 86 percent of the nonwhite population in 207 cities across the country would have to be redistributed in order to entirely eliminate residential segregation.[21]

The prevalence of residential segregation cannot be solely attributed to racist attitudes among American whites. Eunice and George Grier[22] found that implicit in the postwar residential development patterns of major cities was a societal decision to allow the private enterprise system to satisfy the booming housing need. The activities of real estate agents, finance companies, banks, and local governments—in the form of zoning laws, land use restrictions, and building codes that effectively shut low income housing out of peripheral urban areas—fostered the flight of affluent and middle-class whites from central cities.

Further, the containment of Blacks in compact central city ghettos has been due to an adherence by the federal government to policies and procedures that were discriminatory in nature. Not only has the federal government conspicuously failed to enforce nondiscriminatory clauses in laws providing for the disbursement of federal funds,[23] but also

> it is a simple fact that the federal government has actively fostered, implemented and buttressed discrimination housing. . . . It is a matter of fact, not fancy, that the FHA through its procedures, the Veterans Administration through its mortgage loans . . . and the Federal Home Loan Board have all adhered to policies strengthening segregation, supporting discrimination, continuing the ghetto, constructing and tightening the "white noose" around the central cities.[24]

For example, an FHA underwriting manual in use for several years after World War II warned that "if a neighborhood is to retain stability, it is necessary that properties shall continue to be occupied by the same social and racial group."[25] Indeed, essentially similar warnings appeared on FHA forms until 1967.[26]

Wealth

Because there are significant differences in Black-white savings patterns,[27] white Americans, on the average, hold

61

approximately 4.5 times as much wealth as Black Americans, as compared to 1.5 times as much income.[28] A recent examination[29] of the wealth position of Blacks, utilizing investment portfolios and various wealth categories, reveals that at equal levels of income and wealth Blacks invest more in consumer durables, specifically houses and cars, than do whites (even among the highest income Blacks). Blacks may be forced to invest more of their wealth in housing because barriers in other investment markets are greater than in the housing markets, and also because they are less familiar with the knowledge of obtaining investment and how to evaluate the little information they do have. George Joyce and Norman Govoni summed up the wealth problems of ghetto Blacks (and Blacks in general) when they wrote that "Negroes have poorer job security; when they are employed, their jobs are generally those yielding lower incomes. Consequently, their assets are not great. Their incomes are not high enough for them to accumulate much savings."[30]

Prices of Goods and Services

Higher prices of goods and services in Black low-income areas (as opposed to white residential neighborhoods) result from such factors as racial discrimination, pilferage, higher rentals, higher insurance costs, and generally the higher cost of doing business in the ghetto. It costs more to do business, thereby costing the Black consumer more to shop in ghetto areas.[31]

Poorer families have less access to credit outlets because of their low income, insufficient savings to buy goods and services, or previous bad credit records. Most of these families are uneducated about the nature and operation of credit purchases and unaware of their legal rights as consumers.

Low ownership of automobiles in the ghetto compels its residents to buy at nearby markets, which generally provide poorer services and higher prices than markets located in white residential areas. Exploitative practices by ghetto merchants are not uncommon. When a customer falls behind in his payments, the ghetto merchant usually threatens or uses garnishment practices, which are permitted without a hearing or trial. Other practices that exploit ghetto residents include high-pressure selling; "bait" advertising (advertising products at unusually low prices); substituting old and used goods for new ones; "switch-selling" (selling a much more expensive article instead of a low-priced advertised one); misrepresentation of prices; and door-to-door salesmen selling poor quality goods at very high prices.[32]

Epstein and Hampton studied the behavior of merchants whose stores are located in or adjacent to low-income areas, and whose advertising practices are not directed on a citywide basis. They provide us with the following findings:

1. Ghetto merchants make most of their sales through credit. Installment credit transactions account for over 90 percent of total sales. Most of the general market retailers (nonghetto retailers) make most of their sales through cash transactions or through noninstallment credit (mostly revolving credit accounts).

2. Prices and gross margins (the difference between the wholesale cost of a good and total revenue received from the sale at retail as a percent of selling price) are higher for ghetto merchants than for general market retailers. Goods with the greatest margin are appliances such as sewing machines (66.3 percent), radios (60 percent), washing machines (51 percent), and television sets (46.4 percent).

3. Finance charges (the extra cost charged by a retailer when merchandise is sold under the installment plan) are generally higher for ghetto merchants than for nonghetto merchants.

4. The higher gross margin for ghetto merchants does not result in higher net profit as a percentage of sales. About 39 percent of the gross margin is spent on salary and commission expenses. This item is approximately 21 percent of total sales for ghetto retailers as compared to 17.8 percent for nonghetto retailers. The use of outside salesmen by ghetto retailers (who are often paid

commissions on sales as well as on house-to-house collections from customers with installment credit, and on home demonstrations) may account for their spending more for salary and commission than nonghetto retailers.

5. Bad-debt losses account for 6.7 percent of the total sales for ghetto merchants, while nonghetto retailers have bad-debts losses of less than one percent of total sales. The higher bad-debt losses of ghetto retailers account for 24 percent of gross margin.

6. Ghetto retailers spend a substantial amount of their expenses for legal and professional assistance, reflecting the cost involved in filing suits for collection of delinquent accounts.

7. Net profit is approximately 3.9 percent of total sales for ghetto merchants, as compared to 2.3 percent of total sales for nonghetto merchants. This difference of 1.6 percent is not a substantially higher net profit. It accounts for only 6.1 percent of the total difference in gross margin. The business methods utilized by ghetto retailers involve higher costs, which offset the higher charged prices.

8. Average net profits after taxes for ghetto retailers is 12.7 percent, as compared to 8.1 percent for nonghetto retailers.[33]

The terms of obtaining credit have significance regarding the *consumption patterns* of ghetto residents. By conventional standards, these residents are considered "bad risks" because of their low income, unstable employment, and other unfortunate circumstances. As noted above, ghetto residents rely on sources that grant easy credit—the merchants in and adjacent to the neighborhood. This fact explains the frequent purchases of appliances and furniture from the ghetto retailers, where the markup may be two to three times higher than those of general market retailers located "downtown" and in suburban shopping centers.[34]

Outflow of Resources[35]

Despite the Black ghetto residents' frequent purchases of goods and services from ghetto merchants, one of the principal reasons for poverty in the Black ghetto is the lack of money remaining to generate income for its residents. Purchases of goods and services made outside the ghetto constitute a major source of cash drain. Other such cash drains are retail payments to absentee landlords, tax payments, loan repayments to non-ghetto residents, savings and investments of ghetto residents held outside the ghetto, and patronization by ghetto residents of rackets operated by nonghetto residents (i.e., the numbers racket and other illegal activities). As a general rule, the outflow or resources far surpasses the inflow[36] in the Black ghetto.

STRATEGIES FOR CHANGE

So far in this chapter we have discussed the problems of Blacks in American ghettos. We would be wise to remember that the plight of ghetto Blacks in the 1970s and beyond will continue unless there are special efforts made on a micro and macro level to change conditions. In the sections that follow, we will discuss various strategies proposed for bringing about ghetto economic development.

Microstrategies

Investment in the Ghetto:
Case for Ghetto Buildup

One way in which ghetto economic development could be approached is presented in the case for ghetto rebuilding.[37] This case is based primarily on the belief that if money could be retained in the ghetto, it would be possible to revitalize the ghetto economy. Such an economy would help ghetto inhabitants overcome their powerlessness and gain control of public and private institutions governing their lives. By establishing businesses owned and run by Blacks in the ghetto, the argument is that it would be possible to circulate capital in this area, which would be the basis of the socioeconomic improvement of its residents.

65

It is further argued that employment, a serious problem for ghetto residents, would be an outcome of developing businesses in the ghetto. Through training, skilled and technical as well as managerial and executive positions could be filled by ghetto residents. The principal aim would be to increase the number of Black businesses, make them more efficient, and increase their employment of ghetto residents. The supporters of ghetto economic development realize that any improvement in the structure of the ghetto cannot be accomplished with the present predominance of service-type establishments ("Ma and Pa" stores). It is manufacturing, wholesale trade, and other such enterprises that would enable ghetto entrepreneurs to accumulate capital for investments in a more expansive and diversified economy. This part of an approach to ghetto economic development would also aid in the renewal of the central city, where economic stagnation is caused in part by the exodus of white businessmen. Ghetto businesses of various types and sizes would create the capital and the economy for a vibrant central city.

Investment in the Ghetto:
Case Against Ghetto Gilding

An alternative approach to ghetto economic development criticizes rebuilding the ghetto and makes a case against ghetto gilding.[38] Emphasis in this approach is on the insufficiency of the ghetto environment to support businesses that would create capital investment or a vigorous economy. It is argued that the present economic base in the ghetto is so low as to ensure the failure of various market activities. There is also the lack of experience in business management among potential ghetto entrepreneurs, many of whom have been exposed to only service-type enterprises, which will not serve as impetus for economic development in the long run. The ghetto entrepreneur must be able to establish businesses that will allow him to obtain large amounts of capital and operate in a competitive society.

The supporters of the case against ghetto gilding believe that

66

to build up the ghetto as an economic unit is to isolate it and further its destruction. Geographical isolation of the ghetto from the suburbs, it is argued, has caused its social and economic deprivation. Opportunities are occurring on the fringe of metropolitan areas, and ghetto inhabitants must not be separated from them. The solution therefore is for inhabitants of the ghetto to be integrated into the larger society where employment opportunities and resources are located. Efforts to increase productivity and income in the ghetto must be geared toward the destruction of barriers between it and the larger economy. Three of these barriers are: (1) inadequate job information in the ghetto; (2) transportation costs and difficulties in reaching suburban jobs; and (3) discrimination by suburban employers.[39]

Corporate Policies

In the application of corporate policies to the development of the ghetto, the approach has been from two different views. One policy prescription is based on investment in the ghetto, and the other on extending the ghetto entrepreneur into the larger economic framework.[40] Regarding the former, the argument extends to ghetto inhabitants sharing a significant part of the corporation and having a voice in its management decisions. The corporation has the responsibility of training Blacks for administration and managerial positions, and providing employment for the hardcore unemployed. As soon as a sufficient number of Black residents have been trained, and the corporation has been successfully established, corporate personnel and resources are withdrawn from the ghetto. The corporation, in effect, becomes a subsidiary of a parent organization.

On the other hand, corporate policies could be aimed at strengthening Black enterprises so that they are able to compete in the larger economy. Black businessmen are provided with managerial skills and new credit sources, for the purpose of establishing sizable Black-owned banks, motels, supermarkets, and manufacturing plants. It is argued that these kinds of

67

enterprises will make Black businessmen better equipped to compete with their white counterparts in terms of prices, quantity, quality, and services.

Community Development Corporations

Organizationally, efforts to bring about ghetto economic development have been through community development corporations (CDCs). Their value is outlined in the following:

> CDCs can be multi-million dollar shopping centers and apartment complexes, gleaming Esso franchises on dull ghetto avenues, or McDonalds Drive-Ins brightening dark and foreboding street corners. But perhaps the most heartening aspect of the CDCs is that they involve people. They represent a place to voice one's opinions and promote one's ideas. CDCs seek to actively involve a core of community leaders and residents who have become shareholders in the corporation. They attempt to prove to ghetto residents that community ownership and direction of business enterprises is within their immediate reach, applying the general philosophy that the need for the psychological life of the ghetto residents cannot be underestimated.[41]

The most critical role of CDCs in terms of impact upon the overall life of the community is in the creation of resident-owned and operated businesses. The process of establishing these businesses requires: (1) adequate publicity for contact with prospective entrepreneurs; (2) skilled technical assistance to help the applicant create an acceptable proposal; (3) contact with banks or other funding agencies; and (4) a system of ongoing technical assistance in keeping business accounts and in production and marketing techniques.

The primary importance of a CDC is its capacity to serve as a model for Black economic development on a large scale. Each community can choose its own direction according to its greatest needs and highest aspirations, and finds itself limited only by its collective enthusiasm and industry. The best method for measuring the worth of a CDC is to examine how close it comes to achieving its stated objectives.

Macrostrategies

In our discussion of macrostrategies, we will center our attention on the federal government, which, over the past two decades, has increased its expenditures on the poor in an attempt to reduce the large poverty income gap.[42] These expenditures have come in the area of health services, with Medicare and Medicaid; in education, primarily with the Elementary Education Act of 1965; and in increased aid to the aged and to the public assistance recipients, with the Social Security Amendments of 1965, 1967 and 1974. Yet, the government's problems continued to rise due to a lack of resources—money and people, we are told—to do the job. The government's programs of various sorts have continually been faced by the fact that for every ten persons in need of programmatic assistance only one is reached, and by the fact that in almost every case, people receiving financial assistance are not elevated above the poverty level.

It has been thought that poverty could be reduced by providing urban poor with more and better-paid jobs. Yet, the jobs requiring people with modest skills are presently located in the suburbs, miles away from the urban poor. Furthermore, there is an increasing demand for people with better educational backgrounds and sophisticated skills—both of which many of the urban poor are without. To attempt to bring industry back into the city, although a sound suggestion, faces several problems: (1) it runs up against the present-day powerful decentralization trend in America; (2) the ghetto population is often so dense that there is very little vacant land for new industries; (3) the kinds of industries most likely to recruit for development programs would be those paying relatively low wages with limited chances for advancement, and the firms themselves might very well be unstable.

To bridge the geographic gap between ghetto residents and

jobs, better transportation from the ghetto to places where jobs are concentrated has been suggested. Critics argue that this is undesirable, however, because it would require the poor to travel long distances and spend large amounts of money and time in travel. Even with lower fares, the traveling would prove expensive in monetary terms. To attempt to provide housing for ghetto residents in the suburban areas would also be difficult due to the high prices of much of suburban housing, and discriminatory practices.

The federal government has developed programs for manpower training, in the hope of minimizing the effects of poverty. "Street academies" for high school dropouts, programs attached to ghetto schools, and various new kinds of training schemes[43] have been devised to train ghetto residents for fruitful employment. The government has also made grants of up to $4000 per employee to private firms to help subsidize salaries of the poor, as well as guaranteeing jobs for hardcore unemployed ghetto residents. Under the Scheurer-Nelson Amendment to the Economic Opportunity Act of 1966, the federal government will even pay up to 90 percent of the salaries of previously unemployed people put to work in new state and local government jobs that have opportunities for advancement. These cash programs of prejob remedial work and on-the-job training have, however, reached few of the hardcore unemployed poor population.

For the 50 percent of the urban poor unlikely to make up the labor force, income maintenance policies—providing more income by direct payment from the government—have been utilized. These policies have not proved effective because they involve a maximum amount of surveillance by case workers, thereby eliminating the time the case workers could use for counseling the recipients in areas necessary for their personal enhancement. The income maintenance policies have been criticized because they provide a maximum deterrent to work efforts.[44]

Recognizing that there is a direct relationship between poverty and the number of children in a family, family allowances—a specified payment from the government for each child in the family—have been posited as a means for reducing poverty. This allowance would be given to every family as a matter of right. It is felt that with the proper amounts of money, family allowances could readily overcome poverty among families with children.

The problems related to doing away with poverty, that state which cripples Black labor, rest not in the financial dimensions of the situation, but in the development of concomitant programs required to prevent poverty from reappearing and perpetuating itself. It is precisely at this point that the federal government can play a vital role. Over the next ten to twenty years, the federal government must: (1) improve the performance of the nation's educational system with respect to the poor; (2) provide adequate family incomes through employment for adults, improved income-maintenance programs, cash help for the poorest of the poor, and increased public assistance minimums in the low-income states; (3) devise a strategy to reduce the rate of in-migration into the large central cities, possibly by employment in southern cities and in smaller metropolitan areas; and (4) successfully manage the economy to keep a vigorous state of economic growth.

CONCLUSION: WHAT CAN WE EXPECT FOR THE FUTURE?

It is clear from the analysis in this chapter that the problems of the ghetto are complex, and it will require massive effort to solve them. And while there are strategies proposed to eliminate these problems, especially those originating in the public sector, Black Americans must not wait for or rely on white prosperity to trickle down to the Black community in order to deal with problems of the ghetto. Proponents of this view are members of the Congressional Black Caucus. In a joint statement, which came out of a conference at Harvard University in 1972, the Black congressmen noted:

1. Blacks should make better use of their economic and political power. If political action and boycotts are not sufficient, they should consider organizing a half million unemployed Blacks for a march on Washington.

2. More Blacks must get into personnel and hiring offices.

3. Black workers should organize new unions as well as join existing segregated unions.

4. A national job information center should be founded and run by Black community organizations to give Blacks information about available jobs throughout the country.[45]

The statement by the Black congressmen presupposes something very basic: that the American people are themselves desirous of significant reduction of poverty in the inner city. There are signs to the contrary,[46] and because of these signs, it is unlikely that the strategies outlined in this chapter will have any significant impact on the lives of ghetto Blacks. This is for all practical purposes assured, if revolutionary changes are not made in the American system, changes that will allow strategies for change, whatever they are, to have a chance of working.

NOTES

1. See *Report of the National Advisory Commission on Civil Disorders* (Washington, D.C.: U.S. Government Printing Office, March 1, 1968).

2. Ibid, p. 6.

3. See Lee Rainwater, *Behind Ghetto Walls* (Chicago: Aldine, 1970), p. 2.

4. Anthony Downs, *Urban Problems and Prospects* (Chicago: Markham, 1970), p. 27.

5. U. S. Department of Commerce, *The Social and Economic Status of the Black Population in the United States, 1972* (Washington, D.C.: Department of Commerce, 1973), pp. 9-14.

6. Ibid., pp. 17-34.

7. Ibid., pp. 9-14.

8. Ibid.

9. Ibid.

10. Ibid., pp. 17-34.

11. See "Black Progress and Liberal Rhetoric," *Commentary* (April 1973): 5. See also Harrington Bryce, "Putting Black Economic Progress in Perspective," *Ebony* (August 1973): and "The Black Middle Class Majority: Is it Enough?" *Focus* (May 1973), p. 5.

12. *The Social and Economic Status of the Black Population,* pp. 37-57.

13. Ibid. See also *Report of the National Advisory Commission on Civil Disorders,* chap. 7.

14. *Report on the National Advisory Commission on Civil Disorders,* chap. 7.

15. *The Social and Economic Status of the Black Population,* p. 49.

16. See S. C. Drake and H. Cayton, *Black Metropolis* (New York: Harper & Row, 1962).

17. G. Osofsky, *Harlem: The Making of a Ghetto* (New York: Harper & Row, 1968).

18. Ibid., p. 35.

19. *The Social and Economic Status of the Black Population,* p. 78.

20. See Karl E. and Alma F. Taeuber, *Negroes in Cities: Residential Segregation and Neighborhood Change* (Chicago, Aldine, 1965), p. 28.

21. Ibid., pp. 32-34.

22. See Eunice and George Grier, "Equality and Beyond; Housing Segregation in the Great Society," in Bernard J. Frieden and Robert Morris, eds., *Urban Planning and Social Policy* (New York: Basic Books, 1968).

23. Whitney M. Young, Jr., "Desegregation: What Impact on the Urban Scene," in Brian J. L. Berry and Jack Meltzer, eds., *Goals for Urban America* (Englewood Cliffs, N.J.: Prentice-Hall, 1967), p. 104.

24. Ibid., p. 108.

25. Quoted in Donald Canty, *A Single Society: Alternatives to Urban Apartheid* (New York: Praeger, 1969), p. 26.

26. Ibid.

27. See Howard Birnbaum and Rafael Weston, "Home Ownerships and the Wealth Position of Black and White Americans" (Cambridge: Harvard University, March 1972), Discussion Paper No. 73.

28. Ibid., p. 6.

29. Ibid., pp. 1-34.

30. George Joyce and Norman Govoni, *The Black Consumer* (New York: Random House, 1971) p. 257.

31. Ibid., p. 262.

32. Edwin Epstein and David Hampton, *Black American and White Business* (Encino: Dickerson Publishing Co., 1971), pp. 60-72.

33. Ibid., pp. 65-66.

34. Carolyn Shaw Bell, *The Economics of the Ghetto* (New York: Western, 1970), pp. 156-177.

35. This section is based on Robert S. Browne, "Cash Flows in a Ghetto Community," *The Review of Black Political Economy* (Winter/Spring 1971), pp. 25-35.

36. Inflows constitute (1) earnings of exported labor; (2) earnings from goods and services exported by ghetto residents; (3) earnings of ghetto residents employed in the ghetto on public payrolls; (4) transfer payments; (5) gifts from outside the ghetto; (6) loans from outside the ghetto; (7) capital investment from outside the ghetto; and (8) earnings from nonghetto property by ghetto residents.

37. See Frank G. Davis, *The Economics of Black Community Development* (Chicago: Markham, 1972).

38. See John F. Kain and Joseph J. Persky, "Alternatives to the Gilded Ghetto," *The Public Interest* (Winter 1969).

39. See John F. Kain, "Housing Segregation, Negro Employment and Metropolitan Decentralization," *Quarterly Journal of Economics* (May 1968); and "The 'Big Cities' Big Problem," *Challenge* (September/October 1966).

40. See Robert B. McKersie, "Vitalize Black Enterprise," *Harvard Business Review* (September/October 1968); Alfonso J. Cervantes, "To Prevent a Chain of Super Watts," *Harvard Business Review* (September/October 1967); U. S. Department of Commerce, *Franchise Company Data for Equal Opportunity in Business* (Washington, D.C.: U. S. Government Printing Office, 1966); Richard S. Rosenbloom "Corporations for Urban Development," in Richard S. Rosenbloom and Robin Marris, *Social Innovation in the City;* Frederick D. Sturdivant, "The Limits of Black Capitalism," *Harvard Business Review* (January/February 1969); Carl E. Hangen, "Short-term Financing," Eli Gingberg, ed., *Business Leaderships and the Negro Crisis* (New York: McGraw-Hill, 1968); and Frank Hoenemeyer, "Long-term Financing," in Ginsberg, *Business Leaderships and the Negro Crisis.*

41. Gil Serota and James Hefner, "Community Development Corporations: Hope for Blacks in American Ghettos?" (Atlanta: Southern Center for Studies in Public Policy, 1972), p. 1.

42. See Joseph A. Kirshaw, *Government Against Poverty* (Chicago: Markham, 1970).

43. Ibid. See also Robert J. Lampman, *Ends and Means of Reducing Income Poverty* (Chicago: Markham, 1971), chaps. 8-9; Dick Netzer, *Economics and Urban Problems* (New York: Basic Books, 1970), part 2.

44. Lampman, *Ends and Means of Reducing Income Poverty,* chap. 9.

45. Congressional Black Caucus, "What Our National Priorities Should Be," (Cambridge: Harvard University, April 5, 6, 7, 1972), p. 15.

46. A sign that was contrary to alternatives "freedom" for Black Americans, and that has real world policy implications toward the maintenance of the present structure of the ghetto is seen in the following words of Daniel P. Moynihan in a memo to President Richard M. Nixon:

> Your administration represents the first significant opportunity to change the direction in which events move. Your task, then, is clear: to restore the authority of American institutions. . . . The problem is not that one group in the population is beginning to react to centuries of barbarism by another group. [In fact, this was exactly what was happening.] The problem is that this cultural reaction among Black militants is accompanied by the existence of a large disorganized urban lower class which, like such groups everywhere, is unstable and essentially violent. (See "69 Moynihan Memo to President Urged Jobs for Negroes," *The New York Times,* March 1, 1970, p. 1.)

Another sign was President Nixon's first fight against a $2.20 an hour minimum wage bill. Carl Rowan, a syndicated journalist, writes: "How in the name of heaven does the President of the rich United States, himself raking in 200,000 bucks a year, with plush pads in California, Florida and elsewhere, tell the Congress that it may not guarantee the grimiest, sweatingest workers in this land a piddling $88 a week" ("Veto of Wage Bill," *The Atlanta Constitution,* September 12, 1973, p. 8). Recent talk of the Ford administration about slashing social services is another sign of the federal government's posture toward poor people.

3

BLACK POLITICS
IN THE SOUTH:
PROJECTIONS
FOR THE
COMING DECADE

Hanes Walton, Jr.

Hanes Walton, Jr. is Professor of Political Science at Savannah State College. His major books are: *The Negro in Third Party Politics; The Political Philosophy of Martin Luther King, Jr.; Black Political Parties: A Historical and Political Analysis;* and *Black Politics: A Theoretical and Structural Analysis.* He has also written numerous articles on Black politics.

INTRODUCTION

To what extent can electoral politics solve major problems facing Black people in the coming decade? This is a central concern and a question that is much discussed, debated, acted on, and analyzed in the Black community. And there are many divergent views among Black politicians, activists, and theorists, North and South.

One leading Black politician, now mayor of Fayette, Mississippi, Charles Evers, asserts in his biography: "I tell my Black brothers, 'Let's take our town and country politically and then share it with our white brothers—even though they never did it with us. If Negroes can get together, they can *control* and *rule* something. My advice is to control something . . . control the ballot of the country, the politics of the country—in other words, control the entire country where we are predominant'."[1] For Evers, electoral politics offers the solution.

Another Mississippian, Fannie Lou Hamer, agrees. She writes: "I expect a drastic change to occur in this country, particularly in the Deep South, as Blacks become more aware of the importance of entering into politics and developing the skills necessary to find the solutions to the problems of 'mass confusion'."[2]

However, not all Blacks consider politics to be as meaningful as do Evers and Hamer. Political activist H. Rap Brown sees electoral politics as self-defeating. He writes, "History shows that politics as it is defined by America is undesirable and dangerous to Black people."[3] Black political scientist Mack Jones believes that "The key to Black liberation lies somewhere external to electoral politics."[4] Although Evers and Hamer see electoral politics as a meaningful tool, Brown and Jones are doubtful of its possibilities. They see electoral politics as a dead end.

Georgia assemblyman and national political figure Julian Bond combines the opposing positions. In his first book he tries to come to grips with the issue by noting, "I have concluded that elective politics and the radical revolutionary change needed in American society are virtually incompatible, however, politics can offer some victories, and ought never be ignored by Black people as one weapon in a presently rather empty arsenal."[5]

In sum then, many Blacks feel that politics is a solution and are proceeding to practice it, others see it as a waste of time, and a third group sees electoral politics as a partial solution to the problems facing Blacks, especially in the South.

This essay will analyze the potential for Black politics in the South in the coming decades, and assess some possibilities and some limitations, some avenues of hope and some goals that cannot be achieved via electoral mechanisms.

SOUTHERN BLACK POLITICAL HISTORY

Since the era of disenfranchisement (1891-1901) the thrust of Black political activity in the South has been primarily toward reentering southern politics.[6] Although this struggle has intensified in recent years, it has nevertheless been constant, unending, and loosely organized. Blacks throughout the South have tried through various political mechanisms to regain the right to vote, which was taken away by numerous legal and illegal devices including the famous Grandfather Clause, the white primary system, the reading and interpretation test, poll taxes, racial gerrymandering, the malapportionment of the state legislatures, the closing of registrars' offices, economic sanction, and violence (which inspired fear and political apathy).[7] Although each system used its own techniques and devices to keep Blacks out of politics, the efforts overall were nevertheless systematic, unified, and *near comprehensive.* (A small number of Blacks did vote, participate, and hold office,[8] but for the mass of Blacks politics was out of reach.)

The struggle of Blacks to reenter southern politics is not as well coordinated, comprehensive, or systematic as are the efforts to keep them out of the political sphere. Thus, success has been limited and short lived. The struggle to reenter, or as Charles Hamilton has called it, *the politics of participation,* did not begin to make meaningful progress until the mid 1940s and early 1950s. The Supreme Court's *Smith* v. *Allwright* decision in 1944 abolished the white primaries; and its decision in 1961 in the *Gomillion* v. *Lightfoot* case abolished racial gerrymandering.[9] Earlier in *Guinn and Beals* v. *U.S.* (1915) the Court had outlawed the Grandfather Clause. One-day registration was done away with by the *Lane* v. *Wilson* decision.

But as nonelectoral or pressure politics removed most legal barriers to Black participation in southern politics, state efforts to forestall registration got under way. As has often been noted, when the courts (and to a certain extent Congress) established the rights of Blacks to vote, the foes of Black voting then turned to the registration process as their chief weapon against Black electoral majorities or substantial Black turnout. In some areas the registrar would constantly move his office, or close it when Blacks came to register. In other areas the registration process was slowed down to one a day, a week, or month. In other sections economic sanctions or violence were employed against would-be Black voters. Individual or group efforts by Blacks in most localities had little or no success. The number of registered Black voters in state after state remained low, and actual participation was, for the most part, even lower than the actual number who had registered.[10] Yet the rationale behind the herculean effort to participate in southern politics, that is, the notion that those problems that face Blacks as a race can be solved through voting and the acquisition of political power, continues to move Blacks efforts to attempt to reenter southern politics.

As the sixties moved along, Black registration efforts intensified. In Mississippi the Council of Federated Organization (COFO) tried to register Black voters, but had only very limited success; and when these efforts sagged, new techniques and strategies were devised to bring the federal government into the area of voter registration. Although Congress had passed the 1957, 1960, and 1964 Civil Rights Acts, only a few thousand Blacks had been added to the voter rolls as a consequence of these laws. The first tactic to involve the government was the formation of the Mississippi Freedom Democratic Party,[11] which failed in the 1964 Democratic convention and its subsequent congressional seating challenges. When political reform efforts failed, Dr. Martin Luther King, Jr., fresh from his Birmingham marches, employed the method of nonviolent civil disobedience to protest white denial of Black voting rights. President Lyndon B. Johnson responded to the Selma march of Dr. King by urging Congress to pass the Voting Rights Bill of 1965. The law authorized the attorney general to send federal registrars to assist Blacks in those southern counties where registration denial was greatest.[12] As a consequence of this law, Black political participation in southern politics increased immediately, and in less than three years Black officeholders in the South had risen from 76 in the early sixties to more than 800 in the early seventies. Blacks became participants in the political arena. They became elected to public office on the local, county, and state levels. The officers range from mayor and aldermen to county commissioners and state legislators. And each subsequent office saw a larger number of Black elected officials. As Table 3.1 indicates, Blacks hold a wide range of political offices in the states of the old Confederacy.

SOUTHERN BLACK POLITICAL STRATEGIES

Although pressure politics had established a foundation for Black politics in the South, political participation by Blacks took two basic forms: (1) independent or separatist politics and (2) coalition politics. This phase of Black southern politics, growing out of the older era, can be dubbed the *politics of electioneering*, that is, the election of Blacks to public office.

Table 3.1. Black Elected Officials in the South (January 1973)

State	Total	U.S.		State		County			City			Law Enforcement						Education		
		Senators	Representatives	Senators	Representatives	Commissioners	Election Committees	Others	Mayors	Council Members	Others	Judges	Magistrates	Constables	Marshalls, Sheriffs	Justice of Peace	Others	Superintendents	School Bd. Presidents	School Bd. Members
Alabama	144				2	9		10	8	48		1		50	4				1	11
Arkansas	140			1	3			1	8	46	12					19			2	49
Florida	51				3	1			3	36	4	1								3
Georgia	104		1	2	14	8		2		43	1	1				5		1	1	26
Louisiana	127				8	26			3	24		2		7	5	15			1	36
Mississippi	145				1	8	15	5	4	39	7			21	1	19				26
North Carolina	108				3	7			4	64		1							1	28
South Carolina	98				4	14		1	5	39			12							23
Tennessee	69			2	7					18	2	2	15	1		11				12
Texas	98		1		8					38						4			2	45
Virginia	60			1	2	17		2	3	27	7	1								
Total	1144[1]		2	6	55	90	15	21	38	422	33	9	27	79	10	73		1	8	259

[1] Four of these 1144 officials hold two offices. In Tennessee a state senator also serves as a city council member. In Arkansas, Georgia, and Mississippi a city council member also serves on a school board.

Source: Voter Education Project, "Black Elected Officials in the South: January 1973" (Atlanta, Georgia, 1973).

Black Separatist Politics

Due to the fact that some of the normal political mechanisms were closed to Blacks (e.g., the major political parties, some pressure organizations and political clubs), Blacks began a strategy of going it alone. This tactic, which numerous authors have called "separatist politics," has been seen as a no-win or dead-end strategy.[13] Using as an example the experience of the first serious Black separatist effort, the Lowndes County Freedom Organization, with its Black Panther label, many white and Black political observers indicated that it was a perfect illustration of the potential for failure in separatist Black political efforts. Although the Hamilton and Carmichael volume (*Black Power*) indicated clearly that in some instances Blacks could expect no allies and would find themselves outside of the regular political mechanisms and thus would have to go it alone,[14] cries and pronouncements of failure and reverse racism abound from scholars and political analysts.[15] However, despite those theoreticians who saw failure, it was necessary for Black political activists and leaders in numerous localities in the South to develop separate or independent political mechanisms. Among these mechanisms have been the Black political parties, the Black statewide voters league, political associations, racial candidates (i.e., those who sought only Black voters), and numerous Black community-level pressure groups.

Black parties have learned from each other's failures. The Mississippi Freedom Democratic Party (since the failure of the Lowndes County Freedom Organization in the 1966 election) reorganized itself and elected its first Black candidates in 1967 and thereafter.[16] This was four years after its inception. In Alabama Blacks who could not join the regular state Democratic Party, because of the type of leadership exemplified by George Wallace, formed the largely all-Black National Democratic Party of Alabama (NDPA). The NDPA has helped to elect numerous Black candidates and has established an all-Black county government in Greene County, Alabama.[17] The party has endorsed candidates for governor, mayor, and nearly every state, county and local office. Its leader, John Cashin, has made it one of the most viable Black parties to date.[18]

Blacks in South Carolina, following the examples set by the MFDP and the NDPA as well as a tradition in the state (Black South Carolinians had created a separatist party in 1944—the South Carolina Progressive Democratic Party) established in 1970 the United Citizens Party (UCP). The UCP had several candidates in the 1970 and 1972 elections and won some offices on the local level. In the main, Black parties operating either as independent or satellite organizations (in the orbit of a major national party) have been an important separatist thrust of contemporary Black politics and have succeeded in various localities in putting Blacks into political offices.

Another separatist political mechanism has been the statewide voting league. Blacks in Georgia set up such an organization in 1970 and ran Black candidates for all of the major state offices. Although the Black gubernatorial candidate got only seven percent of the votes cast, he nevertheless said that his candidacy was serious and hoped to make the major white candidates consider the poor political situation of Blacks in the state.[19]

Blacks in Louisiana tried the same technique in 1971 when they met in New Orleans, formed the Black Louisiana Action Committee (BLAC), and held a statewide convention on July 16-17. The League nominated its own candidates for all of the major state offices and supported them at a level similar to that of the Georgia league. The Louisiana gubernatorial candidate received about six and a half percent of the Black vote. In both states, the leagues underwent internal splits caused by political jealousy just before the election, and so each state had two Black candidates for governor.

In Arkansas and North Carolina independent Black candidates for governor emerged, but made little impact on the Black electorate. Other areas of the South have seen numerous Black community pressure groups and organizations seeking to place Blacks in power on the local and community levels. These organizations, like the parties, have achieved varying degrees of electoral success. Separatist Black politics, despite some denials to the contrary, has put many Blacks into public office.

Black Coalition Politics

In many southern localities Blacks have not had to go it alone or be shut out from participation in the normal political mechanisms. Blacks in these areas have achieved political offices with the aid of Black and white votes. The elections of Black mayors and vice-mayors of such cities as Atlanta, Georgia and Chapel Hill, North Carolina are good examples of success when Blacks unite with white allies to win public office. The elections of Blacks to the state legislature, aldermanic boards, and county commission posts have come in part due to the backing of white allies. The recent election of three Black congresspersons from the South is a further indication that the coalition strategy works. In each instance the Black candidate won with the aid of white votes. The results of these coalition efforts have led many analysts to view this as the wave of the future. "In politics it has long been a truism that no single group can win by itself. Each group needs allies. . . . Black power must be coupled in some degree with white power."[20] In their autobiographies, numerous Black politicians in the South (notably Julian Bond and Charles Evers) have stressed that coalition politics is the most important tool for Blacks to use in their struggle to gain more political offices in their communities. These leaders and others have, for the most part, eschewed separatist politics, except in very isolated cases. Alliances with whites are stressed and seen as the most viable method to get and maintain Black political power.

The politics of electioneering has taken two basic routes in the South, with both political avenues providing Blacks with political power and public offices: Both separatist and coalition techniques have proven successful and viable in certain areas.

Black Political Strategies
and Population Mix

At this point, however, the main concern is the difference between those who represent electoral districts with predominantly Black populations, and those representing districts where victory is dependent upon a sizable portion of the white vote.

86

To date, there is little scholarly analysis of the matter, but current literature suggests that Black elected officials from Black areas tend to take more militant stands and stronger positions on policy matters of interest to Blacks than do those with mixed districts. For instance, in his study of Greene County, Alabama (which is predominantly Black) Milton Lee Boykin found that Black candidates took a hard line on racial matters and sought to improve in a very specific fashion the housing, income, and welfare conditions of Black inhabitants.[21]

Journalist L. H. Whittemore, in his study of Black politicians in nine states found that campaign organization and policy concerns tend to fluctuate as the population mix changes.[22] He shows that Richard Austin, candidate for mayor of Detroit, Michigan, and Thomas Bradley, Edward Brooks, and Andrew Young in other racially mixed areas, ran entirely different campaigns and had a much broader focus than did candidates from predominantly Black districts (e.g., Julian Bond and Lonnie King in Georgia, and Imamu Amiri Baraka in Newark.[23] Even Julian Bond—in his pamphlet on Black candidates—hinted that campaign styles and platforms varied as the political unit's population structure changed. Much more research needs to be done on this matter. But at present, the literature and the nature of coalition political strategy indicate that expediency, compromise, and balanced platforms must be employed if an electoral victory is to be achieved. More dangerous than ideological dilution and compromise necessitated by racially mixed constituencies are direct efforts to constrain and contain Black political participation. We now turn to examine white resistance.

SOUTHERN WHITE RESISTANCE TO BLACK POLITICAL POWER

Some whites in the South are still trying to halt new Black political advances made since the 1965 Voting Rights Act. The present southern white aims to limit Black political power are: (1) repeal of the Voting Rights Act, (2) annexation, (3) consolidation, (4) regional government, (5) making elected offices appointive, and (6) a shift from ward and district elections to at-large and areawide elections.

The struggle by white politicos to retain their control of southern politics did not disappear with the enactment of the 1965 Voting Rights Act. In fact, the Civil Rights Commission Report on Black political participation revealed that the white effort to stymie Black politics was anything but over.[24] On the national level, southern congressmen tried to have the Voting Rights Act killed when it came up for renewal in 1970. The act is effective only for five years, and has to be renewed after each five-year period if it is to remain in effect. Thus, in 1970, when the act was up for renewal the southern congressmen tried to kill it or water it down with amendments. Their attempt failed in 1970 and in 1975 but might succeed in 1980. The nonrenewal of the Voting Rights Act would mean the disappearance of federal registrars and federal monitoring of the electoral process in southern states. Hence, the number of Black voters might once again decrease, and with their decline would be the concomitant vanishing of numerous Black elected officials.

Some southern whites have begun to align themselves with the Republican Party and their law and order candidates to stop desegregation efforts, repeal the Voting Rights Act and halt Black equality drives.[25]

On the state and local levels is the politics of annexation: the attachment of a predominantly Black area to a predominantly white area in order to dilute Black power and decrease the number of Black elected officials. In numerous localities throughout the South the process of annexation is well under way.[26]

Coupled with annexation is the politics of consolidation—combining the county government with the various local governments in the county to make a large *metrogovernment*. While annexation brings together one or two areas, consolidation unites *all surrounding areas* and sections and creates a large political unit. Under metrogovernmental schemes, Black representation generally decreases.[27] In the metropolitan charter proposed for Charleston, South Carolina, the mayor of the proposed metrogovernment would have full appointive power for all boards, commissions, and department heads. In addition, only three of the proposed eighteen aldermen could be elected from central cities, where Blacks are a majority.[28]

The metrogovernment has been a new device for further dilution of Black voting strength and the blunting of Black attempts to gain control of central cities in the urban South.

Recently, through the A-95 Review Process (a federally mandated procedure that requires participation in a regional planning process by local government units in a given region) the Federal government has made it mandatory for the five or six counties and cities in and around a metroarea to create a regional board to decide what impact new projects (e.g., housing, airports, health care centers) will have on the overall growth of a particular region. And this new regional board is to coordinate and review all areawide projects. This board, with members appointed by the local mayors and county commissioners, could veto or recommend the federal funding of projects in Black dominated areas or in cities where Blacks are a substantial portion of the region.[29]

Beyond regional governmental schemes are the efforts to have city and county elections at large, rather than by wards, which also in effect decrease Blacks' power to elect a large number of political officials and to concentrate their voting power. In this way, the number of Black elected officials would decline.

These new tools and many of the older techniques are in operation or are being put into practice to halt recent Black political advancements; and much of the political efforts of Blacks have been to thwart these new political devices.

In addition, a great deal of Black political energy has been focused on trying to get the Black electorate involved and activated. According to recent figures released by the Voter Education Project, more than 45 percent of the Black voter-age population in almost all of the southern states is still not registered and involved. Thus, political motivation and stimulation has absorbed the efforts of many Black elected officials. In this manner, then, defensive measures and techniques rather than offensive and corrective measures in the area of public policy have been a central thrust of Black politicians. Voter registration and turnout are defensive tactics. The entire rationale behind Blacks' efforts to secure the right to vote in the first place was seen not only as a device to improve their lot, but "the sovereign remedy for all . . . his grievances."[30] In the words of W. E. B. DuBois, the vote was the tool that Blacks needed for "sheer self-defense."[31] In the words and rhetoric of Black organizers and strategists, the vote became the political mechanism with which Blacks could protect themselves from continued encroachment by whites in their community. In the final analysis, then, voter registration and turnout, which has absorbed much of the energy and input of Black politics in the South, is a defensive measure.

In addition to the defensive measure of voter participation, the racial composition of many political units in the South has become important. It has further complicated Black political advancement because Black politicians and candidates are forced to modify their stand on politics and policy concerns to get white votes. Although public policy has been important to many Black officials, it still has not been the main concern due to the existence of these inhibiting factors. Thus, the Black community has not always reached the full benefits of political participation. The simple increase in Black decision makers has been, by and large, the chief reward. But the prospects for the future indicate a change of focus and emphasis from the politics of electioneering and defensive strategy to the politics of governance, decision making, and policy concern. Before we look at the prospects of Black politics in the future, we will examine southern Black politics in a specific case.

SOUTHERN BLACK POLITICS IN PRACTICE: THE ATLANTA MAYORALTY ELECTION OF 1973

On October 16, 1973, Atlanta became the first major metropolitan city in the South to elect a Black mayor. Although other southern cities, such as Raleigh and Durham, North Carolina had Black mayors, these were not major urban areas. Therefore, the election of Maynard H. Jackson as mayor of Atlanta has been hailed by most observers—both in and outside of the South—as a new step in the right direction for the state and the nation, if not a major turnabout in race relations. *The Pittsburgh Press* noted: "Voters may not be free of prejudice, but they know the color of a man's skin is a poor gauge of whether he's qualified to govern a modern American city." An analysis of the election will reveal many of the forces that have been present in southern politics from the past until the present.

Historically, the Black voter in Atlanta faced the same uphill battle to get the right to vote as did Blacks in other areas of the South. In the late 1930s, only about 25,000 Blacks in the city had the right to vote. And these voters were under the control of the city's only Black attorney, A. T. Walden, who also controlled and headed the local NAACP, YMCA, and Urban League. Later, Walden combined his small group of Democratic voters with those of the Black Republicans in the city to fashion an organization called the Atlanta Negro Voters League.[32]

Walden led this organization into a coalition with conservative whites in the city and kept a white mayor in power for twenty-three years, with no significant reward being granted to Blacks, who were an important base of support for the white power structure.[33] Walden died, the white mayor retired, and the old coalition began to crumble in the early 1960s. Moreover, the rise of the sit-in in Atlanta, and the efforts of Martin Luther King, Jr. and the Southern Christian Leadership Conference (SCLC) offered a new political awareness and structure.

In 1962, due to reapportionment, Atlanta elected the first Black to the Georgia legislature. A few years later it elected its first Black alderman; and then in the late 1960s the number of Black elected officials in the city slowly began to increase.

In 1969, a year after the death of Martin Luther King, Jr., Atlanta (whose motto is "a city too busy to hate") elected a Jewish mayor (Samuel Massell) and a Black vice-mayor (Maynard Jackson). Massell won precisely because of Black support; but in his first term in office he proposed to the state legislature an annexation plan that would have increased the number of whites in the city and significantly decreased Black political power. The plan was never called up in the state legislature.

In local politics, Massell appointed only a few Blacks as city government and department heads. The city government remains highly white dominated. Massell appointed a white police chief, who soon came down hard not only on Black policemen, but on the Black community as well. In one highly publicized incident, the police chief accused a Black alderman who headed the police committee of being a racket king and put him under 24-hour surveillance. The atmosphere became so heated that a grand jury ordered the chief to produce evidence to back up his accusation or publicly apologize to the alderman. When the date came for the revelation of the evidence the chief had none but refused to apologize.

The Black vice-mayor, Jackson, had no vote in council matters. In many instances he found himself opposing the mayor on policy positions whether he wanted to or not, because the mayor saw him as a potential threat and constantly tried to press him into positions that were seemingly antiwhite.

Hence, early in 1973, Jackson and two other Blacks announced their candidacy for mayor. Jackson, not being the heir to the old Walden machine, found himself trying to put together a Black-white coalition. As Table 3.2 indicates, Jackson significantly defeated the white incumbent, with four-fifths of his votes coming from the Black community. In fact, Jackson's total Black vote was double that of Massell. Nevertheless, a runoff was required by law and it was held on October 16, 1973.

In the runoff election Maynard Jackson received 95 percent of the total Black vote and 17.5 percent of the white vote. In a city that had mourned the death of Martin Luther King, Jr., and had told the nation that it was too busy to hate, Jackson was able to get only 17.5 percent of the white community into a coalition with him. Moreover, Massell's campaign was overtly racist—he claimed that a Black takeover spelled doom for Atlanta's financial future. Yet only 17.5 percent of the white voters left rank to aid and join Jackson.

Overall, the election results show that Jackson could have won even without a single white vote and in only a close election would white votes have made much difference.

In the race for president of the city council, a grassroots Black leader and outspoken militant, Hosea Williams, was opposed by a white business leader, Wyche Fowler. In this

✳ **Table 3.2. The 1973 Atlanta Mayoralty Election Results**

Total Registration (Sept. 20, 1973)	206,270	
Black	101,091 = 49%	
White	105,179 = 51%	

	October 2, 1973	*October 16, 1973*
MAYOR		
Total Votes Cast in Race.	102,069 = 49.5%	125,641 = 60.9%
Black	55,522 = 54.9%	67,550 = 66.8%
White	46,547 = 44.3%	58,091 = 55.2%
Votes for Maynard Jackson	47,609 = 46.6%	74,404 = 59.2%
Black	44,040 = 79.3%	64,216 = 95.0%
White	3,569 = 7.7%	10,188 = 17.5%
Votes for Samuel Massell	20,263 = 19.8%	51,237 = 40.7%
Black	3,888 = 7.0%	3,334 = 5.0%
White	16,375 = 35.2%	47,903 = 82.5%
PRESIDENT OF CITY COUNCIL		
Total Votes Cast in Race.	96,728 = 46.9%	122,226 = 59.2%
Black	50,772 = 50.2%	64,164 = 63.5%
White	45,956 = 43.7%	58,062 = 55.2%
Votes for Wyche Fowler	30,006 = 31.0%	78,209 = 63.9%
Black	5,218 = 10.3%	21,918 = 34.2%
White	24,788 = 53.9%	56,291 = 96.9%
Votes for Hosea Williams	29,009 = 29.9%	44,017 = 36.1%
Black	27,882 = 54.9%	42,246 = 65.8%
White	1,127 = 2.4%	1,771 = 3.1%

Source: Adapted from data collected by Clarence Bacote of Atlanta University.

race, the white community cast few ballots for the Black candidate. Even a significant portion of the Black community failed to support the Black militant.

The Atlanta election is a classic example of the numerous forces operating in southern politics, Black and white. It suggests that even a moderate Black candidate with a proven track record who works diligently to effect a Black-white

93

coalition will get only a small number of white supporters, not many more than twenty-five percent. Secondly, it reveals that the Black community will respond in a nearly unified manner if it has been significantly outraged.

The results also reveal that within the Black community there are numerous economic and social cleavages which impact voting. The upper- and lower-class Black wards in Atlanta voted for the white candidate, while the middle-income Black wards and a small percentage of the Black lower-class wards voted for the militant Black candidate.

Finally, the results show that under no circumstances would the white community (no matter how liberal its claims) support a Black militant to any significant degree. Outspoken Black militants in the South cannot hope in the near future to get any appreciable support from the white community.

BLACK POLITICAL PROSPECTS

To analyze the future of Black politics in the South one must distinguish "between having power and being associated with those who have it, between participating in the decisional process and actually influencing the outcome of that process, and between the symbolic trappings of political power and political power itself."[34] In other words, having Black representation and Black elected officials is not necessarily having power. One must be able to bring this power to bear upon the party who has it and persuade it to act in one way or another. To meet the tremendous social, political, economic, and welfare requirements of the Black community it is necessary to develop specific policy options and obtain the power to achieve them. This process, known as the setting of a Black agenda, has not been carried out in most Black communities; nor have Black representatives agreed on Black priorities and needs.

It has been difficult to operationalize Black power in most instances because Blacks do not have enough representation or control in the local, county, and state decision-making agencies. As a result, political payoffs have been slow, unsystematic, poorly coordinated, lacking in continuity, and partial in results.

94

In other words, in some places Blacks having gotten better lighted and paved streets and an increase in police protection; in other Black areas there are new industries, jobs, and more Blacks in public employment; and in other areas there is nothing but a Black public official, that is, symbolic recognition. In short, present Black political representation has not meant an increase of public policy decisions that are sufficient to solve all the problems inherent to Black communities after centuries of segregation and discrimination.\

The number of Black elected municipal officials in the South has steadily increased, but the socioeconomic position of Blacks has not increased proportionately. In South Carolina, where Black elected officials are up 62.1 percent, Black male unemployment has risen from 3.6 percent in 1960 to 4.6 percent in 1970. The picture for Mississippi reveals that unemployment was 7 percent in 1970, but was only 3.1 percent in 1960. Since the unemployment rate in some states has increased, the median income has risen only slightly, and not in proportion to the rise in Black elected officials. In Mississippi the rise in Black officials has been 31 percent but the rise in median Black family income does not anywhere approximate this increase in representation. At the present time there is not much data on this subject, but what there is suggests a low correlation between the rise in Black representation and improvement in the socioeconomic conditions of the Black masses. As Graph 3.1 shows, the median income of white families in the southern states is much higher than that of Black families in the Black majority counties. In fact, the number of Black families in the Black dominated counties with incomes below the poverty level is double that of the whites in the white dominated counties. Therefore it follows that the number of Black families in the Black counties who need public assistance is also very high.

The trend is similar for education and other socioindices in the Black dominated counties. Economically they are now, and have been historically, the most in need in terms of social services, economic relief, and employment opportunities. This means that the per capita outlay to improve these areas will need to be higher than it will in white communities. This money will have to be raised at the state, federal, or private level,

95

Graph 3.1. Median Income for Southern Families by States

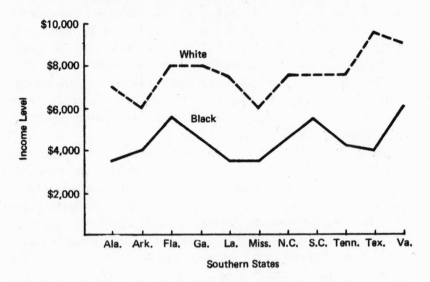

Southern States

because to increase the taxes of people already below the poverty line to improve their economic condition would be a self-defeating policy.

Thus, Black politicans coming to power in predominantly Black areas will have to develop new and innovative economic policies if they want to put Blacks on a level with whites.

Because the immediate impact of the Black political thrust has been noticeable only in the area of political representation, it does not mean that long-range payoffs in other areas will not be forthcoming.

The number of cities in the South with more than 35 percent Black population is indeed large. Based on 1972 projections and growth rates, Blacks could be the majority policy and decision makers on the governing bodies in 14 of these urban areas before the end of the decade. In addition, the number of Black congressmen from the South could rise before the end of the century, and Blacks could control more than 10 counties in Alabama, 4 in Arkansas, 2 in Florida, 21 in Georgia, 13 in Louisiana, 26 in Mississippi, 6 in North Carolina, 14 in South Carolina, 1 in Tennessee, 1 in Texas, and 12 in Virginia. It can be seen that the number of southern cities, counties, and congressional districts that Blacks can control by the end of

96

the century is quite large. These are primarily areas where separatist politics can be pursued with a significant degree of success. In other areas in the South where Blacks can pursue coalition political strategies to achieve victory are 17 cities, 115 counties, and 22 congressional districts.

Therefore, through coalition and separatist political strategies Blacks in the South can come to dominate a significant amount of political power. Once Black representation on decision-making boards begins to approach the level of parity, policy decisions reflecting the priorities of the Black community have the potential for tremendous creative impact. Moreover, the major state services in the areas of education, health and welfare, law enforcement and public protection, natural resources, planning, housing and development, labor and industrial relations, will begin to reflect this political impact.

A systematic analysis of the 1972-73 volume of the *The Book of the States,* which summarizes expenditures and services, does not reveal such an impact after 7 years of participation.[35] However, before the decade is over, state services for Blacks and other minorities in the South will become a major concern and a major recipient of public funds. The political institutions of state and local governments cannot possibly absorb the coming increase in reform-orientated Black elected officers without reflecting these new concerns in public policy and administration.

SUMMARY

In summary, the politics of electioneering in the South has created avenues of both separatist and coalition politics. These political strategies have achieved only a very small portion of their potential impact, but as they begin to reach their optimum levels, the policies needed by the Black community will emerge and possibly create a new southern political revolution. Areas where separatist politics flourish should experience the greatest socioeconomic impact first. In areas where Blacks are majorities, the greatest payoff and impact of electoral politics will be seen first because Blacks will control the policy boards and the

97

decision-making apparatus and will formulate and implement economic policies that will affect Blacks. The two greatest contemporary examples are Fayette, Mississippi and Greene County, Alabama, where the Black community has benefited economically from the influx of new jobs, federal projects, and foundation funds as a result of Black control. In these areas the presence of economic rewards can be seen with greater clarity than in areas where Blacks are a smaller part of the political units and must share more of the benefits given to the community at large. Both areas will operate as spurs to each other and help make political promises a reality in the coming decades. If there is a rise of Black policy makers, the South will see numerous governmental reforms and political improvement. The thrust of contemporary Black political activity has been reformist and corrective in nature, and southern political institutions need much improvement and change if progressive measures are to benefit its inhabitants.[36]

NOTES

1. Charles Evers and Grace Halsell, *Evers* (New York: World Publishing, 1971), p. 11.

2. Fannie Lou Hamer, "If the Name of the Game is Survive, Survive," in Nathan Wright, Jr., ed., *What Black Politicians Are Saying* (New York: Hawthorn, 1972), p. 44.

3. Quoted in Hanes Walton, Jr., *The Poetry of Black Politics* (London: Regency Press, 1972), p. 15. See also H. Rap Brown, *Die Nigger, Die* (New York: Dial, 1970).

4. Mack H. Jones, "Black Officeholders in Local Governments of the South: An Overview," *Politics 1971* (March 1971): 72.

5. Julian Bond, *A Time to Speak, A Time to Act* (New York: Simon & Schuster, 1972), p. 148.

6. Hanes Walton, Jr., "Black Politics in the South," *Ebony* (August 1971): 141-142.

7. For a discussion of a variety of these tactics see Charles Hamilton and Stokely Carmichael, *Black Power* (New York: Random House, 1969); and Reese Cleghorn and Pat Walters, *Climbing Jacobs Ladder* (New York: Harcourt Brace Jovanovich, 1967).

8. See Hanes Walton, Jr., *Black Politics: A Theoretical and Structural Analysis* (Philadelphia: Lippincott, 1972).

9. Bernard Taper, *Gomillion vs. Lightfoot* (New York: McGraw-Hill, 1962).

10. See Donald Matthews and James Prothro, *Negroes and the New Southern Politics* (New York: Harcourt Brace Jovanovich, 1966).

11. Walton, *Black Politics,* p. 124.

12. See U.S. Commission on Civil Rights, *Political Participation* (Washington, D.C., U.S. Government Printing Office, 1968), pp. 202-211 for the full text of the law.

13. For an explanation of this point of view see Harry Holloway, *The Politics of the Southern Negro* (New York: Random House, 1969), pp. 310-357.

14. Hamilton and Carmichael, *Black Power,* pp. 58-84.

15. Hanes Walton, Jr., *Black Political Parties* (New York: Free Press, 1972), pp. 131-157.

16. Ibid.

17. L. H. Whittemore, *Together: A Reporter's Journey into the New Black Politics* (New York: Morrow, 1971), pp. 265-287.

18. Walton, *Black Parties,* pp. 149-157.

19. See Hanes Walton, Jr. and Delacy Sanford, "Black Governors and Gubernatorial Candidates 1868-1972," forthcoming article.

20. Holloway, *Politics of the Southern Negro,* p. 356.

21. Milton Lee Boykin, "Black Political Participation in Greene County, Alabama," *Politics 1973* (March 1973): 51-56.

22. Whittemore, *Together.*

23. Ibid., pp. 302-316.

24. See Commission, *Political Participation,* pp. 19-132.

25. Earl Black and Merle Black, "The Changing Setting of Minority Politics in the American Deep South," *Politics 1973* (March 1973): 42-45. See E. Baseman, "Deep South Republicans, Profits and Positions," in B. Baseman and R. T. Huckshorm, eds. *Republican Politics* (New York: Praeger, 1968).

26. On this matter, see Lee Sloan and Robert M. French, "Black Rule in the Urban South?" *Transaction* 19 (December 1971): 32; and Joseph Zimmerman, "Metropolitan Reforms in the U.S.: An Overview," *Public Administration Review,* (October 1970): 537-538.

27. On this matter see Richard L. Engstrom and W. E. Lyons, "Black Control or Consolidation: The Fringe Response," *Social Science Quarterly* (June 1972): 161-167.

28. Walton, *Black Politics,* p. 223.

29. Such a regional board has just been created in the Atlanta metro-county area and has a 31 member board with no provision for Black representation.

30. Walton, *Black Politics,* p. 3.

31. Ibid.

32. Ibid., p. 67.

33. Edward C. Banfield, *Big City Politics,* (New York: Random House, 1965), p. 34.

34. Mack H. Jones, "Blacks and Politics in Atlanta: Myth and Reality," 1972 (Unpublished paper), p. 1.

35. Council of State Government, *The Book of the States, 1972-73* (Kentucky: Council of State Government, 1972).

36. See Robert Sherrill, *Gothic Politics in the South* (New York: Grossman, 1968).

4

LEGAL STRATEGY
FOR BLACKS IN
THE COMING DECADES
Freedom—the Goal;
Legal Redress—the Tool

Lois B. Moreland

Lois Baldwin Moreland is presently Professor and Chairman of the Political Science Department, Spelman College, Atlanta, Ga. Her book, *White Racism and the Law*, is in current use in a number of colleges and universities in graduate and undergraduate courses. Dr. Moreland is a former Dean of Instruction at Spelman College.

The challenge to develop legal strategy for Blacks in the coming decades involves a review of the major problem areas and issues that plague the lives of Black Americans. It involves a determination as to whether some problems are more devastating than others and a judgment as to which of these require priority attention. The procedure further involves an assessment of the powers inherent in the legal process and the judicial branch of government that can be addressed to these problems and that can effect significant change in the lives of Black Americans. It involves awareness of the political realities and constraints intermingled with these powers. For example, the Supreme Court of the United States cannot enforce its own decisions. The executive branch must enforce them. Attention is drawn to the distinction made between the law, per se, and application of the law.

The purpose of this article is to propose a legal strategy (theory) which, when applied, will aid in eliminating racism, its vestiges, and the deprivations that flow therefrom.

In reviewing the multiplicity of problems that denigrate the Black community, no objective standard was found that could be used as a guide to determine which areas are most critical. The establishment of priorities would have required arbitrary choice. It also appeared from the investigation that in developing legal strategy using a problem-area approach, it would be necessary to propose specific strategies to accommodate specific problems. This approach seemed piecemeal and ineffective. Moreover, it probably could not be applied universally because of local situations.[1] Thus, the approach to develop an issue-oriented legal strategy was abandoned. Nonetheless, it is informative to review some of the gross inequities experienced by Blacks as reflected in selected statistical data:[2]

Blacks own only 2 percent of all business

Blacks account for only 3.5 percent of all housing equity

Blacks account for only 6.6 percent of all personal income

Blacks account for only 6.6 percent of all college enrollment

Blacks account for 25 percent of all unemployment

Median family income for Blacks is about 60 percent of white family income; stated another way, the average Black family's income is about 40 percent less than the average white family's income

Forty-two percent of Blacks 20 and 21 years old have not completed high school

One-third of all Blacks are still below the poverty level, which for a nonfarm family of 4 was $3,743 in 1969

Since 1964, Blacks have been less than 1 percent of all Ph.D.'s granted

Black banks handle less than 1 percent of the total banking business

Summer unemployment of Blacks ages 16-21 during summer 1969 and July 1970 was 30.2 percent compared to whites of the same age and same time period of only 16 percent

Blacks comprise only about three-tenths of the total number of elected public officials, although 10 percent of the voting population is Black and Blacks comprise at least 40 percent of the population in 14 major cities

Still other kinds of problems confront Blacks. For example, that portion of the Black community that purchases items such as clothing, furniture, stereos, and televisions from neighborhood credit stores pays as much as 200 percent to 300 percent

104

more when paying on an installment basis.[3] Blacks pay over 10 percent more for housing in ghetto areas than do their white counterparts.[4] There are also problems in the administration of criminal justice. The personnel is preponderantly white.[5] Only 1 percent of all lawyers are Black; there is one Black lawyer for every 8,000 people; in the south there is one Black lawyer for every 28,000 people. Black enrollment in law schools is only 1.3 percent. There are "only 65 Black state judges;" and only "15 out of over 300 federal judges."[6] Double standards of justice are imposed, such as exorbitant bail, surety bonds, and harsh sentences for frivolous charges.[7]

The issue that receives the most public attention, however, is school desegregation. Because of its high visibility, because of its fundamental importance to the Black community and its crisis potential, a specific legal strategy will be proposed.

Perhaps it was naive for the Black community to believe that justice and fairness would prevail in implementing the Supreme Court's school desegregation decision[8] and decree[9] almost 20 years ago. Surely, it was not expected that racism would disappear, but it was expected that in a country that believes in "law and order" the law would be enforced. Instead, it has been 19 years of hypocrisy and deceit via evasive techniques, despite the Court's ruling that no evasive tactic would be approved.[10] Recently there has been a flurry of activity in opening new white private schools; there has been the white flight to the suburbs; even closing an entire school system[11] was attempted to avoid the comingling and education of Black children with white children. More recent are the political attempts to merge county and municipal systems and political districts.[12] Merger would attenuate the political power of a growing Black municipal population and decrease the overall ratio of Black-white students. Consolidation probably would result, in most instances, in retention of the white majority power position. Consolidation presumably is to improve utilization of resources and to solve community problems that transcend existing boundaries. As an overall political scheme, it looks like the same evasive design.

In the controversy over busing students and in developing quotas to determine when a school is or is not in compliance

105

with the Court's requirement, the decision seems always to be that Blacks are to be transferred to the white school.[13] Why must it always be the Blacks who transfer? Blacks have lost Black principals and Black schools in the desegregation process because the Black high schools have been closed and Black principals made assistants in the white schools. This loss decreased the number of important positive role models necessary in the socialization of Black children. In an editorial *The Voice* said:

> State and local officials used desegregation as a tool with which to fire and demote Black school educators. . . . Since the 1954 Supreme Court decision some 31,000 Black teachers have lost their jobs. In [sic] 1970 alone, the Black community lost a quarter of a billion dollars in income because of this. Many Black principals were either forced out of the system, or had white principals placed above them while their own title and responsibilities shrank to the assistant principal level.[14]

Another dangerous development appears. "Pressures to merge the Black state colleges in the south with the predominantly white colleges may result in a new purge of college teachers and administrators."[15] Desegregation could be the tool to achieve it.

It seems from the current debate over busing,[16] that some of the original reasoning as understood by the writer for projecting school desegregation as a means to achieve equal education for Black children has been lost. It should be resurrected and placed into the debate. Perhaps this will put into perspective the issues of busing, Black-white quotas, and the like. These should be viewed as tools or techniques to be used, if necessary, to implement the 1954 decision. Busing and quotas are not ends in themselves, although they may appear to be. Even the concept of desegregation as an end or goal is questionable, although actual realization of the goal—equality— may result in desegregation. Desegregation should be viewed as a means or tool to achieve equal educational opportunity.

Some of that original reasoning, from this writer's view,

was that having gone through a "separate but equal" society since 1896,[17] it seemed unlikely in 1954 that the concept of equal education would be realized through continued segregation of Blacks and whites into separate communities. The separate but equal doctrine had not been enforced. Separation was enforced but equal educational facilities and opportunities had not been made available to Blacks despite the *Plessy* ruling.[18] There was little reason to believe that the money to develop equal facilities would come to the Black schools. The means to expose Black children to equal education, it appeared, would be to place Black and white children together into the schools. A disproportionate sum of the available money to develop educational facilities, historically, had been given to those schools where white children attended. The money followed the white children. There was little reason to believe this practice would not continue.

The goal of equal education apparently was unacceptable to the white community because the mechanism to achieve the goal was desegregation "with all deliberate speed." There has been little, if any, objection to giving "quality education." Efforts were made to thwart the decision. Subsequent evasive techniques seem completely to have displaced the original goal by emphasizing techniques to avoid it. Thus, the Court was placed in the unusual position of a continuing supervision of an implementation decree. That 1955 decree was in itself unusual. Vindication of a right should be immediate. It appears that the Court was making a political judgment as well as a judicial judgment when it said the right should be vindicated "with all deliberate speed." That term did not carry with it a specific time period by which schools were to be desegregated. "With all deliberate speed" meant that local school boards should make "a prompt and reasonable start" with "good faith compliance" toward desegregation, or begin "as soon as practicable."[19]

It is not the percentage of students and faculty, Black or white, in a school that determines whether equal education is available there. That goal is determined by another level: by those who run the school system in the decisions they make about money, current student-teacher ratio, etc. In 1954 it was unlikely that Blacks could be a part of that policy-making administrative coterie. In 1976 it is possible and desirable.

The Atlanta, Georgia school desegregation case[20] suggests a legal strategy different from that previously employed. Its approach coincides with the analysis above.

The National Association for the Advancement of Colored People (NAACP) and the Legal Defense Fund are the major architects of the legal strategy used to desegregate the public schools. Lonnie King, President of the Atlanta branch of the NAACP, summarized that strategy.[21] In preparation for the Atlanta school desegregation case, he traced the twenty years of Legal Defense Fund and NAACP school cases. He found that most were directed toward pupil desegregation, and in the late 1960s the thrust was toward faculty desegregation. Some of the problems that Black Atlanta children face involved suspension of Black students by white administrators for petty reasons, teacher-student relations, poor reading scores, lack of qualified personnel to operate the new equipment in the schools. He asked rhetorically: "How could these problems be solved by increasing the number of Blacks in white schools or vice versa? What do you do in a school system where more money is being spent on the Black child and the child still isn't reading?"

The NAACP legal strategy had been based on an assumption that the money follows the white child. Even with more money, King reasoned, Atlanta's unequal educational opportunity persists. After assessing the Atlanta problems and NAACP strategy, he concluded that the Black-white numbers game yielded no solution because the Atlanta difficulties stemmed from administrative problems: school assignment plans, selection of sites for new schools, curriculum development, personnel, appropriations for particular schools. Although school boards make policy for the systems, boards are, in fact, rubber stamps of the administrative apparatus that runs the school. This is not negligence; it is not their fault. School board offices are part-time jobs. The administrative apparatus has information and facilities that the board does not have. Boards must rely on the information given to them by this administrative source. The "root and branch of the problem" is found in the administrative apparatus. What was needed was "administrative desegregation." Perhaps it was not the complete answer, but in King's judgment, the better approach would be to put someone in an administrative position who is committed to eliminating the problems. To the extent that white racism had contributed to the educational problems of Black children, placing Blacks on the administrative staff could neutralize the racism and eliminate its effects.

The Atlanta case struggled through the courts for years. It was originally filed in January 1958. The Fifth Circuit Court of Appeals told the Atlanta school board that it must come up with a plan to totally desegregate the schools. According to King, that mandate set in motion the kind of climate necessary to gain approval of a plan for administrative desegregation—a plan for Black parity in the administrative apparatus. It was fear of coming into the inner city, King suggested, which prompted the white community, after much jockeying and submission of alternate plans, to give up some of its power, its control of the administrative machinery. He said it was not easy.

There were three facets to the plan:[22] administrative staff desegregation, teacher changes, and pupil transfer in a majority to minority (M & N) plan. M & N means that a student may transfer from a school in which he or she is in the majority to one in which he or she will be in the minority. Such transfer will be on a voluntary basis and transportation will be provided by the school system. A coordinator and citizens' advisory group will be responsible to the board for the success of the M & N program.

Below are copies of data taken from the brief, which present the nucleus of the plan.

Administrative Desegregation[23]

The school system will be headed by a Black Superintendent, the first in Atlanta's history.

	Number of Positions	Race
Superintendent	1	Black
Associate Superintendent — Administration	1	White—New Staff Position

Administrative Desegregation (Continued)

	Number of Positions	Race
Associate Superintendent — Operations	1	Black—New Staff Position
Assistant Superintendent — Community Affairs	1	Black
Assistant Superintendent — Administrative Services	1	White
Assistant Superintendent — Personnel	1	Black
Comptroller — Finance	1	White
Deputy Comptroller — Finance	1	Black—New Staff Position
Assistant Superintendent — Plant Planning	1	White
Director of Plant Planning	1	Black—New Staff Position
*Assistant Superintendent — Research and Development	1	New Staff Position
Director of Research and Development	1	Black—New Staff Position
*Assistant Superintendent — Vocational Education	1	New Staff Position
*Assistant Superintendent — Intergovernmental Programs	1	New Staff Position
Assistant Superintendent — Instruction	1	Black
Area Superintendents	5	3 Black, 2 White
Staff Attorney — Director Level	1	Black
Coordinator — Liaison Services	1	Black—New Staff Position
Director of Payroll and Certification	1	Black—New Staff Position
Coordinator of Vocational Personnel	1	Black—New Staff Position
Deputy Director of Educational Broadcasting	1	Black—New Staff Position

*At least one of these positions must be filled by a Black.

Administrative Desegregation (Continued)

	Number of Positions	Race
Food Service Coordinator	3	Black—New Staff Position
Assistant Area Superintendent	5	2 Must Be Black—New Staff Position
Director of M to N Transfers	1	Black—New Staff Position
Coordinator of M to N Transfers	1	White—New Staff Position
Directors	2	Black

Teacher Changes[24]

Note that the total number of changes for Blacks and whites is the same.

TEACHER CHANGES RESULTING FROM PROPOSED STAFF INTEGRATION PLAN

[ ] Denotes teachers removed. Nonbracketed number denote teachers added.

ELEMENTARY

	B	W
Ben Hill	3	[3]
Bethune	[3]	3
Birney	4	[4]
Continental Colony	5	[5]
English	[2]	2
Fain	[2]	2
Home Park	3	[3]
Hope, R. L.	3	[3]
Hutchison	2	[2]
Inman	3	[3]
Jackson	3	[3]
Kimberly	3	[3]
Morningside	2	[2]
Pitts	[2]	2
Wesley	[3]	3
Changes Required (Persons Involved)	43	43

111

Teacher Changes (Continued)

| | *HIGH* | |
	B	*W*
Archer	[6]	6
Dykes	12	[12]
Fulton	4	[4]
Grady	4	[4]
Howard	[5]	5
North Fulton	4	[4]
Northside	10	[10]
O'Keefe	3	[3]
Price	[5]	5
Roosevelt	4	[4]
Turner	[5]	5
Washington	[5]	5
Changes Required (Persons Involved)	67	67
TOTAL	220	

Majority to Minority Transfer[25]

The following criteria are guidelines for the M & N program.

1. No school would contain less than 30 percent Black students.
2. No exceptions unless a school was shown to be stable and integrated 20 percent or more Black.
3. White students would be transferred only into white schools where the resulting enrollment would be 30 percent white.
4. All Black schools unaffected or left "untouched" would be determined according to agreed upon objective criteria such as condition of the building, classroom space, distance to other schools, and phasing out.
5. Rules 1 through 4 would be applied in all effort to maximize integration of all students.

It was further agreed that the following methods would be employed toward reaching the above in the listed order of priority:

1. Redrawing of zone lines
2. Closing of schools
3. Pairing with the closest schools of the opposite race

The plan concludes with a statement that attempts to justify the allocation of jobs on a racial basis. It is a statement that might be used to justify other goal-implementing tools such as affirmative action, preferential treatment, and reparation. These, too, sometimes loom as ends in themselves. The statement reads:

> The racial designations indicated in the plan for desegregation of administration are made to remedy alleged past discriminatory practices with respect to the hiring of administrative personnel. These racial designations are for a one-time basis only and all future hiring, firing, promoting, demoting and recruiting shall be based on non-discriminatory individual qualifications without regard to race.

Along with the Atlanta branch, the above court-approved plan was submitted as a compromise by plaintiffs, defendants, and a court-appointed biracial committee. The national office of the NAACP sent a telegram to Lonnie King in which he was informed that the Atlanta branch settlement did not conform to the policy established by the NAACP 1971 national convention. The plan requires only a small amount of busing and according to King will not greatly change the present Black-white ratio in 80 percent or more of the schools. Ultimately, King, the other officers, and board members of the Atlanta branch were suspended by the national office. The Atlanta branch has been put on notice that the settlement will be appealed by The Legal Defense Fund. The survey below indicates that a majority of the Atlanta Black community supports the plan.[26]

113

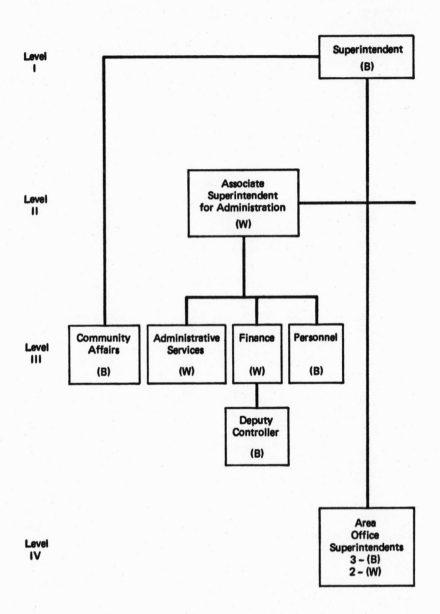

Level
I
Superintendent
(B)

Level
II
Associate
Superintendent
for Administration
(W)

Level
III
Community
Affairs
(B)
Administrative
Services
(W)
Finance
(W)
Personnel
(B)

Deputy
Controller
(B)

Level
IV
Area
Office
Superintendents
3 – (B)
2 – (W)

Graph 4.1. Administrative Organization

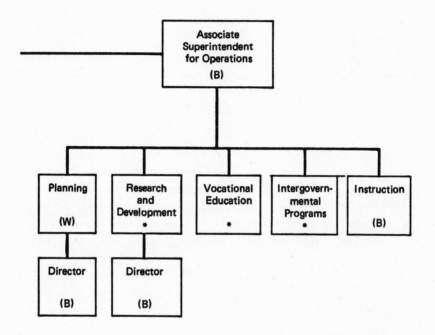

*At least one position to be Black.

TABLE 4.1. Opinion of Proposal on Education and Busing[1]

	WHITES BY OCC				BLACKS BY OCC	
	City-wide	Bus-Prof	White Col	Blue Col	Manual S/skld	Bus-Prof/ White Col	Blue Col/ Man/S-skld
	%	%	%	%	%	%	%
Approve	42	40	25	21	31	56	55
Disapprove	38	35	49	53	51	31	28
Depends	13	18	18	12	11	9	10
Don't know	7	7	8	14	7	4	7
	100	100	100	100	100	100	100

[1] *"A proposal:* Through a compromise between the NAACP and the Atlanta school board, it has been proposed that a Black be appointed as the superintendent of schools and that there be only a small amount of busing of school children."

King said that the Legal Defense Fund challenges the Atlanta plan because it is in violation of *Swann* v. *Charlotte-Mecklenberg,*[27] in which the expectation is that each school will reflect the ratio of Blacks to whites in the school district. In Atlanta, Black school children comprise 79 percent of the 94,000 students.[28] King's observation was that even with massive busing, given the present 79:21 ratio, "What is the difference between having 80 percent students Black and 90 percent students Black?" The "plan increases the number of students in desegregated schools from 27,239 to 37,605. It increases the number of desegregated schools from 47 to 64."[29] He stated that because Atlanta's situation is unique, a unique remedy was necessary.

It would seem, in this writer's view, that despite local situations, the legal strategy that seeks the acquisition of power for Blacks to significantly participate in those decisions that affect the Black community is an approach that is applicable to school desegregation cases, per se. For example, this strategy eliminates the court's self-imposed need to distinguish between de jure and de facto segregation. The state action limitation inherent in the de jure distinction results in focusing attention on southern school desegregation as opposed to northern desegregation requirements. The *Swann* busing decision is limited to areas where there has been a history of de jure segregation. In northern cities, the problems stem more from de facto segregation and *Swann* need not apply. Yet, the problems of unequal educational opportunity result from both de facto and de jure separation. Further, it has been in the administrative apparatus that decisional information was compiled to justify the closing of Black high schools, then sending Black children to the white high schools. It was at this level that it was decided that Black high school principals be demoted to assistant principals in the white high schools. And it was at the administrative level that decisions were initiated to make Black high schools into junior high schools. One result of such decisions is the loss of role models for Black students. Another is the loss of a layer of leadership in the Black community. A political by-product of this strategy might be the appeal it would have to that group of Blacks who distrust the system and who want racial segregation because the system has been unjust in its implementation of the 1954 decision; it might also appeal to that group of Blacks who still believe desegregation can work. At least in this approach the opportunity for more equitable implementation should be increased.

For the first time, the U.S. Supreme Court in a major decision addressed itself to school desegregation in the north.[30] This decision relates to what has been said about the Atlanta case. In the Denver, Colorado case, "the court held 7 to 1 that once a school system has been caught in significant acts of discrimination, it has a heavy burden of showing why it should not be compelled to desegregate all the schools in the district."[31] The Court applied the de jure-de facto distinction. What were the "significant acts of discrimination?" The acts were those made by the school board. Lower courts had found that it had manipulated attendance zones to retain a predominantly Black and Mexican-American school attendance in the Park High neighborhood; and that there was deliberate segregation in selecting the site for the new elementary school in the middle of a Black community. Such choice would retain segregation. Denver had exaggerated the amount of school desegrega-

117

tion by counting "Hispanos" as part of the anglo population. By proving discrimination in one section of the city, it was to be presumed that discrimination existed elsewhere, according to the courts. The burden of proof rested on the school board to prove it had no "discriminatory motive in the core area." If it does not so prove, then it must show "that its past acts had not contributed to or created the current center-city condition."

While the Court shifted the burden of proof onto the board (which is where it should be), the board, no doubt, had based its decisions on information and recommendations made by the administrative staff of the school system. It is at this level, as previously stated, that school sites are selected, curriculum developed, and the like. Employment of Blacks in key positions on the administrative staff could conceivably relieve the Court of looking at these administrative decisions to determine whether they were racially motivated; whether the schools' racial patterns exist because of intentional segregation or historical actions; and whether the patterns result from de jure or de facto reasons. The school desegregation plans would be drawn, presumably, without racism because Blacks in key administrative positions would have power to neutralize that element. "Racial balance" is merely a tool and is not to be confused with the goal of equal education. Another tool, and the one proposed, is the acquisition by Blacks of administrative power in the school system. The legal strategy is "administrative desegregation."

The Denver decision was decided by the "Nixon Court." On the same day that it was announced, the Court handed down a series of 5-4 decisions. While it broke new ground by deciding a northern case based on de jure factors used in southern cases, this Court made a significant departure in one of these decisions in a due process principle established by the "Warren Court." New law was made. In past years the Court has been accused of "making law" in race relations and by so doing has been attacked as acting beyond its area of jurisdiction, as being activist. What is the role of the Court in making law?

THE COURT AS A POLITICAL AGENCY

Political strategy is often given a narrow definition, which excludes judicial activity. Political strategy as narrowly defined might be directed toward activities such as increasing the number of Black voters, increasing the number of Black public officials, developing temporary and shifting political coalitions between Blacks and others who share mutual interests and needs, exerting political pressures upon legislators and other elected officials, employing economic boycotts, organizing and mobilizing protest and confrontation demonstrations, employing creative disruption techniques, and utilizing guerilla warfare techniques.

Furthermore, it has been asserted that there already are sufficient laws and court decisions to give Blacks all the rights of first-class citizenship. The problem, it is suggested, is that the laws and court decrees have not been enforced. Since the executive branches on both state and national levels of government have the responsibility of enforcement, "administration of the law is nine-tenths of the law." It will be enforced at the will of these executives. This charge of judicial impotence highlights the need for examining the scope of and limitations on the powers of the judicial branch.

Also legal strategy is often ignored because of the lingering belief that the judicial branch of government is outside the political process, that the law is not political in its application, that "justice is blind," that all that is required of the objective judge is to determine the will of the legislature and apply the statute, or base the decision on history and precedent, using the principle of stare decisis. This belief is unsubstantiated when examined. In interpretating the law and in deciding cases, judges do make subjective decisions.[32] Their judgments necessarily involve choices between competing values, claims, and interests.

Because this belief appears to be so widespread, because of the respect in which the Supreme Court is held, and because of the pervasive influence, if not power, of the Court upon the American belief system and lifestyle as keeper of the "constitutional conscience,"[33] it is important that an examination of this question be made an integral part of this article.

119

The distinguished jurist and Supreme Court Associate Justice, Benjamin Cardozo, wrote, "It is when . . . there is no decisive precedent that the serious business of the judge begins. He must then fashion law."[34] He wrote further, "Finally, when the social needs demand one settlement rather than another, there are times when we must bend symmetry and ignore history and sacrifice custom in the pursuit of other and larger ends."[35] He stated that the method for filling the "gaps in the law" is sociological. Its emphasis is on social welfare. Quoting from Dean Pound, Justice Cardozo wrote: "The emphasis has changed from the content of the precept and the existence of the remedy to the effect of the precept in action and the availability and efficiency of the remedy to attain the ends for which the precept was devised."[36] It is the ends, the goals to be reached, that determine the just choices between competing claims.

Cardozo's words should be remembered when seeking to achieve the goal of equal education. The remedies of busing and quotas seem inadequate to achieve the goal; another remedy should be sought. Administrative desegregation was suggested. Focusing upon the goal allows for greater flexibility in seeking a remedy.

The political role of the judiciary may be illustrated by examining the part it played in the reapportionment of the state legislatures and the Congress of the United States. There was a significant increase in the number of Black legislators following legislative reapportionment.[37] In 1960 there were only 36 Black state legislators. As of the 1970 elections there were 205.[38] That increase should not be totally credited to the rise in the percentage of Black voters. There were 3.3 million Blacks registered in the 11 states in the south as of the 1970 elections.[39] Most Black elected officials come from these states (one-third of the total or 684 of 1769). In 1968 there was a total of only 643 Black elected officials.[40] Nor should this significant increase be attributed exclusively to passage of the Voting Rights Act of 1965.[41] It was the initial reapportionment and related decisions[42] by the Supreme Court that ordered that state legislatures and the Congress must be reapportioned to reflect their respective population shifts. These decisions precipitated activities that resulted in increased numbers of Black legislators. Because Blacks were moving to urban areas in large numbers (in 14 major cities Blacks constitute 40 percent of the population),[43] because whites are moving to the suburbs and if the Black birthrate continues to be much higher than that of whites,[44] Black acquisition of political power through elective officials should continue to grow.

It should be apparent that the consequences of the Court's decisions that legislative assemblies must reapportion themselves to reflect these population shifts had significant political impact. What may be less apparent is that the Court played a political role because it answered a political question. The Court had refused to rule on a reapportionment case in 1946[45] when the issue was brought before it. The Illinois state legislature had not redrawn its legislative district lines since 1901. It was alleged that great disparities in equal representation in the House of Representatives was the result. The Court had refused to answer political questions previously. It said that such questions were "nonjusticiable" and were to be decided by the political branches—the executive and legislative branches.[46] It is not clear why reapportionment was a political question and nonjusticiable in 1946 but was justiciable in 1962, almost 20 years later.

The political consequences of reapportionment decisions by the Court become dramatically clearer when the earlier cases are compared with the reapportionment cases[47] of the Nixon Court.[48] In describing the Nixon Court's actions on criminal procedure decisions, one article assessed the Court this way:

> In replacing retiring members of the activist Warren Court with men of conservative views on the rights of persons accused of crimes and of "strict constructionist" views of the court's own role, Nixon kept his promise to change the direction of the Supreme Court. He appointed men who saw their role as interpreting, not making, the law.[49]

The court has been criticized for both its activism and its restraint.[50] The Warren Court has been described and criticized as "activist."[51]

121

Although the 1973 Court is called the "Nixon Court" it does not mean it is a "new" court.[52] When the Court changes, it inherits case precedents, some of the judges who were part of the former Court, "the intellectual apparatus—the framework of concepts and vocabulary—developed along with that precedent," ligitants' expectations, organizations committed to championing certain values, "the objective logic of many problems, which must be perceived the same way no matter who happens to be on the Court." Finally, the new Court inherits the necessity of justifying its decisions to the public. With such a large inheritance, the changes in public law are likely to be subtle.[53] Nonetheless, precedents are shattered, and change can be abrupt: "basic concepts rise and fall over time (indeed, watching that phenomenon is one of the fascinations of constitutional law)."[54] The Nixon Court has already shifted directions. These will be discussed later. When these constitutional concepts change, the Court is sometimes accused of assuming a political role, a role, it is asserted, best assumed by the executive and legislative branches of government.

In fact, in reviewing the 1970 term of the Supreme Court, Harry Kalven, Jr. said that the Court "exercises great political power." He suggested:

> The Court thus has a hybrid role; and the arresting thing is that were its role to be purified in either direction—by having it become more simply a court and nothing more, or by having it become, bluntly, a political agency and nothing more—it would lose its power and its purpose. The special burden of the Court, then, is to exercise great political powers while still acting like a court.[55]

The Court's political role is inescapable. In discussing the reapportionment cases, Archibald Cox, who was Special Prosecutor in the Watergate investigation, wrote that if the Court had declined jurisdiction for reasons stated in 1946 that the question was political, that declination, per se, would have "put some stamp of legality upon malapportionment regardless of the technical limitations of the judicial rationale."[56] No matter what action the Court had taken in these cases, its position could not be neutral. "Occasionally problems for which the right solution has no rational basis in identifiable sources of law must be resolved in constitutional terms."[57] If the Court's ruling in *Reynolds* v. *Sims*[58] (the one man, one vote principle must be the basis of representation in state legislatures), which had no judicial precedent, is valid in "its claim to be law," Cox says, then its validity rests on the ability of the Court to accurately perceive the "dominant theme in American political development. . . . Out of such a *coup de main* great legal principles may occasionally be created."[59] Justice Cardozo called it "filling in the gaps."

Perhaps, it is to be concluded, that since the Court's political role is inescapable, it is not that the Court is more political when it is accused of being activist, it is that its decisions do not coincide with the values of those who disagree with its decisions. Is the Court "interpreting" law rather than "making law" simply because it is a conservative Court? Conservative is used here to denote locus on the political continuum. The conservative position indicates a desire to retain the status quo or to return to a previous way of doing things rather than to be flexible, innovative, or experimental with new methods or remedies. The term does not connote meanings of "good or bad," "right or wrong."

To illustrate: The Nixon Court is not less political in its reapportionment opinion; it is more conservative than the Warren Court. In three 1971 decisions the Court retreated from its "one man, one vote" equal protection decisions. In *Whitcomb* v. *Chavis*[60] the Court upheld the multimember district system of representation for Marion County in the Indiana legislature despite previous decisions that had held them unconstitutional if they decreased the political power of racial elements in the population.[61] A multimember district system of representation has two or more representatives elected at large. Black ghetto dwellers challenged the representational scheme, asserting that their voting strength was diluted. County dwellers received a disproportionate share of the voting power. Justice Harlan said that the *Whitcomb* decision "bears witness to the morass into which the Court has gotten itself by departing from sound constitutional principle in the electoral field."

123

In *Abate* v. *Mundt*,[62] the Court approved the reapportionment plan for the Rockland County, New York, legislature, which provided for a total deviation from population equality of 11.9 percent. This was the largest deviation allowed by the Court and it was reasoned that "slightly greater percentage deviations may be tolerable for local government reapportionment schemes." Further, there was no "built in bias."

Black political power greatly increased with the one man, one vote concept. The Court is retreating from that concept. It remains to be seen what the political impact of these decisions will be, but that the decisions are not politically neutral should be apparent.

Given then, that the Court is a political agency, another question arises regarding the wisdom of developing legal strategy as the means to the end, when there is ample evidence that the Court itself has sometimes stripped Blacks of the very constitutional rights for which Blacks petition.[63] There also is a question regarding the Court's power vis-à-vis the executive and legislative branches. The Court has been called the "arbiter of the federal system."[64] The system is sometimes referred to as one of "judicial supremacy." As arbiter, the Supreme Court may declare unconstitutional laws passed by Congress. This is the power of judicial review.[65] It is a power the Court took upon itself via constitutional interpretation. The Court reviews decisions of state courts when a federal question is involved.[66] The Court also reviews state legislation to determine whether it conforms to the requirements of the U.S. Constitution and to determine whether it conflicts with congressional legislation. Under Article III of the Constitution, the Court is delegated the power to settle disputes between the states.

One writer challenges the view that this is a system of judicial supremacy or that the Court is the final arbiter, because its decisions are not self-executing.[67] They may be nullified because of two constitutional structures: checks and balances and federalism.

What then, is the power of the Court to effect a remedy for Blacks? Although its decisions are not self-executing, the Court's strength is in establishing goals that are constitutional, legal, morally right. The Court "shapes as well as expresses our national ideals. . . . Its opinions are often the voice of the national conscience. . . . The educative force of its opinions cannot be ignored in the process of decision."[68]

The rights of Blacks cannot be vindicated until that which is being petitioned is declared to be a right. The Supreme Court defines the rights protected under the Constitution. Once the right is defined and established as a right of American citizenship, the Court's role is to maintain scrutiny where there are plans to implement these rights. Both these roles have been illustrated through the school desegregation and reapportionment cases. Both sets of cases involve political as well as legal questions. There also are moral and ethical questions. The Court translates into constitutional rights those moral principles embedded in the Constitution.[69] These include the "self-evident" truths of the Declaration of Independence. These principles are part of the natural-law philosophy. That philosophy is the rock bed of the democratic belief system. The concepts of justice, freedom, and equality inhere in that belief system. These are rights (goals) that Blacks seek. The legal strategy of Blacks may be directed toward either of the two roles of the Court—that by which it establishes or creates a right of citizenship or that by which it maintains scrutiny of the plans (tools) to implement these rights.

It is not suggested that Blacks should rely exclusively on the Court as the means by which their rights are to be vindicated. When the other branches of government do not set new constitutional goals, the Court may. "If one arm of government cannot or will not solve an insistent problem, the pressure falls upon another."[70]

LEGAL STRATEGY IN THE COMING DECADE

Since the first step is to establish the right, the legal strategy that should be given priority is the establishment of rights not yet articulated. This does not mean that legal strategy should not also be developed around affirmative action, reparation, preferential treatment, quotas, and the like.

The right that has not been established is the right against

125

discrimination by private persons. To date, the rights of Black Americans are, with rare exception, in the public domain.[71] They are rights against discrimination by government or government related action whether the specific activity be in employment, transportation, education, jury selection, salary, housing, finance, or public accommodations. The right against discrimination by private persons is a broad right, which subsumes specific activities (e.g., education, housing, employment, finance). Admittedly, this is a very controversial right; resistance and opposition surface.[72]

The reasoning behind the decision to seek establishment of a right against racial discrimination by private persons is that it is a broad, pervasive right, which subsumes subsidiary, specific activities that involve private racism. Attainment of this goal could have results analogous to the school desegregation case.[73] Although it was a decision that involved schools, per se, the principle established was applied to all publicly owned or operated places and establishments. Having established the principle, it was necessary to devise methods (strategies) for its implementation in specific activity areas. We are now in that era. That decision was revolutionary; and there is reason to believe that establishment of the right sought herein would be equally revolutionary. It is reasoned that once having established the right against private discrimination, a period of devising strategies to implement that right would follow. It probably would arouse no less opposition and potential disorder.

One strategy has already been projected. It is based on a legislative remedy that has been available for 102 years: a personal damage suit. At this point it should be noted that for more than a hundred years, the Court overlooked law derived from Reconstruction acts and still in force which could have eliminated private racism in specific activities. Had this been done through the years, how different our culture would be.[74]

It has been suggested that Title 42 U.S.C. § 1983, derived from the original Reconstruction Act of April 20, 1971,[75] passed under authority of the Fourteenth Amendment, be used to file Court actions to collect damages when Black Americans have been deprived of constitutional rights for racist reasons.[76] The suggestion that such action is synomous with "reparations" is debatable. Section 1983 reads:

Civil Action for Deprivation of Rights

Every person who, under color of any statute, ordinance, regulation, custom or usage, of any State or Territory, subjects, or causes to be subjected, any citizen of the United States or other person within the jurisdiction thereof to the deprivation of any rights, privileges, or immunities secured by the Constitution and laws, shall be liable to the party injured in an action at law, suit in equity, or other proper proceeding for redress.

Two questions, historically, had commanded much of the Court's attention in opinions about the Fourteenth Amendment. One was the scope of congressional power to enforce the provisions of the amendment. The other was whether congressional power extends to the regulation of private activities that deprive citizens of civil rights. When there is an available law to redress grievances motivated by private racism, the Court appears only since 1966[77] to be disposed to apply it. This is the antithesis of its actions between 1873 and 1883, when it declared unconstitutional most of those protective laws passed by the Reconstruction Congress.

In *Griffin* v. *Breckenridge,* 1971,[78] the Court used 42 U.S.C. § 1985(3), derived originally from the Reconstruction Act of April 20, 1871, to assert that Black Americans may sue for damages those private persons who conspire to deprive the parties of citizenship rights. The damage suit had been brought by Black American citizens of Mississippi who had been riding in a car driven by a Tennessee citizen. The car was stopped by white citizens of Mississippi. The riders were held by firearms with threats of murder, clubbed, and physically brutalized. Allegedly, the whites mistakenly believed them to be civil rights workers. Section 1985(3) reads in part:

127

Conspiracy to Interfere with Civil Rights—
Preventing Officer from Performing Duties

Depriving Persons of Rights or Privileges

(3) If two or more persons in any State or Territory conspire or go in disguise on the highway or on the premises of another, for the purpose of depriving, either directly or indirectly, any person or class of persons of the equal protection of the laws, or of equal privileges and immunities under the laws; or for the purpose of preventing or hindering the constituted authorities of any State or Territory from giving or securing to all persons within such Territory or State the equal protection of the laws.

This provision had been interpreted by the Court since *Collins* v. *Hardyman* 1951[79] as applying only to those who act "under color of law," persons who are agents of the state. There is nothing in the law itself that limits application to those acting "under color of law." Indeed, § 1983, which has the color of law stipulation would seem to make § 1985 redundant. Both the district court and the court of appeals had dismissed the suit, relying on *Collins* v. *Hardyman.* Justices Burton, Black, and Douglas had dissented in *Collins* v. *Hardyman* and spoke to this redundant interpretation: "[t]he language of the statute refutes the suggestion that action under color of state law is a necessary ingredient."[80] Nine Justices, including Justice Harlan, who, except for Part V-B, filed a concurring opinion stated, "On their face, the words of the statute fully encompass the conduct of private persons."[81]

Yet another indication that the Court may enforce protection against private racism when a legislative remedy is available is seen in *Jones* v. *Mayer.*[82] The case involved a couple who tried to buy a house from a private land developer. They were refused sale. The Court invoked 42 U.S.C. § 1982, a law derived from Section One of the Reconstruction Act of April 9, 1866. Section 1982 reads:

Property Rights of Citizens

> All citizens of the United States shall have the same
> right in every state and territory, as is enjoyed by
> white citizens thereof to inherit, purchase, lease, sell,
> hold, and convey real and personal property.

This law was passed under authority of Section Two of the
Thirteenth Amendment and reenacted in Section 16 of the May
30, 1870 law under authority of Section Five of the Fourteenth
Amendment. The entire 1866 law was reenacted in Section 18
of the May 30, 1870 law. In 1906 the Court had invalidated use
of the conspiracy statute[83] to punish persons who conspire to
deprive Blacks of the right to be employed.[84] In *Jones* the
Court overruled *Hodges* and said the right to make and enforce
contracts was secured. The Court did not resolve the question
as to whether the 1870 reenactment placed a state action limitation on the reach of § 1982 so that private actions could
not be reached. "But it does not follow that the adoption of the
Fourteenth Amendment or the subsequent readoption of the
Civil Rights Act was meant somehow to limit its application to
state action."[85] Of this it spoke no more. It does not speak to
the issue under the Fourteenth Amendment. It said, "We find
it unnecessary to decide whether that discrimination also
violated the Equal Protection Clause of the Fourteenth Amendment."[86] Much of the opinion was devoted to the legislative
power of Congress under the Thirteenth Amendment. Justice
Douglas' concurrence stated that a relic of slavery, race prejudice, still persists. The law was an attempt to remove some of
the "badges of slavery." Although the Court upheld the power
of Congress to pass the law, it clearly indicated that only the
discrimination to which § 1982 was addressed was prohibited.
If carried to its limits, however, *Jones* could reach all goods
placed on the market. Further, it provides a route via the Thirteenth Amendment by which private racism may be reached.
It is not encumbered with the state action limitation.

By using Titles 18 U.S.C. § 241,[87] 42 U.S.C. § 1982[88] and
42 U.S.C. § 1985(3)[89] as illustrated, to reach acts of private
racism since 1966, the Court has reversed the trend it set in

129

motion in the 1880s and culminated in the state action doctrine in 1883[90] —because of the federal structure, Congress could not directly protect the civil rights of Blacks since states were to assume that responsibility. The state action concept, enunciated in 1883, and the Court's emasculation of Congress' legislative powers to protect Blacks will be discussed at a later point. While once a heated and controversial issue, it now seems to be settled, at least for a while (since constitutional principles rise and fall), that Congress has ample authority via both the Thirteenth and Fourteenth Amendments to reach acts of private racism.

However, the issue is not settled. One of the basic problems for contemporary race relations is that some Americans, Black and white, feel they have a right to discriminate against other Americans when they act as private individuals in a social capacity. They feel this is a right. It is not the "feeling" that is being assailed in this article. What is problematic is that there is no clear distinction as to what is a "social" right as opposed to a "civil" or "legal" right. For example, in 1883 the Court said in the *Civil Rights Cases*[91] that private owners of restaurants, inns, motels, places of amusement and recreation, and public transportation carriers had the right to exclude Blacks from their places of business. Blacks had no right of admission to these places. Admission was not a civil right but a social right. Justice John Harlan dissented from that decision and said that Blacks had a legal right to be admitted. Since that decision Congress, in the Civil Rights Act of 1964,[92] made it a legal right of Blacks to be admitted to places of public accommodations. The Court upheld the legislation on the basis of Congress' power to regulate interstate commerce.[93] It still is not a "right" in the same sense of the word, as for example, the right to jury trial, free speech, and assembly. Rather, it is an incident in the regulation of commerce.

Two Justices in concurring opinion raised doubts about regulating human behavior in the same manner as goods or commodities via the commerce clause. Mr. Justice Douglas stated that the right

> occupies a more protected position in our constitu-
> tional system than does the movement of cattle,

fruit, steel and coal across state lines . . . the question deals with the constitutional status of the individual not with the impact on commerce of local activities or vice versa.[94]

Mr. Justice Goldberg stated that it "is the vindication of human dignity and not mere economics."[95]

The fact that racial discrimination is a moral problem was recognized, but the commerce clause was invoked as the constitutional authority to reckon with racism. It was easier for the Court to use Congress' regulatory powers over interstate commerce than to embroil itself in the disputed and potentially divisive issues of state action and protection from private discrimination. The commerce clause, however, lacks the moral force needed to combat racism in this country.

To reach the public accommodations decision via the Fourteenth Amendment would have necessitated speaking to the *Civil Rights Cases* of 1883. That case established the principle that Congress cannot pass

> general legislation upon the rights of the citizen, but corrective legislation, that is, such as may be necessary and proper for counteracting such laws as the States may adopt or enforce, and which by the amendment, they are prohibited from making or enforcing.[96]

The scope of Congress' power to pass protective civil rights legislation had been severely curtailed. Section Two of the 1875 Act, which granted admission to Blacks to places of public accommodations, was similar to Title II of the 1964 Civil Rights Act. The Court declared Section Two unconstitutional because it was general legislation. The difference between "corrective" and "general" legislation is not clear. Moreover, the means by which Congress was to enforce the Fourteenth Amendment was unresolved. Federalism was a political as well as a legal issue. At the time the amendments were ratified, great debate centered around the distribution of powers between the national and state governments.[97] The civil rights acts were considered to be

131

nationalistic. There was public reaction against them. In fact, as the Supreme Court stripped Black Americans of newly acquired rights, one press response read:

> Deeply as we sympathize with his [Black Americans] wrongs, we have no . . . hope of seeing them righted, by hounding on his old masters to acts of violence and lawlessness, by the passage of equally violent and lawless Acts of Congress.[98]

Nevertheless, the four dissenting Justices in the first Fourteenth Amendment case, affirmed that a revolution in the federal system had been wrought by the Fourteenth Amendment.[99] The rights, privileges, and immunities of the Fourteenth Amendment asserted the primacy of national citizenship. Protection of these rights would require very little congressional legislation, according to Justice Bradley;[100] they would be judicially enforceable. The case was not a race relations case. The dissenters wanted national regulation of property. The Justices were not staunch defenders of the rights of ex-slaves. For example, Justice Field, one of the dissenters, stated in a subsequent concurring opinion that the Fourteenth Amendment provided no protection against private acts of discrimination.[101]

When the private right of white Americans to discriminate in various ways against Black Americans can result in an unemployment rate of 25 percent, then the private right to discriminate is of such public consequence and significance that it requires public regulation. It has been argued that such regulation would invade privacy, that when whites lose the right to discriminate, Blacks also will lose this right.[102] It has been stated that if Congress does not legislate in this area, the Court is unlikely to develop a judicial remedy to prohibit private racist actions, even when such actions deprive Blacks of basic human rights. The right must be sought, nonetheless, because Congress may fail to act, despite its new judicially sanctioned authority to provide legislative protection to Black Americans. A right should not be dependent upon the ebb and flow of political whim.

Notwithstanding present constitutional and statutory

protections, Blacks in 1973 are still second-class citizens. For example, banks, mortgage firms, loan and insurance companies, are owned by private people who refuse to lend money to Blacks. Money is needed to build or buy homes, initiate or improve business enterprises, finance a college education. These private refusals deny the Black community the opportunity to become a source of economic influence and power. Blacks are denied jobs by private persons who work in government or in privately owned companies despite legislation to the contrary. Private persons exclude Blacks from apprenticeship and on the job training programs. They practice unfair promotional policies for racist reasons, and intimidate and brutalize Blacks. Add to these overt acts the severe, irreversible psychic damage that results from these humiliations. At present, there is no constitutional protection against these private acts of racism unless there is a specific statutory remedy, or if it can be shown that they involve state action or take place within interstate commerce.

Protection via these routes is insufficient. Present statutory remedies are few. Even a proliferation of statutes would not be as forceful as would be the acknowledged existence of a right against discrimination. Existence of a right carries with it pervasive moral force, which is absorbed into the culture. Dependence upon statutory remedies would make vindication subject to the political climate of Congress and the country. Use of the state action concept, as a practical device, leaves too many areas of private racism untouched.[103] It, too, lacks the moral force intrinsic in rights.[104] But most important, it bypasses discussion of the fundamental problems in human relationships. Finally, admission to places of public accommodation as an incident of commerce begs the question. As Justices Goldberg and Douglas stated in *Heart of Atlanta*, it is a question of "human dignity," the "constitutional status of the individual." To strive for a judicially enforceable right raises the specter of judicial activism.

Freedom from racism is a fundamental, inherent human right. What is needed is a decision by the Supreme Court that clearly establishes the right to be free of racial discrimination. "The law cannot change attitudes, but it can control

133

behavior."[105] The law has an educative function. As long as the belief persists that there is a constitutional right to discriminate against Blacks, racism will last. The right to be free of racial discrimination is asserted, in this article, to be a right of citizenship. Despite its civil rights decisions in recent years, until the Court declares that there is no legal right of white Americans to discriminate against Black Americans, the Court was and continues to be a significant force in contributing to the racist climate that exists in this country. What follows is the development of a suggested legal theory by which the judicially enforceable right to be free of private racism is to be established.

Because a legal theory must be developed within the intellectual framework of the Court's milieu, a brief history (previously alluded to in parts) of the judicial status of the right against private discrimination will be summarized.[106] The most important concepts, vocabulary, doctrine, and precedents surround the Court's interpretation of the Thirteenth, Fourteenth, and Fifteenth Amendments and the seven Reconstruction Acts.[107] It is as important to understand what those who wrote these amendments and statutes intended as it is to analyze the Court's interpretations and their consequences in 1973.

Controversy over what protections were intended abounds.[108] For purposes of this article, discussion of the controversy will be limited to questions related to racial discrimination. Most of the questions speak to these broad areas: What new rights were created to protect the former slaves and their descendants? Are these rights to be protected against violation by the government? Private persons? Both? Because of the federal system, which rights are to be protected by the national government? The states? Both? What is the power of Congress to enforce the protection of civil rights? Are these rights judicially enforceable? Does prohibited state action, the judicially developed concept in the *Civil Rights Cases*[109] include the illegal actions of government officers? (State action means the hand of government is involved in the action.) Does it mean that the state is responsible for the discriminatory action even when it has not mandated or sanctioned the action performed by others? Is failure to provide enforcement of civil rights

134

prohibited state action? Does state action mean government has an affirmative obligation to protect civil rights? Is state action limited only to legislation and actions by public agents? Does state action ever include the actions of individuals acting in private capacities?

Beginning with the first case brought under the Fourteenth Amendment,[110] the Court began to eradicate the newly acquired rights of ex-slaves. The Court limited the authority of the national government to protect the rights of Black Americans. It was not a race relations case. In a 5-4 decision, emphasis was placed on the limited powers of the national government, states' rights, and the nature of dual citizenship rights. Fundamental rights are derived from state citizenship and protected by the states. States' privileges and immunities "embraces nearly every civil right for the establishment and protection of which organized government is instituted."[111] The privileges and immunities clause of the Fourteenth Amendment did not authorize the national government to protect these fundamental rights. According to the Court, states have primary responsibility for protecting civil rights.

The Slaughter-House Cases so closely followed ratification of the Fourteenth Amendment that when the Justices, contemporaries of the amendment's debates, examined its legislative intent, they agreed that the "one pervading purpose" of the amendment was "the protection of the newly made freeman and citizen from the oppressions of those who had formerly exercised unlimited dominion over him."[112] It was in stating that the amendment's privileges and immunities clause does not provide national protection of fundamental rights that the Court, in an apparently overlooked inconsistent reasoning, first limited the potential protection the national government could give to its Black citizens, despite the "one pervasive purpose." Since Confederate states were not disposed to protect the ex-slaves, it was necessary that such power reside in the national government.

Two years later, in *U.S.* v. *Cruikshank*[113] and in subsequent cases[114] through the *Civil Rights Cases*[115] when the state action limitation clearly emerged, the Court systematically took from Black America some of the citizenship rights intended by the three amendments and legislation passed thereunder. The Court destroyed much of the force of the legislation by declaring the following provisions unconstitutional: The May 30, 1870 Act,[116] in *U.S.* v. *Reese*,[117] Section Three, which punished public officials for failure to enforce the right to vote, and Section Four, which made private persons liable for interfering with the right to vote; the May 30, 1870 Act, in *James* v. *Bowman*,[118] Section Five, which stipulated punishment for private persons for interfering with the right to vote; the April 9, 1866[119] law was reenacted in Section 18 of the May 30, 1870 Act. Section 16 was a partial reenactment of Section One of the 1866 legislation. Section 17 was a reenactment of Section Two. In *Hodges* v. *United States*,[120] Section 16 of the May 30, 1870 Act was invalidated. It, in part, granted to all persons the right to "make and enforce contracts, to sue, be parties, give evidence" and enjoy "the full benefit of all laws and proceedings."[121] The April 20, 1871 Act,[122] in *Baldwin* v. *Franks*[123] and *United States* v. *Harris*[124] in Section Two, which punished private persons for conspiracy against the United States and conspiracy to deprive persons of equal protection of the laws, was invalidated. This law was specifically directed against the Ku Klux Klan. Also invalidated in the *Civil Rights Cases*[125] were Sections One and Two of the March 1, 1875 Act.[126] In Section One Congress stated its duty "to enact great fundamental principles into law." Section Two granted to all citizens equal enjoyment of all privately owned places of public accommodation and transportation conveyances.

Another means by which civil rights protections initially granted to Black citizens were taken away was by the Court's omission from its opinions those statements in its previous cases that could be used to show that there is constitutional protection against "race prejudice" and the remaining vestiges of slavery.

Some of these omissions include: "Is not protection of life and property against race or color prejudice a right, a legal right, under the constitutional amendment?"[127] In that case the Court said yes. It was speaking about the Fourteenth Amendment. In the *Slaughter-House Cases* it had said states were responsible when state laws were insufficient or unenforced.

This suggests state responsibility for failing to provide positive protection of civil rights—an inaction concept. It further stated that Congress had power to provide this positive protection. If states do not enforce the equal protection clause, then under "the 5th section of the article . . . Congress was authorized to enforce by suitable legislation." This directly contradicts the decision rendered ten years later in the *Civil Rights Cases.* In the *Civil Rights Cases* it was held that Congress is not authorized under Section Five to pass civil rights laws in areas within the protective powers of the states.[128] Congress can pass only "corrective" legislation.[129] Further, Fourteenth Amendment rights of U.S. citizens are protected only from violations of a "particular character" by state legislation and public officers. This is the state action concept. There was no protection against private racism. Fourteenth Amendment rights are found in the privileges and immunities clause; the life, liberty, and property due process clause; and equal protection of the laws clause. The limits of Congress' power were established. The judicially enforceable aspects of the amendment were not discussed.

Justice John Harlan was the lone dissenter. It is that portion of his dissent in 1883 quoted below that this article urges should be adopted as the majority view of the Court at the present time:

> Exemption from race discrimination in respect of civil rights which are fundamental in citizenship in a republican government is, as we have seen, a new right created by the nation....[130]

Freedom from race discrimination was a newly created right, but his dissent also enlisted, like the majority view, the state action doctrine. This article suggests abandoning the state action approach. It is not certain whether it was for purposes of the cases before him, or in an effort to bring conformity to the majority-minority position, that Justice Harlan used the state action concept. He found state responsibility in privately owned places of public accommodation through the state's licensing procedure. Conceivably, the licensing requirement would leave few relationships that involve any commercial transaction beyond the scope of federal regulation. His state responsibility doctrine also could reach commercial transactions beyond the scope of 42 U.S.C. § 1982. The majority's state action concept has been problematic, not only in the sometimes strained distinction between public and private actions in race relations cases,[131] but also in others.[132] Discussion of the application of Harlan's view to non-race relations cases is beyond the scope of this paper.

Adoption of Harlan's state action finding would eliminate obstacles that limit judicial enforcement of the civil right as asserted in *Moose Lodge No. 107* v. *Irvis* in June 1972.[133] His concept was not used. Such decisions contribute to the racist climate that exists, and perpetuate the belief held by white Americans that they have the "social" right to discriminate against Black Americans.

The Court did not adopt Justice Harlan's state action concept. The plaintiff argued that the private club, Moose Lodge No. 107, was within the scope of state action because of its liquor license. This was the same route suggested by Harlan in 1883. Irvis, a Black guest of one of the members of the club, was denied service because of his race. He was not applying for membership. He asserted that issuance of a state liquor license to the club made the state a party to the discrimination in violation of the Fourteenth Amendment's equal protection clause. Irvis asked for injunctive relief, but not damages, under 42 U.S.C. § 1983.[134]

The case was discussed in state action terms. Moose Lodge No. 107 was conceded to be a private club. The Pennsylvania Liquor Control Board "plays absolutely no part in establishing or enforcing the membership or guest policies of the club which it licenses to serve liquor,"[135] said the Court.

> The only effect ... [it] can be said to have on the right of any other Pennsylvanian to buy or be served liquor on premises other than those of Moose Lodge is that for some purposes club licenses are counted in the maximum number of licenses which may be issued in a given municipality.[136]

138

The Court held that the Board was not so involved in the club's racist guest policy as to bring it within the realm of prohibited state action under the equal protection clause.

Two dissenting opinions were filed. The first was written by Justice Douglas, joined by Justice Marshall. They, too, argued in state action terms. Speaking immediately to the question of the private right to choose one's associates, they said that the Bill of Rights creates

> a zone of privacy which precludes government from interfering with private clubs. . . . So the fact that the Moose Lodge allows only Caucasians to join or come as guests is constitutionally irrelevant, as is the decision of the Black Muslims to admit to their services only members of their race.[137]

But the fact was not irrelevant. It is central to the whole question of citizenship rights. Is such exclusion a "social" right? The right in question is not the narrow right suggested by the majority—to buy or be served liquor. The constitutional right to be established is the right against racial discrimination. It is important to state here that this article is not arguing the merits of *Moose Lodge*. It is asserting that the state action concept is an inadequate tool for considering questions of private discrimination.

It is suggested that when the right against racial discrimination is invoked, a balancing of competing constitutional rights is required. This right interferes with the right to discriminate. But as one author states, "The right to discriminate, taken alone, cannot outweigh the right to Negroes to be treated fairly."[138] The right to discriminate frequently "occurs in conjunction with the interests in privacy, free association, or free expression."[139] These interests must be balanced against the right to be free from racism. Which right is more fundamental would be determined by the particular activity involved. Identification of the right to be free from racism requires a different kind of interpretation of the Fourteenth Amendment.

One of the difficulties in the Court's present application of the state action concept is that it seems to be using a balancing of interests approach without declaring which private interests are being weighed.[140] To look for the presence of the state in these private interests necessarily complicates and confuses the meaning of state action. To state explicitly which rights are being balanced would require judicial delineation of which rights inhere in the Fourteenth Amendment. The listing would open up for discussion the earlier questions of what new rights were created therein—questions judiciously avoided.[141] It is suggested that the balancing test be used in conjunction with the new interpretation of the Fourteenth Amendment.

Because *Moose Lodge* was argued in state action terms, perhaps the question of private choice was "irrelevant." In footnote reference, however, the dissenters recognized that a definition of what is "private" as distinct from what is "public" was a key issue:

> There was no occasion to consider the question whether, perhaps because of a role as a center of community activity, Moose Lodge No. 107 was in fact "private" for equal protection purposes. The decision today, therefore, leaves the question open.[142]

Two primary factors led to their state action finding. The result of the Pennsylvania Liquor Control Board's Regulation No. 11309 was as if there were a Board "provision that the license may not be used to dispense liquor to Blacks, Browns, Yellows—or atheists or agnostics."[143] Regulation No. 11309 stated that club recipients of licenses must enforce their respective club's bylaws and constitution. The dissenters looked at the result or effects of the license regulation to reach its conclusion that "Regulation No. 11309 is thus an invidious form of state action." It had been the *effects* of the segregated white primary that brought the Court to state in *Terry* v. *Adams*[144] that the Jaybird Association, a private club, organized since 1889, was within the ambit of prohibited state action. It said:

> It is immaterial that the state does not control that part of this elective process which it leaves for the

Jaybirds to manage.... The effect ... is to do precisely that which the Fifteenth Amendment forbids.[145]

The second reason, as stated by the dissent, was that because of a liquor license quota system, the "scarcity of licenses restricts the ability of Blacks to obtain liquor."[146]

The second dissent was written by Justice Brennan, joined by Justice Marshall. They opined that "something is uniquely amiss in a society where the government, the authoritative oracle of community values, involves itself in racial discrimination."[147] Apparently, the prohibited state action is not present merely because of the issuance of a license to the club. Quoting from the District Court, they said the state liquor license is

different in nature and extent from ordinary licenses ... the power to grant licenses for the sale of intoxicating liquor was an exercise of the highest governmental power, one in which the state had the fullest freedom inhering in the police power of the sovereign.[148]

To qualify for a license, the club must meet extensive statutory requirements. Although the state's license power "has no relation to the traffic in liquor itself,"[149] the state permits the license power "to be exploited in the pursuit of a discriminatory practice."[150] The dissent concluded by holding that

the mere existence of efforts by the State, through legislation or otherwise, to authorize, encourage, or otherwise support racial discrimination in a particular facet of life constitutes illegal state involvement in those pertinent private acts of discrimination that subsequently occur.[151]

As stated in this minority opinion, the Court had ample precedent in previous decisions to reach a different result. In addition to those cited by the minority, the state action concept had been expanded to include private activities even when the state's involvement is not "exclusive or direct."[152] The Court had even found state responsibility where the state was not actively involved in the discrimination. A privately owned coffee shop in Wilmington, Delaware, operated segregated facilities in space leased in a building owned by the Wilmington Parking Authority. The Court ruled that the private coffee shop could not operate a segregated facility because the state's involvement in the discrimination was "significant." Public ownership of the building was "significant state involvement."[153]

Emerging from *Burton* is the principle that when a state fails to provide civil rights protection, the state is responsible. An inaction criterion for state responsibility is in keeping with the affirmative obligation of the national government to provide equal opportunity to all its citizens.[154] "Today . . . the duty of government to provide jobs, social security, medical care, and housing extends to the field of human rights and imposes an obligation to promote liberty, equality and dignity."[155]

The author of the quotation hastens to add that the responsibility for framing and administering the remedies is best lodged in the executive and legislative branches. This writer responds with the author's own statement that when these branches do not fulfill their duty "the pressure falls upon another."[156] He also said that in constitutional law cases, counsel

> is to aid the Court in that mysterious process by which decisions meet new needs yet are shown to have legal roots needed to maintain the rule of law.[157]

As Justice Cardozo indicated, these are the "gaps" in the law. When the Court bridges these gaps to fill new social needs, it is called "activist" or "political." The pressing social need is to enforce protection of human rights found in the equal protection clause of the Fourteenth Amendment. Protection from both public and private violation is necessary when the effects of such violation are indistinguishable; be it public or private, regulation of each is required. As previously stated, it is not suggested that legal redress is the only route to freedom. This article is an attempt to demonstrate that it is an available route.

Even with the more inclusive concept of state action, the doctrine is inadequate to the purpose, for the reasons already stated. Additionally, it offers no clear guidelines for future cases, as illustrated by the minority's opinions in *Moose Lodge.*

The legal theory proffered is that the right to be free from racial discrimination is a constitutional right. In the absence of its specific enumeration in the Constitution, it will be necessary to demonstrate how and where that right was created. Rights that are found in the Constitution or in some national law are "secured" rights. Secured rights may be protected from both public and private violation.[158] It is asserted that Congress already has secured the right in 42 U.S.C. § 1981, derived from the Reconstruction Act of May 31, 1870. Section 1981 reads:

Equal Rights Under Law

All persons within the jurisdiction of the United States shall have the same right in every State and Territory to make and enforce contracts, to sue, be parties, give evidence, and to the full and equal benefit of all laws and proceedings for the security of persons and property as is enjoyed by white citizens, and shall be subject to like punishment, pains, penalties, taxes, licenses, and exactions of every kind, and to no other.

The right against private racism is found in the words "all persons . . . have the same right to . . . the full and equal benefit of all laws and proceedings . . . as is enjoyed by white citizens." The word "law" is interpreted by the writer to include more than statutes. Whites have the right to be free from racial discrimination. Such freedom is a human right. It comes from the natural law, moral law. If whites have the right, then under § 1981, Blacks also have it. If the Court continues its recent invocation of Reconstruction Act provisions to reach acts of private racism,[159] then § 1981 is a broadbased remedy. Any

143

right that whites have, Blacks also have. That the provision was passed under authority of Section Five of the Fourteenth Amendment, which had been encumbered with the state action limitation, is no longer an obstacle. Six Justices rejected the principle established in the *Civil Rights Cases* that Congress may pass only "corrective" legislation. Congress may also pass protective, affirmative legislation.[160] On the basis of *U.S.* v. *Guest,* the Court could uphold the constitutionality of § 1981, passed under the Fourteenth Amendment to reach acts of private racism. *U.S.* v. *Guest* portends a revolutionary change in federal-state relations if Congress chooses to act.[161]

It would seem from these recent cases that the Court would prefer to invoke a congressional statute than to declare that the right to be free of racial discrimination is a judicially enforceable right under Section One of the Fourteenth Amendment. This is an area in which the Court has disagreed. The *Civil Rights Cases* did not speak to whether the state action limitation applies also to Section One. Rights in the Fourteenth Amendment had been interpreted as "protected" rights and not saved from violations by private persons.[162] They were protected only from state action. In *U.S.* v. *Guest,* concurring Justices disagreed with the Court's view that 18 U.S.C. § 241, the criminal conspiracy statute, reached private persons only because there was "indirect" state involvement in the conspiracy to interfere with the right to equal utilization of public facilities. The Court held that the Fourteenth Amendment of its own force, did not prohibit the conspiracy. Section 241 was applicable because it was national law. The disagreement was over what is meant by "secured" right (as distinguished from "protected" rights). Justices Brennan and Douglas and Chief Justice Warren stated that a right is secured "if it emanates from the Constitution, if it finds its source in the Constitution."[163] They held that this was the source of the right to equal utilization of public facilities, since there was no law or expressed constitutional provision that prohibited private interference with the right to equal use of public facilities. It was because the right "emanated" from the Constitution that it was secured. It was protected against private conspiracy. There was no need to find state involvement—the right was judicially enforceable.

Returning to the suggested legal theory, then, what is gleaned from *U.S.* v. *Guest* is that the right to be free from racial discrimination need not be expressly enumerated in the Constitution. It can emanate from or "find its source in the Constitution." That rights emanate from the Constitution had been reasoned by Justice John Harlan in his *Civil Rights Cases* dissent. In the absence of expressed power, Congress had passed the Fugitive Slave Laws to protect the rights of property. He cited three cases to support his view that what had been done to protect slavery and slave masters could be done "for human liberty and the fundamental rights of American citizenship."[164] Similarly, in *Logan* v. *United States*,[165] where six prisoners were taken from the custody of a federal marshal by a lynch mob, the Court held that a right not expressed in the Constitution could be protected against violation by private persons. The right was a national right to a fair trial unfettered by mob violence. The concurring opinion *U.S.* v. *Guest, Logan* v. *U.S.,* and Justice Harlan's dissent demonstrate that the right to be free from racial discrimination can emanate from or find its source in the Constitution. The Ninth Amendment states that there are other rights of citizenship that are not enumerated in the Constitution. The primary source for constitutional rights is natural or moral law. These cases illustrate the source of an unexpressed right. They also illustrate the Court's power to "create" rights. One of the best-known judicially created rights one not expressed in the Constitution, is the right to privacy. The Court explicitly established this right in *Griswold* v. *Connecticut*.[166] The First, Third, Fourth, Fifth and Ninth Amendments were used to locate the right to privacy.

The constitutional provision appropriate to the right to be free of racial discrimination is the Fourteenth Amendment's equal protection clause. This clause is the one most used in race relations cases. This legal theory proposes that it be rendered a substantive interpretation instead of the reasonable classification interpretation presently used.[167] Reasonable classification means that there must be a reasonable relationship between the goals to be governmentally implemented and the classes (groups) into which people are thereby divided. A substantive interpretation would be read to incorporate citizenship rights. It is not new to nonrace cases.[168] Two notable cases are: *Reynolds* v. *Sims*,[169] in which the Court held that all citizens have the right to equal participation in state elections; and *Griffin* v. *Illinois*,[170] in which the Court held that the state must provide transcripts for indigents in criminal appeals cases. The concurring opinion cited in *U.S.* v. *Guest* rendered a substantive interpretaion. *Brown* v. *Board of Education* may be viewed as employing both reasonable classification and a substantive reading. Using the reasonable classification scheme it is held that there is no relationship between the goal–education–and the separation of groups into Black and white. Using the substantive interpretation, the Court said that separation is inherently unequal. This may be seen as a move toward the ideal of normative equality. Normative equality is an attribute of citizenship that comes from the natural law. This view leads to questions of moral law as well as constitutional law, which leads to discussions about judicial activism and the proper role of the Court.

SUMMARY OF THE LEGAL THEORY

It has been asserted that the right to be free from racial discrimination is a judicially enforceable right under the equal protection clause of the Fourteenth Amendment. The proposed legal theory has:

1. established that in the absence of an enumerated right, the source of the right to be free from racial discrimination "emanates" from the Constitution, citing the Ninth Amendment and especially *United States* v. *Guest, Logan* v. *United States,* and Justice John Harlan's dissent at two points: (a) a right against racial discrimination was created, (b) in the absence of an expressed power, rights may be protected
2. demonstrated the authority of the Court to "create" rights, citing especially *Logan* v. *U.S., United States* v. *Guest, Griswold* v. *Connecticut*
3. established that the right is judicially enforceable, citing the concurring opinion in *United States* v. *Guest*

4. established that where a right is secured it may be protected against private invasion, citing especially *Logan* v. *United States* and *United States* v. *Cruikshank*
5. established that the Fourteenth Amendment can be given a substantive interpretation, as opposed to reasonable classification, making it the appropriate constitutional provision to locate the unexpressed right to be free of racial discrimination, citing especially *Reynolds* v. *Sims, Griffin* v. *Illinois, Brown* v. *Board of Education* and concurring opinion cited in *United States* v. *Guest.*

The proposed creation of "new law" would subject the Court to continued allegations that it has become a political agency. It is both a court and a political agency. That political role is circumscribed by legal precedent, procedure, and process. The Court is further constrained by the separation of powers principle and federalism. These procedures and structures, in themselves, provide the necessary "judicial restraint."

NOTES

1. That the Supreme Court of the United States may be inclined to look at local situations is indicated in the obscenity case decided the week of June 17, 1973.

> The court made clear that "community standards" of decency may be those of a locality and not a national community, so that the same film may be banned in one city but shown freely in another. States are free to establish statewide standards but may also permit local option. (*The Washington Post,* June 22, 1973.)

2. For basic information on problems confronting the Black community, read *Civil Rights Progress Report 1970* (Washington, D.C.: *Congressional Quarterly,* 1971). The statistics cited above are found in this volume.

3. Louis L. Knowles and Kenneth Prewitt, eds., *Institutional Racism in America* (Englewood Cliffs, N.J.: Prentice-Hall, 1969), p. 26.

4. Ibid.

5. Ibid., p. 59.

6. Ibid., p. 64.

7. Ibid., p. 67

8. *Brown* v. *Board of Education of Topeka,* 347 U.S. 483 (1954).

9. *Brown* v. *Board of Education of Topeka,* 349 U.S. 294 (1955).

10. *Cooper* v. *Aaron,* 358 U.S. 1 (1958).

11. *Griffin* v. *County School Board of Prince Edward County,* 377 U.S. 218 (1964).

12. See *Civil Rights Progress Report 1970,* p. 71; and *Political Participation* (Washington, D.C.: United States Commission on Civil Rights), pp. 25-35.

13. *U.S.* v. *Montgomery County Board of Education,* 395 U.S. 225 (1969).

14. *The Voice,* July 7, 1973, p. 1.

15. Ibid.

16. See "What is the Law of the Land," by Louisiana Democrat John Rarick; "Busing," by President of the United States, Richard M. Nixon; and "Busing in Perspective," by Minnesota Democratic Senator, Walter F. Mondale. These articles are found in Richard M. Pious, ed., *Civil Rights and Liberties in the 1970s* (New York: Random House, 1973), pp. 35-50.

17. *Plessy* v. *Ferguson,* 163 U.S. 537.

18. *Cummings* v. *Richmond County Board of Education,* 175 U.S. 528 (1899).

19. *Brown* v. *Board of Education of Topeka,* 349 U.S. 294, 300-301 (1955).

20. *Calhoun et al.* v. *Cook et al.,* Civil Action No. 6298. U.S. District Court, Northern District of Georgia.

21. The following statements on the Atlanta, Georgia, school desegregation case are taken from oral interviews with Mr. King in June 1973.

22. The plan submitted by the Atlanta Branch, NAACP, was submitted as the brief itself. The charts are copied from *Calhoun* v. *Cook,* Civil Action No. 6298. U.S. District Court, Northern District of Georgia.

23. Ibid., pp. 4-5 and Exhibit A.

24. Ibid., Schedule A, pp. 8-9.

25. Ibid., p. 16.

26. "A Survey of Public Opinion in Atlanta (Washington, D.C.: William R. Hamilton and staff, June 1973), p. 26.

27. 397 U.S. 1 (1970).

28. Unpublished statement submitted by Lonnie King to the National Office of the NAACP, 1973, p. 1.

29. Ibid., p. 3.

30. *The Washington Post,* June 22, 1973, pp. A1, A11.

31. Ibid., p. A1.

32. Benjamin N. Cardozo, *The Nature of the Judicial Process* (New Haven, Conn.: Yale University Press, 1954).

33. James Burns and Jack Peltason, *Government of the People,* 8th ed. (Englewood Cliffs, N.J.: Prentice-Hall, 1972), p. 405.

34. Cardozo, *Nature of Judicial Process,* p. 21.

35. Ibid., p. 65.

36. Ibid., p. 73.

37. There are 172 Black elected state representatives; 13 state senators; now 14 members of the House of Representatives of the Congress of the United States; 1 senator of the Senate of the United States. These figures are based on totals given in "Negro Elected Officials Continue to Grow in Number," *Civil Rights Progress Report 1970* (Washington, D.C.: *Congressional Quarterly,* 1970), p. 70. The number of Black legislators in the House of Representatives has increased from the number published in *Congressional Quarterly* in 1971. The actual figure was given in this footnote.

38. Ibid., p. 73.

39. Ibid., p. 72.

40. Ibid., p. 69.

41. 42 U.S.C. § 1973, 79 *Stat.* 437 (1965).

42. *Baker* v. *Carr,* 369 U.S. 186 (1962); *Gray* v. *Sanders,* 372 U.S. 368 (1963); *Wesberry* v. *Sanders,* 376 U.S. 1 (1964); *Reynolds* v. *Sims,* 377 U.S. 533 (1964); *Lucas* v. *Colorado,* 377 U.S. 713 (1964); *Kirkpatrick* v. *Preisler,* 349 U.S. 526 (1969); *Wells* v. *Rockefeller,* 394 U.S. 542 (1969); The Court addresses itself to questions of reapportionment in local government in *Avery* v. *Midland County* 390 U.S. 474 (1968); *Hadley* v. *Junior College District,* 397 U.S. 50 (1970).

43. *Civil Rights Progress Report,* pp. 69, 73.

44. Ibid., p. 69. The article states, "And the Negro birthrate is far higher than that of whites (25.8 births per 1,000 for Blacks, 16.3 per 1,000 for whites)."

45. *Colgrove* v. *Green,* 328 U.S. 549.

46. See *Luther* v. *Borden,* 7 Howard 1 (1849). For a brief discussion of "The Doctrine of Political Questions" see C. Herman Pritchett, *The American Constitution* (New York: McGraw-Hill, 1959), p. 151.

47. *Whitcomb* v. *Chavis,* 403 U.S. 124 (1971); *Abate* v. *Mundt,* 403 U.S. 182 (1971); *Gordon* v. *Lance,* 403 U.S. 1 (1971).

48. Four vacancies occurred on the Supreme Court since President Richard M. Nixon was elected to office. These appointees are Chief Justice Warren E. Burger, Harry A. Blackmun, Lewis F. Powell, Jr., and William H. Rehnquist. See "The Nixon Court: 'To Interpret, Not Make, Law' " *Current American Government* (Washington, D.C.: Congressional Quarterly Service, Fall 1972), p. 104.

49. Ibid.

50. For a discussion of attacks on the Court because of its activism or

restrain, see "Supreme Court Power to Rule Legislation Unconstitutional Exerts Deterrent Effect," *Current American Government* (Washington, D.C.: Congressional Quarterly Service, Fall 1972), p. 99; William Ebenstein et al., *American Democracy in World Perspective,* 3rd ed. (New York: Harper & Row, 1973), pp. 127-131.

51. Wallace Mendelson, "From Warren to Burger: The Rise and Decline of Substantive Equal Protection," *The American Political Science Review 56* (December 1972): 1226.

52. Harry S. Kalven, Jr., "The Supreme Court 1970 Term," *Harvard Law Review* 85, no. 3 (1971): 5.

53. Ibid., p. 6.

54. Ibid., p. 5. Decisions handed down on the same day saw a division of Nixon appointees on one side and Warren Court judges on the other. Some of these decisions reversed the trend of the Warren Court.

> In a dissent [criminal due process case], Justice William J. Brennan wrote that the Court's decision is another step towards the complete evisceration of the fundamental constitutional principles established by this Court only six years ago (when the right to a lawyer at a lineup was established). (*The Washington Post,* June 22, 1973, p. A11).

A new direction was established in a 5-4 obscenity case decision (*The Washington Post,* June 22, 1973, pp. A1, A10. See also *Harris* v. *U.S.,* 401 U.S. 222 (1971); *Johnson* v. *Louisiana;* and *Apodaco* v. *Oregon,* 39 U.S. *Law Week* 3566 (June 28, 1971). *Moose Lodge No. 107* v. *Irvis,* slip opinion; *James* v. *Valtierra,* 402 U.S. 137 (1971); *McKiener* v. *Pennsylvania,* 403 U.S. 528 (1971); *Palmer* v. *Thompson,* 403 U.S. 217 (1971); *Younger* v. *Harris,* 401 U.S. 37 (1971); *U.S.* v. *White,* 401 U.S. 745 (1971).

55. Kalven, "Supreme Court 1970," p. 3.

56. Archibald Cox, "The Supreme Court 1965 Term Foreword: Constitutional Adjudication and the Promotion of Human Rights," *Harvard Law Review* 80 no. 91 (1966): 98.

57. Ibid.

58. 377 U.S. 533 (1964).

59. Cox, "Supreme Court 1965 Term Foreword," p. 98.

60. 403 U.S. 124 (1971).

61. *Fortson* v. *Dorsey,* 379 U.S. 433 (1965); *Burns* v. *Richardson,* 384 U.S. 73 (1966).

62. 403 U.S. 182 (1971).

63. Lois B. Moreland, *White Racism and the Law* (Columbus, Ohio: Merrill, 1970).

64. Richard M. Pious, ed., *Civil Rights and Liberties in the 1970s* (New York: Random House, 1973), pp. 10-13.

65. *Marbury* v. *Madison,* 1 Cranch 137 (1803).

66. *Martin* v. *Hunter's Lessee,* 1 Wheaton 304 (1816).

67. Pious, *Civil Rights and Liberties,* pp. 10-13.

68. Cox, "Supreme Court 1965 Term Foreword," p. 97. His statement about the Court's role in the sit-in demonstration cases speaks to the political as well as moral questions inherent in decision making:

> Had the Court affirmed the convictions of the sit-in demonstration, for example, a lawyer might accurately have said that the decision had nothing to do with morality or policy but resulted from the limited function of a constitutional court. To the layman and legislator, however, the Court's decree would have legitimatized the convictions and even the racial discrimination that lay behind them. The force of legality would have influenced both the national consciousness and the debate upon legislative measures. In short, whatever the legal conception, affirmance of the convictions would have aided the advocates of segregation. (p. 97)

69. Edward S. Corwin, *The "Higher Law" Background of American Constitutional Law* (Ithaca, N.Y.: Great Seal Books, Cornell University Press, 1955); Alan P. Grimes, *American Political Thought* (New York: Holt, Rinehart & Winston, 1960), pp. 98-127.

70. Cox, "Supreme Court 1965 Term Foreword," p. 122.

71. It seemed that the right against governmental discrimination had been established and the trend was toward implementation. However, as Professor Kalven stated ("Supreme Court, 1970"), these concepts change. Several decisions by the Nixon Court raise doubts: *Palmer* v. *Thompson,* 403 U.S. 217, in which the Court (1971) did not examine the motives of Jackson, Mississippi officials in closing a municipal swimming pool; and *Whitcomb* v. *Chavis,* discussed earlier.

72. See Notes, "The 'New' Thirteenth Amendment: A Preliminary Analysis," *Harvard Law Review* 82, (1969): 1294; Cox, "Supreme Court 1965 Term Foreword," p. 94.

73. *Brown* v. *Board of Education,* 397 U.S. 241 (1954).

74. That all faith in the Court be not lost, one word of possible defense may be that in rearranging the civil rights laws and separating them for separate chapters in preparation for the Revised Statutes, some of their visibility was lost. See Robert K. Carr, *Federal Protection of Civil Rights: Quest for a Sword* (Ithaca, N.Y.: Cornell University Press, 1947), p. 45.

75. 17 *Stat.* 13.

76. Paper read at conference held at Tuskegee Institute, Tuskegee, Alabama, April 1973.

77. *United States* v. *Guest,* 383 U.S. 745. The Court used 18 U.S.C. § 241 to reach its finding that private persons could be punished for conspiring to deprive a citizen of Fourteenth Amendment constitutional rights. It reads:

If two or more persons conspire to injure, oppress, threaten, or intimidate any citizen in the free exercise or enjoyment of any right or privilege secured to him by the Constitution or laws of the United States, or because of his having so exercised the same; or

If two or more persons go in disguise on the highway, or on the premises of another, with intent to prevent or hinder his free exercise or enjoyment of any right or privilege so secured

They shall be fined not more than $10,000 or imprisoned not more than ten years, or both; and if death results, they shall be subject to imprisonment for any term of years or for life.

78. 403. U.S. 88 (1971).

79. 341 U.S. 651.

80. *Griffin* v. *Breckenridge,* 403 U.S. 88, 95 (1971), citing *Collins.*

81. Ibid., p. 96.

82. 392 U.S. 409 (1968).

83. 42 U.S.C. § 241 (1964 ed.), 16 *Stat.* 140.

84. 203 U.S. 1.

85. Ibid.

86. *Jones* v. *Mayer,* 392 U.S. 409 (1968).

87. *United States* v. *Guest,* 383 U.S. 745 (1966).

88. *Jones* v. *Mayer,* 392 U.S. 409 (1968); also see *Sullivan* v. *Little Hunting Park, Inc.,* 396 U.S. 229 (1969).

89. *Griffin* v. *Breckenridge,* 403 U.S. 88 (1971).

90. *The Civil Rights Cases,* 109 U.S. 3. To be discussed later.

91. 109 U.S. 3 (1883).

92. 42 U.S. C. 1975 (1964 ed.), 78 *Stat.* 422.

93. *Heart of Atlanta Motel, Inc.* v. *United States,* 379 U.S. 241 (1964).

94. Ibid., p. 279.

95. Ibid., p. 291.

96. 109 U.S. 3, 13.

97. Charles Warren, *The Supreme Court in United States History, 1836-1918,* vol. 2, rev. ed. (Boston: Little, Brown, 1926), pp. 455-692.

98. Ibid., p. 605.

99. *The Slaughter-House Cases,* 83. U.S. 36, 88 (1873). See dissenting opinions of Justices Field, Swayne, Bradley, and Chief Justice Chase.

100. Ibid., pp. 111-124.

101. *Virginia* v. *Rives,* 100 U.S. 313, 332 (1880).

102. See Notes, "The 'New' Thirteenth Amendment."

103. See *Moose Lodge No. 107* v. *Irvin,* Slip Opinion, June 1972.

104. Moreland, *White Racism*. Read discussion of the "sit-in" cases in "The Right to Be Served," pp. 127-160.

105. Ibid., p. 4.

106. Ibid., See also chapters 1-9.

107. Enforcement Act of 1866; Enforcement Act of 1870, amended by Act of February 28, 1971; Antilynching Act of 1871; Civil Rights Act of 1875; The Slave and Kidnapping Act of 1866, and the Peonage Abolition Act of 1867.

108. Horace E. Flack, *The Adoption of the Fourteenth Amendment*, extra volume 26 (Baltimore: Johns Hopkins University Studies in Historical and Political Science, 1908); Joseph B. James, *The Framing of the Fourteenth Amendment* (Urbana: University of Illinois Press, 1965); Jacobus ten Broek, *Equal Under Law* (Originally published as *The Anti-Slavery Origins of the Fourteenth Amendment*) New York: Macmillan, 1965); Charles Fairman, "Does the Fourteenth Amendment Incorporate the Bill of Rights? The Original Understanding," *Stanford Law Review* 2, 5 (December 1949); Howard Jay Graham, "Our 'Declaratory' Fourteenth Amendment," *Stanford Law Review* 7, 3 (December 1954); Howard Jay Graham, "The Conspiracy Theory of the Fourteenth Amendment," *Yale Law Journal* 48, 171 (December 1937); and *Yale Law Journal* 49, 371 (January 1938).

109. 109 U.S. 3 (1883).

110. *The Slaughter-House Cases*, 83 U.S. 36 (1873).

111. Ibid., p. 76.

112. Ibid., p. 71.

113. 92 U.S. 542 (1875).

114. *Strauder* v. *West Virginia*, 100 U.S. 303 (1880); *Virginia* v. *Rives*, 100 U.S. 313 (1880); *Ex Parte Virginia*, 100 U.S. 339 (1880); *U.S.* v. *Harris*, 106 U.S. 629 (1882).

115. 109 U.S. 3 (1883).

116. 16 *Stat.* 140.

117. 92 U.S. 214 (1876).

118. 190 U.S. 127 (1903).

119. 14 *Stat.* 27.

120. 203 U.S. 1 (1906).

121. 14 *Stat.* 27.

122. 17 *Stat.* 13.

123. 120 U.S. 678 (1887); and 106 U.S. 629 (1883).

124. 106 U.S. 629 (1883).

125. 109 U.S. 3 (1883).

126. 18 *Stat.* 335.

127. *Strauder* v. *West Virginia*, 100 U.S. 303, 309 (1880).

128. 109 U.S. 3, 11 (1883).

129. Ibid., pp. 14-15.

130. Ibid., p. 56.

131. See, for example, *Griffin* v. *Maryland,* 378 U.S. 130 (1964).

132. See *Black* v. *Cutter Laboratories,* 351 U.S. 292 (1956).

133. Slip Opinion, June 1972.

134. See p.

135. Ibid., p. 12.

136. Ibid.

137. Ibid., dissenting opinion, p. 1.

138. Notes, "The 'New' Thirteenth Amendment," 1313.

139. Ibid.

140. See William Van Alstyne and K. L. Karst, "State Action," *Stanford Law Review* 14, 3 (December 1961); Jerre S. Williams, "The Twilight of State Action," *Texas Law Review* 41, 347 (February 1963); Comment, "State Action under the Equal Protection Clause of the Fourteenth Amendment and the Remaining Scope of Private Choice," *Cornell Law Quarterly* 50, 473 (Spring 1965).

141. *United States* v. *Guest,* 383 U.S. 745 (1966).

142. *Moose Lodge No. 107* v. *Irvis,* Slip Opinion, June 1972, p. 16.

143. Ibid., p. 3.

144. 345 U.S. 461 (1953).

145. Ibid., p. 469.

146. *Moose Lodge No. 107* v. *Irvis,* Slip Opinion, June 1972 (dissenting opinion) p. 4.

147. Ibid., p. 2.

148. Ibid.

149. Ibid., p. 6

150. Ibid.

151. Ibid.

152. *United States* v. *Guest,* 383 U.S. 745, 754 (1966).

153. *Burton* v. *Wilmington Parking Authority,* 365 U.S. 715 (1961).

154. Arthur S. Miller, "An Affirmative Thrust to Due Process of Law," *The George Washington Law Review* 30, 339 (March 1962); *Griffin* v. *County School Board of Prince Edward County,* 377 U.S. 218 (1964).

155. Cox, "Supreme Court 1965 Term Foreward," p. 93.

156. Ibid., p. 122.

157. Ibid., p. 98.

158. C. Herman Pritchett, *The American Constitution* (New York: McGraw-Hill, 1959). p. 619; if the right is an attribute of national citizenship or created by the Constitution it may be protected against private and public violation, *United States* v. *Cruikshank,* 92 U.S. 542 (1875).

159. *Jones* v. *Mayer; United States* v. *Guest; Sullivan* v. *Little Hunting Park, Inc.; Griffin* v. *Breckenridge.*

160. *United States* v. *Guest.*

161. *U.S.* v. *Price,* 383 U.S. 787 (1966), decided on the same day as *U.S.* v. *Guest* that 18 U.S.C. § 241 protected Fourteenth Amendment due process rights. National protection against private invasion was given to fundamental rights.

162. Pritchett, *American Constitution.*

163. *U.S.* v. *Guest,* 383 U.S. 745, 779 (1966).

164. *Civil Rights Cases,* 109 U.S. 3, 53 (1883).

165. 144 U.S. 263 (1892).

166. 381 U.S. 479 (1965).

167. *Yick Wo* v. *Hopkins,* 118 U.S. 356 (1886).

168. See Wallace Mendelson, "From Warren to Burger."

169. 377 U.S. 533 (1964).

170. 351 U.S. 12 (1956).

5

BLACK PEOPLE, TECHNOCRACY, AND LEGAL PROCESS: THOUGHTS, FEARS, AND GOALS

Henry J. Richardson III

Henry J. Richardson III is Associate Professor of Law at Indiana University School of Law. He is the author of articles on international law and on law and Black people and has served as an international legal advisor consultant to the government of Malawi. Professor Richardson is currently visiting Professor of Law at Northwestern University.

INTRODUCTION: MODERN TECHNOLOGY
AND AMERICAN SOCIETY

In a society which applauds its scientific progress, expanding technology (including automation and the pervasive use of computers) is welcomed and hailed as yet another advance of modern civilization. Universal improvements in the standard of living and enormous, if vaguely conceptualized, benefits are expected in the automated, technocratic, post-industrial future. Only a few dissonant voices are heard. One, Theodore Roszak, warns of the approach of a technocratic wasteland, characterized by artificiality and standardization of American society, and the increased military-like training of people to do a growing number of alienating tasks.[1] Roszak sees a militant march of the scientized temperament through the whole of culture:

So, by imperceptible degrees, we license technical intelligence, in its pursuit of all the factors it must control, to move well beyond the sphere of "hardware" engineering—until it begins to orchestrate the entire surrounding social context.[2]

This tends to continue

until we find ourselves surrounded by every manner of scientific technical expert, all of them purporting to know as the scientist knows: dispassionately, articulately, on the basis of empirical evidence of experiment, without idiosyncratic distortion, and if possible by the intervention of mathematics, statistics, or a suitably esoteric methodology. ... In urban-industrial society, nothing enjoys much of a chance of being dignified as knowledge which does not proceed from such an epistemological stance.[3]

In such a situation, systems analysis enjoys much prominence as a mode of thinking, but:

The good systems team does not include poets, painters, holy men or social revolutionaries who, presumably, have nothing to contribute to "real-life" solutions. And how should they when ... the relevant experts are those who understand a people "as members of a system of people, machines, material, and information flow, with specific well-described and often measurable performance requirements?" Above all, the experts are those who can place "quantitative measures on everything—very often, cost and time measures."[4]

In this "suave technocracy"[5] experts become the chief employees and principal legitimators of power, not its possessors. Their dissent may often be passionate but not deep and not heard far away; their chief goal becomes the preservation of intellectual respectability against those who would vulgarize the mysteries of the guild.[6] These experts service an advanced capitalist society in which there is a powerful government-corporate partnership. Through the influence of this corporate-government partnership on educational institutions, and by direct training, corporations insure a supply of the right kind of experts. As the major corporations steadily grow in world influence as multinational corporations their longevity and stability give them and the surrounding society the leeway to seem relatively benign and pluralistic; dissent tends to be dealt with as much by absorption as by strong-arm methods.

Roszak believes that the capacity of the suave technocracy

to absorb dissent and discontent is both its greatest strength and its greatest weakness for it is progressively difficult to know who is outsmarting whom: It may well be that the technocrats will yet have their way with us, outwit or outlast their opposition, and speed us into the Brave New World well ahead of any other society.[7] As an antidote to the technocratic society, the strategy of using countervailing expertise is capable of stopgap success on specific political and social issues, but it leaves wholly untouched one of the basic historical questions of our time:

> It does not challenge the universally presumed rightness of the urban-industrial order of life. Therefore it cannot address itself to the possibility that high industrial society, due to its scale, pace and complexity, is *inherently* technocratic and so inherently undemocratic. At most, it leaves us with the hope that the bastardized technocracies of our day might yet be converted into ideal technocracies. Presumably, then, ... only the requirements of industrial efficiency and the well-being of mankind—the two perhaps conceived to be one and the same—would govern the uses of technology.

> Like good physicians the virtuous experts would advise, counsel, educate and employ their skills with no other end in view but their patients' benefit. So we would begin to approach the "administrative state," where amid the industrial abundance, conflict could only stem from misunderstanding or ignorance....[8]

THE HISTORICAL QUESTION: BLACK SURVIVAL IN THE TECHNOCRATIC WASTELAND?

Obviously Roszak sees modern technology as extremely and pervasively dangerous. Whether or not one is in complete agreement with Roszak, he focuses our attention on a key development of the contemporary period: the political, cultural, social as well as economic transformations in society as a result of modern technology. Roszak asks if automation, computerization and indeed the urban-industrial order of life is inevitable. Are technocracies inherently undemocratic? Is the standardization of individual and cultural group identity and autonomy an inevitable component of a technocratic society? These constitute Roszak's historical question. These are also crucial issues for Blacks. While agreeing that the rise of technocratic patterns of management has important ramifications for all Americans, it raises questions which go to the very heart of Black American survival. The question of Black survival in an age of technology centers around two linked but analytically separable issues: first, maintenance of Black collective identity (and by extension the fate of Black nationalism) in the face of cultural sterilization and bland standardization according to a white American model; and second, protection and enhancement of individual Black liberties to cope with the redefinition of traditional Black roles (as well as traditional white roles) by the exigencies of a new technocratic era. Concretely, this includes such things as protecting Black employment opportunities in the face of automation, finding better strategies to combat attacks on the right of privacy, and so on.

Fears have been expressed that increasing industrial automation will, according to the age-old American employment policy toward Blacks of "last hired, first fired," eliminate a large number of semiskilled and moderately skilled jobs currently held by Afro-Americans and thus raise Black unemployment drastically.[9] More ominously, if the trend continues, Samuel Yette argues that increasing automation of industry will erase the economic role of Black people from the American economy and thus make them a prime candidate for genocide.[10]

With standardization comes cheap and more frequent shallow diversions for, and mass escapist behavior by, those persons standardized. The threat of psychic brutalization is general to all "victims" in the technological wasteland. In terms of who Afro-Americans are, where they come from historically, and where they must go to achieve liberation, the prospect of this standardization for whatever social purpose promises, on its face, special injury. The unique history of Blacks in American

162

society, including their strength under oppression and their distinct collectivity are valuable resources for Black people. Uniformity and standardization are a threat and indeed perhaps a devastating blow to these resources necessary for development of Black institutions based on a collective Black identity.

This brings us to a pertinent tendency in Afro-American thought. When Afro-Americans as a group historically have been confronted by external and internal threats, the tendency has been to turn reflexively inward to examine, strengthen, and criticize *our own* institutions, as opposed to turning *both* inward *and* outward to also perceive trends in and take action against the surrounding American political and economic context. The rise of the Black church as the early major social institution,[11] the Marcus Garvey movement, and the emphasis on developing internal Black consistency (e.g., "buying Black") all stand as examples of this inward turning, and nationalism as a body of strategic thinking is a prime intellectual stimulus and reflection of this historical trend. It may be immediately argued that turning inward is *the* most effective way of dealing with both internal and external threats: as in and of itself a way of turning simultaneously both inward and outward. There is merit to this claim, especially in considering W. E. B. Du Bois' thinking, the history of the Pan-Africanist movement, and the American lynching propensities of the nineteenth and early twentieth centuries. But at rock bottom it remains a narrow way of dealing with threats, especially if pursued as an exclusive strategy, so long as Afro-American migration to another continent (including Africa) is not a real mass possibility or even desirable for most Black people, and inward turning is not a preparation for the departure.

Calling it "narrow" is by no means meant to denigrate the survival necessary today, and especially in earlier years, of a strong Black church and other internal institutions. Not only can such solidarity not be denied, but it was fundamentally necessary for those conditions and remains so. But the world is becoming increasingly complex. That such inward turning was and is necessary for Black survival does not escape the concomitant need for deliberate inquiry and foreseeing of social trends. Such additional strategies would focus deliberately on

163

the relationship of outside pressures to the Black community and in that light examining and modifying internal institutions.

A thoughtful answer to this problem may be that resources are not sufficient to allow Blacks to turn both inward and outward at once, and therefore they must, in the main, choose to turn inward, in part for the very survival reasons that have historically required us to do so up to now. The point here is, however, in light of our historical question about technocratic society, that the above "answer" is not one at all but *rather an issue to be resolved.*

THE LEGAL PROCESS AND THE HISTORICAL QUESTION

To recapitulate the argument thus far: I have suggested that despite the focus on the benefits of technological society by most scholars and others, a number of caveats must be entered based on Black priorities and the Black experience. Following Roszak, I have highlighted two problems for Blacks: standardization and destruction of Black identity and excessive suffering (if not elimination) of Blacks in the technological transformation of society. To be more specific: It is not altogether clear that Blacks would enjoy the prosperity and increase in living standards which is the supposed overarching benefit of technological advance and automation. Sidney Willhelm has stated the issue: In the past Blacks had a specific, if degraded, economic role—slaves, then exploited laborers and indeed a reserve labor supply.[12] Once unskilled and semiskilled jobs are eliminated by automation, what role, if any, will Blacks occupy? Does lack of an economic role provide, as Yette and Sidney Willhelm contend, create the potential for elimination of Blacks? Does the present high Black unemployment and underemployment rate presage just that process?[13] Are Blacks moving into positions as technocratic managers fast enough to begin to offset these possibilities? Is it worthwhile for Blacks to advance in a system that promises to standardize away their cultural autonomy? Blacks might find the new technocracy another form of the old oppression with the potential for forced idleness (at best) and/ or cultural debasement.

164

The immediacy of the technological danger requires Blacks to "look outward"—to develop strategies to impact the larger society. Since one of the major themes in Black political thought has been constitutionalism[14] (involving the attempt to use the law and the legal system to attain Black rights or to protect rights already won), it is only natural that Blacks would seek to use legal strategies to protect against these new dangers. But can legal strategies be developed to prevent Blacks from suffering psychic and/or economic destruction in the technocratic wasteland? That is the historical question for Blacks as it pertains to the legal system.

The historical question cannot be answered solely through empirical research (although research on the many issues pertinent to Blacks is sorely needed) precisely because it is historical in the sense that its resolution will depend upon the dialectics of the historical process. Crucial to this process will be public policy decisions emphasizing the importance of a high quality of life and protecting specific social values. The historical question underscores an underlying, fundamental concern of Blacks: In what ways can the legal system be used to ward off technocratic destructiveness when Blacks have been traditionally excluded from major roles in the legal system as they have been elsewhere structurally isolated in American society? Thus the problem is two-fold: Blacks must continue to seek methods of utilizing the legal system contemporaneously to achieve present goals (which are often as minimal as mere Black representation within the legal system) and at the same time Blacks must shape survival strategies relevant to the technocratic future.

In the remainder of this essay I shall examine the state of legal process (in various areas of law) as it affects Blacks in order to discuss the potential for legal strategies to cope with the larger technological problem. I shall examine constitutional law, commercial law, criminal law, Torts, and International Law, briefly summarizing Black legal strategies and goals and outlining the present extent to which legal doctrine protects identifiable Black interests. Having thereby laid the foundation for discussing Black legal strategies against technological destructiveness, I shall conclude by suggesting a direction for Blacks in general and particularly Black lawyers.

Constitutional Law

On the local day-to-day level, Afro-Americans have partici-
pated in the American legal process in many of the same ways
as have white people, in making individual legal claims in some
capacity or other for them to be accepted, rejected, or modified
by the courts. But there is, of course, much more to it than this.

As far back as the American Revolution, Blacks were
oppressed by racist legislative and judicial treatment—an accurate reflection of their political, economic, and social treatment
as indentured servants, slaves, and general targets of white
oppression.[15] This can be seen as the major component of a
larger spectrum of American racist oppression also against
Indians, Japanese, Chinese, and Mexicans. To briefly review
pertinent history, we may note the southern colonial state slave
codes; the federal Fugitive Slave Acts; the *Dred Scott* decision
by the U.S. Supreme Court in 1857, which confirmed the status
of slaves in American law as merely property and capped many
years of proslavery judicial decisions in which Black people
were no more than pawns for white interests;[16] Lincoln's
Emancipation Proclamation at the close of the Civil War, which
gave faint hope that was quickly nullified by the southern Black
codes with their grandfather clauses that defied the Reconstruction Amendments to the Constitution;[17] the continuous reality
and threat of lynchings that obtains to the present day; and
Plessy v. *Ferguson* in 1896, where the Court upheld racism on
the spurious doctrine of "separate but equal."[18] The list could
easily be extended, but the point is that by 1900 there was
an impressive array of legal machinery arrayed against Afro-
Americans designed to keep them ensnared in the coils of
racism.[19]

In a wider arena, there were corresponding manifestations
in international law. The pernicious Eurocentric distinction in
legal doctrine between "civilized" and "noncivilized" nations
generally meant white and nonwhite, with correspondingly
decreased rights and duties applicable to the latter. The
mandate system was established after 1918 to "bring civilization" with appropriate European discipline. The legal
machinery of colonialism, largely founded on doctrines enabling

166

valid territorial title to be conferred by conquest and coerced treaties, was already in place. Concurrently, the doctrine of national responsibility ensured appropriate excuses for European and American intervention to protect economic and political interests in those nonwhite or developing nations that had attained juridical independence, and in states otherwise too weak to resist.[20]

Thus, an absolutely crucial task for Afro-Americans was to begin as soon as possible to dismantle this backlog of racist legal machinery, a task not yet complete. In contrast to an individual cause of action scenario, it was early apparent that each case brought in this dismantling process involved the interests of the race as a whole; that these particular legal claims, confrontations, and decisions were signally to affect Blacks as a group and therefore would have lasting impact. Such confrontations have occurred especially in cases challenging the validity under the federal Constitution of statutes and judicial decisions adverse to Black people. The federal courts were major arenas, with claims being made on the basis of the Thirteenth, Fourteenth, and Fifteenth Reconstruction Amendments to the U.S. Constitution,[21] and especially based on the Fourteenth Amendment guarantees of equal protection and due process of law. These claims were only part of a long process of Black judicial struggle against racism dating back to the late eighteenth century. More specifically, early in the twentieth century a chain of litigation was begun by the NAACP to reverse the *Plessy* separate-but-equal doctrine. This arduous effort reached one culmination point in *Brown* v. *Board of Education,*[22] the 1954 Supreme Court decision that abolished the separate-but-equal doctrine, desegregated schools on the grounds of the guarantee to Black children of equal protection of the law, and became the most notable example of judicial confirmation of Afro-American interests.[23] Simultaneous to opening this campaign, an intense, ultimately unsuccessful effort of legislative lobbying was begun by the NAACP in an attempt to get Congress to pass anti-lynching legislation. These are probably the two most sustained early efforts in this area. The detailed history to the present of Black-oriented constitutional litigation, a struggle in full swing across a wide front, need not be recounted to know that constitutional law has been a major area of American law where major Black interests in and of themselves have been defined in the courts. These interests include the right to vote, the right of access to public facilities, the right to interracial sex and marriage, the right to protest, the right to military service and conscientious objector status, the right to education, the right to housing, the right to employment, the right to be justly protected, and the right to be free from discriminatory juries.[24]

It is also clear that the overall goal of this litigation was to secure "equal opportunity" (the similarity to "equal protection" is not fortuitous). In other words, the aim was to shoe-horn Afro-Americans into the system, in part because it was the only way for the mass of Black people to go, especially after Marcus Garvey's downfall in 1925; and because of the widespread, perhaps inevitable, buying by the same masses of part of the American Dream. A carrying charge of the latter was the belief that the system as a whole was basically acceptable, if it could only be made to function as it was designed in theory for *all* people—so, campaigns of constitutional litigation were launched to make *this* Constitution equitable. The issue for most Blacks was the functioning of this Constitution, not a new constitution, notwithstanding ongoing Black separatist activity from the early nineteenth century through the present.

Constitutional law is the area where Black interests relative to the legal process have been spelled out most clearly—clearly enough to produce "civil rights" courses in law schools across the country and to stimulate similar strategies and attempts to use many of the same case-law precedents to free other victims of discrimination (e.g., women, Chicanos, Indians). Such a clear delimitation of Afro-American interests has generally not yet occurred in other areas of the law, though there are some emerging possibilities. Given the proper research and thinking, there almost certainly will be found the need for similar campaigns to be mounted in other domains of the law, and some of these possibilities are noted in the following discussions.

Commercial Law

In the area of commercial transactions there has been recent emphasis in legal education on "debtors' rights," as well as the traditional focus on "creditors' remedies," somewhat reflecting the frequent contract difficulties Black people in the ghetto find themselves in a vis-à-vis local merchants for goods bought on installment payment plans. Similarly, for the same reasons, but to a lesser extent, there is some increased emphasis on bankruptcy. In the area of property law, increased attention is being paid to the tenant side of landlord-tenant relations, again a ghetto reflection, but also a reflection of other tendentious renting situations, for example, relations between university student tenants and town landlords. In this connection, much litigation has occurred via claims based on both the Fourteenth Amendment and open-housing statutes, in the area where property and constitutional law intersect, to eliminate racial discrimination as a valid condition of a sale, resale, mortgage, lease, or renting of property and dwelling places. Here Afro-American interests, both as individuals and as a group, have provided one doctrinal cutting edge and have been fairly clearly identified. Recent cases against racist real estate developers have successfully secured remedies of injunctive relief and damages for Black victims of discrimination. Much white opposition to Black equal housing opportunity still remains, for example, the problems posed for the above cases by white-initiated referenda.[25]

In the law of contracts, however, a definition of Black interests with respect to basic doctrines has apparently not occurred (e.g., the absence of an examination of Section 90/ *Restatement of Contracts* notion of reliance as consideration to inquire whether current judicial definitions of reliance are consonant with Afro-American commercial needs and expectations); an examination of whether theories of offer and acceptance forming contracts over distances are valid for Black people, given their generally more restricted access to means of modern communication.

However, a defined body of legal inquiry has emerged around the interests of the Black entrepreneur, relating to the desirability and definition of "Black capitalism." In general, this inquiry focuses on legal issues helpful to the particular situations of Black businessmen, and seems to foreshadow and argue for their increasing entry into national wealth processes.

169

In labor law there is a body of litigation both in the courts and before the National Labor Relations Board designed to integrate Black workers into major unions on the same basis as whites and to shield them from combined and conspiratorial union-employer racism. This must be placed in the context of the simultaneous intertwined legislative and judicial struggle to secure equal opportunity in employment. Here again, we can say that a body of Afro-American interests has been defined in legal process for what they are, often with the aid of constitutional principles of equal protection and due process. The overall goal apparently continues to be, even given increasing Black self-help efforts, to integrate Black workers (and managers)[26] into the American mainstream.

Criminal Law

Criminal law presents a special situation. It is a racial frontier in the legal process in that criminal sanctions are generally one of the first tools that any society uses to move against people it does not like and considers antisocial for whatever reasons. In some very real ways, that describes the feelings of this society about Afro-Americans. That Blacks comprise a highly disproportionate number, nationwide, of arrests, convictions, prison population, and recidivists is a commonplace.[27] Thus, litigation to introduce more justice for defendants in these areas does define Black interests to a considerable extent, but for the wrong reasons. Notwithstanding the intersection of criminal process at almost every turn with the Fourteenth, Fourth, Fifth, and Sixth Amendments to the Constitution, and their constant invocation as defenses by most Black defendants with competent legal advice, the goal here is virtually to survive. More so in light of the glaring nationwide across-the-board absence of Afro-Americans in important law enforcement and investigative positions, and in light of the fact that when Blacks have needed the law most—to protect their physical safety—it has failed them entirely: there are literally hundreds of histories of oppression of Blacks by force.[28] When we consider several newly recognized but age-old problems, the

170

irrespective of whether the subject matter of the right ever constituted a tort at common law. Given the use that Black people have heretofore made of constitutional law, the potential of this holding is considerable for getting damages against bureaucratic harassment and political oppression, though there is some dispute as to whether *Bivens* is limited to damage actions arising from violations of Fourth Amendment rights.[35]

With respect to reparations as a general concept, two questions arise, assuming some form of reparations is eventually paid (as Bell Telephone has already done for women and Blacks to a limited extent): (1) Does this use of legal process share Afro-Americans' general goal of getting a more equitable slice of the pie? and (2) is there any relation between reparations and the larger historical questions surrounding technocratic society?

The answer to the first question would on its face appear to be affirmative. This would be so whether the rationale is payment on the grounds of tort damages, or payment on an unjust enrichment contract-law basis as reimbursement for past contributions to the world's richest economy. In light of the inferior economic position held in the midst of plenty by Afro-Americans as a group, the objective of reparations is to transfer a just amount of economic resources to immediately improve the Black financial position so that participation in the economy thenceforth could be done on a more equitable basis. No major economic, social, or political structural changes would seem required to define this claim, since the latter ostensibly rests on past and not contemplated injustices by white people toward Blacks.

On reflection, however, this conclusion, while basically correct, may be somewhat limited. For if the reparations claim against the federal government is successfully implemented, a new economic distribution pattern will have been established on the basis of governmental recognition of Afro-American *peoplehood,* that is a recognition of Black collective interests transcending political boundaries and subdivisions. This would seem to be the case whether the congressionally enacted reparations scheme calls for payments (in money or other benefits) directly to Black people as individuals, to representative Black organizations, or as is more likely, to a combination

focus in this depressing picture becomes even sharper: the detention and incarceration of Blacks as political prisoners; the widespread use of illegal investigations in conjunction with grossly expanded (relative to the lack of evidence required to convict) criminal conspiracy doctrines; the use of judicial disciplinary procedures against Black judges who take direct action from the bench against racist prosecutions and investigations; and the increasing use of the contempt power by white judges against Black lawyers (and some white lawyers) who insist on defending their clients' rights against the racism of both the prosecution and the bench. Criminal penalties have been used more to oppress Black people than to protect their rights.[29]

In light of our historical question, the goals of Black people with respect to criminal law could very likely assume even more urgency than at present. The emergence of a technological wasteland will, if it occurs, quite likely be accompanied by (if present trends and the experience of other societies' use of criminal sanctions are any guide) the prescription of criminal sanctions to enforce such conformity. Such sanctions will exist in conjunction with expanded facilities and greater legal latitude of judges and administrators to preventively detain those arrested, and to isolate and incarcerate persons suffering "mental disorders" as evidenced by their refusal to conform and rest passively in their assigned social slots.[30] These decision makers will be aided by a progressively refined technology of surveillance, already in existence. Because in such an intensely interdependent national society, the social costs of "deviancy" and disruption in any one sector will probably be exponentially higher than is the case today.

This present and projected situation returns us to the particularly damaging psychic effects of social and cultural standardization on Blacks with the approach of the technocratic wasteland. The indiscriminate, unevaluated, detrimental use of arrest records in commercial credit reports on persons seeking credit is one example. To this must be added widespread white fears in major cities today, especially among law enforcement officials, of Black revolutionary groups deliberately sabotaging vital services at crucial times—requiring comparatively little effort and difficult to prevent—causing widespread public breakdown and panic.[31] Interdependence taken as a social presumption in the context of injustice breeds repression. The question would rapidly become (even more so than now) whether Black people as a group can maintain any self-identity at all.

Torts

The law of torts deals with compensation for noncriminal wrongs as between private parties, and stimulates similar questions about Afro-American objectives in law. There has been no general identification of a body of interests specifically relating to Black people coupled with an assessment of the adequacy of tort doctrines. No data have come to light on any distinction between the level of damages awarded comparatively by juries and in negotiated settlements in negligence actions for the same injuries to Black and white plaintiffs, though there are suspicions that such awards may be racially discriminatory. No special causes of action particularly useful to Blacks have been identified in the area of products liability, though these almost surely exist (e.g., those that might redefine the ways in which useful information about products can reach Blacks particularly *before* purchase, either by disclaimer or otherwise). On the whole, participation by Afro-Americans in tort law has apparently occurred on an individualized basis, with Blacks getting the short end of the stick.

There is, however, some indication that damages will lie in tort for emotional distress caused a Black person by racial epithets slung at him by white people. *Alcorn* v. *Anbro Engineering Co.*[32] concerned a Black worker who was verbally abused by an agent of his company, fired on racial grounds, and suffered shock, physical illness and insomnia as a result. He appealed from a lower court dismissal of his case. In overturning the dismissal, the California Supreme Court held that the circumstances were aggravated enough for the plaintiff to have his case survive the dismissal and be presented to the jury, under the common law doctrine of intentional infliction of emotional distress.

This is a step in the right direction, but it is not a complete solution to these kinds of problems because recovery of damages depends on the jury as the trier of the fact determining the plaintiff's susceptibility to racial slurs. Therefore a premium is placed on equitable Black representation on civil (as well as criminal) juries. Further, insult to race was only one of several factors leading the court to sustain the cause of action. Others included the defendant's position of authority over the plaintiff, his presumed awareness of the plaintiff's susceptibility to this kind of slur, his ignoring of the plaintiff's union status, and his termination of the plaintiff's employment, all without just cause or provocation. It is an open question whether the case would have gotten to the jury on the racial slur alone. The question, as framed by the court, is whether the trial judge should conclude that the trier of fact (generally the jury) could reasonably find the defendant's behavior to be "extreme and outrageous." The latter in turn is based on "community" standards, which may diverge considerably from the Black experience. So the real possibility remains of a white person shouting "nigger!", doing real psychic damage to a Black person who, however, has no cause of action for that alone, especially if there was any suspicion that the epithet *unintentionally* slipped out of defendant's mouth.

Two additional broad areas of tort doctrine are also relevant here: (1) the development of a doctrinal basis for a legal claim to reparations to Afro-Americans for past injustices, paid either by corporations or the federal government or both; and (2) the modus operandi of tort law, the concept of the reasonable man. As for the first, the claim has been now on the public table for about seven years since James Foreman's, *Manifesto to the Churches* in May, 1969. More recently, Professor Boris Bittker has published a useful introductory study of the legal basis in tort and constitutional law for the government making such payments, and of possible implementing arrangements.[33] And the U.S. Supreme Court in *Bivens* v. *Six Unnamed Narcotics Agents of the FBI*[34] has recently provided some assistance by holding, in effect, that the violation of a constitutional right can serve as the basis of a cause of action in tort for damages, here personally against the agents under the Fourth Amendment,

of these.[36] To the extent that this concept of peoplehood is buttressed by constitutional claims, the well-known dictum under the Equal Protection Clause of the Fourteenth Amendment that "the Constitution is color-blind" will be reversed. Already the Supreme Court has allowed use of racial classifications for remedial purposes.[37] Conceivably, recognition of peoplehood for these reparations could serve as a wedge for its recognition for additional Afro-American interests, including those diversity issues falling within our historical question. Conceivably also, if past trends are any guide, the successful concerted prosecution (or even a near miss) of a national claim for reparations by Black people[38] will lead to similar efforts by other American groups, as is already increasingly the case for women, Chicanos, and Indians. Other emergences of peoplehood in law may follow, and thus a force for diversity within the social fabric would be released through making out successful judicial causes of action. In such a context, any government trying to enforce social standardization in the name of technological efficiency would presumably find itself enmeshed in contradictions.

The other side of the coin might, however, be posed by the second question above, depending on what the trade-off is for reparations. What burden now presumably owed by the federal government and/or corporations to Afro-Americans will, in order to receive reparations payments, have to certify as discharged? This is yet unclear, but in light of past bitter experience (e.g., Reconstruction) the price of such reparations is likely to be high. And the fact that the agency from which the reparations funds would flow (presumably Congress) cannot escape responsibility for decisions about *who* in the Black community gets what proportionate share of reparations[39] almost guarantees the onset of federal trade-off thinking. Harbingers exist, which may be consulted. In response to Blacks taking to the streets and generally demanding an end to racism, both government and corporate bureaucracies have generally adopted the same off-putting tokenistic racist strategy: to trade moderately high salaries and fancy titles (material benefits) to a few Black individuals for their collective isolation from the real centers of power and influence, and for exclusion from

175

participation in significant decision making; while allowing limited benefits to, and suppressing the protests of, the remainder. Ensuring such a trade-off at the street level in the Black community was a major (and largely successful) objective of the federal "War on Poverty" community action programs, and apparently it is continuing as Blacks move into the echelons of management. It is dangerously possible that a similar trade-off could be attempted on a mass basis using reparations as a lever. Such a trade-off, with the subsequent Afro-American discharge of white corporate and governmental burdens enshrined into legislation, would forge a potentially powerful and destructive tool for technocratic standardization by government of Black political, economic, social, and cultural freedom. All attempts must be made in any reparations negotiations to stifle this possibility.

This brings us to the tort law doctrine of the "reasonable man."[40] As a construct of how an individual would act reasonably in given circumstances, it is *not* based on an example of any one type of person. The historical fact is that the construct has evolved from the cultural heritage of the English common law, and as transplanted across the Atlantic has been updated, redefined, and decided upon by white male judges operating basically on their own standards of WASP reasonableness. It is not claimed here that this tradition of what is or is not reasonable is *totally* alien to that of Afro-Americans; total alienation is prevented by the common bedrock of humanity linking the races, and by some shared internalization of common law norms. But at the edges, which are quite wide, and on the frontiers of doctrine, the differences are likely to be important. Moreover, the difference between "Black reasonableness" and the "reasonableness" currently enforced in U.S. civil courts is founded on cultural distinctions that create significantly diverse ways of ordering day-to-day priorities that have legal consequences.

The source of all the inputs into the minds of judges and juries as to what constitutes reasonableness is as wide as the entire society. It is doubtful that Blacks have much input, though *Alcorn* (after *so* many years), holds out some hope. We may be sure, however, that one source of such inputs are opinions of the Supreme Court. The Court's recent holding in *Laird* v. *Tatum*[41] is relevant both in this connection and to our larger historical question. *Laird* held that the confirmed presence of, and public knowledge about, an extensive Army intelligence apparatus established to investigate "dissenting" social and political groups, did not constitute a "chilling effect" on the First Amendment right to free speech of members of these groups because no "actual harm" had occurred. That the Army had mounted an investigative campaign against them was not considered "actual harm."

This decision establishes a dangerous criterion of reasonableness: that the reasonable citizen who is at all politically active (and some who are not) should now consider it reasonable to be tightly surveillanced and accept the fact that his very loss of privacy is neither compensable nor judicially remediable. The petitioners in this case were mostly white groups, but the holding is subject to weigh even more heavily on Black dissent. The point is that in an extremely interdependent automated technocratic society, supposedly neutral and objective legal constructs such as reasonableness quickly gravitate to serve the ideas of efficiency and public order held by those wielding centralized power. The Watergate revelations confirm this trend in nonmilitary government thinking. Afro-America must take steps to counter such trends; it is an open question whether this can be done consistently with the goal of integration into the American mainstream.

International Law

We next turn in our survey of legal process to international law, to which Afro-Americans have related in largely indirect terms. This has been so in part because international legal principles have not readily been seen by American courts as available to support domestic causes of action, and therefore to aid the Black struggle. But signs within the last decade indicate change in this situation, to be discussed shortly.

However, in another sense, Afro-American have indeed been concerned with international affairs, and therefore implicitly

177

with international law, for a long time. The great scholar W. E. B. Du Bois was one of the early exponents of Pan-Africanism and the organizer of five Pan-African conferences over a period of 30 years beginning in 1899. His name is a symbol for the essential unity of African peoples in Africa and the United States. Similarly, Malcolm X shortly before his death, in the context of Islam, declared the internationalization of the race struggle to be a Black imperative. These and other forces, including the waves of African independence beginning with that of Ghana in 1957, and the advent of an Afro-Asian bloc in the United Nations commanding a voting majority in the General Assembly and responding to the South African and Rhodesian liberation struggles as *world* racial crises, have instilled a heightened international consciousness into the Afro-American community. However, the diffuseness of this consciousness must be kept in mind.

Those groups of a more nationalist persuasion have borrowed international definitions to describe and attempt to shape the Black experience: terms such as "nationhood" and "self-determination." One group, the Republic of New Africa, has openly espoused and is attempting to put into territorial operation the concept of a Black nation in the southern United States. On other levels, increasingly open identification is made with Africa and other nonwhite developing countries (as the term "Afro-American" people indicates). Such identification ranges from Stokely Carmichael's advocacy of dual citizenship or a citizenship exchange by Black people with an African country, to the late Whitney Young's calling for a "domestic Marshall Plan" to aid the Black "nation" in the United States. African governments, such as those of Tanzania and Uganda, have invited professionally trained Black people to emigrate to aid in their development, and some have accepted. Afro-American annual travel to Africa steadily increases, as do a host of other informal contacts. And a network of more formal contacts with African officials has grown up around the United Nations.

A key issue in international law is whether the substantial body of human rights principles, which arguably comprise a kind of "international legislation," can be mobilized into the

American legal process to aid in the struggle to confirm the rights of Blacks. There is some potential for this. These principles, as positivistic legal statements, date back to before 1900, when they were applied to European minorities, and their substance is generally rooted in the natural law tradition deriving from the Romans, the Scholastics, through Grotius and Pufendorf. They thus have a considerable history apart from white-Black racism, especially in light of Nazi genocidal atrocities in Poland and Germany against the Jews, and of Soviet, Spanish, Portuguese, and Greek atrocities in recent years. Refugee problems created by both World Wars (and the Vietnam War) added increased impetus. And it was largely on this non-Black-white basis that such principles were drafted into major international legal instruments, for example, the Charter of the United Nations, the Universal Declaration of Human Rights, and the European Convention on Human Rights. These in turn were partly inspired by such antecedents as the Bill of Rights in the U.S. Constitution and the French Declaration of the Rights of Man. However, all major governments at the time of drafting the U.N. Charter and the Universal Declaration did their best to ensure, by all means known to domestic and international law, that these principles had only *international* application and carried no legal obligation on those governments to be implemented *domestically*. All tacitly realized that for their own discriminated-against domestic minorities to acquire leverage on the basis of legally being able to claim enforcement of these wide-reaching rights would create pressures that would be political dynamite.

But beginning in 1948, with India's claims in the United Nations on behalf of her nationals and kin against South African apartheid, and followed by the commencement in 1950 of litigation by Ethiopia and Liberia against South Africa in the International Court of Justice over the status of (and South African obligations under) the mandate over Southwest Africa, this body of principles began to be formally mobilized by Africans with respect to their rights against colonial and racist domination. This process received a large boost by the role the invocation of human rights principles played in the mobilization of opposition in the United Nations and around the world to

Rhodesia's illegal Unilateral Declaration of Independence beginning in 1965.[42] For the first time, the broad legal principle of maintaining international peace and security was linked to that of protecting human rights. And as an outcome, the binding force of U.N. Security Council resolutions by way of a treaty obligation through the Charter on the U.S. government, was recently invoked in a useful, albeit unsuccessful, attempt to block the importation to this country of Rhodesian chromium ore.[43] Similarly, there are actions being brought in American courts against American companies doing business in South Africa and Namibia on the general theory that such actions violate both international law and American constitutional guarantees. At present, the primary international concern of Afro-America is the liberation of Southern Africa.

Finally, recent changes in U.N. Economic and Security Council resolutions governing submission of individual petitions of human rights violations to the U.N. Human Rights Commission[44] give some hope that a kind of "litigation" on domestic American human rights grievances before the Commission under international law may be possible in the near future. In this connection, the National Conference of Black Lawyers and several other Black organizations have affiliated themselves with the U.N. as nongovernmental organizations, with observer and quasi-operational status, and petitions have been submitted toward fulfilling this hope.

The above, cumulatively, point toward increased, though indirect, pressure on the federal judiciary to allow Blacks and other litigants to bring actions before domestic American courts directly on the basis that treaty provisions are the law of the United States (without first having to prove that such provisions are self-executing) under Article VI Section 2 of the Constitution. While such causes of action are not yet easily allowed,[45] it seems only a matter of time, not only as a result of Black international involvement, but also from the stark prominence of international legal principles as a result of the Vietnam War.[46]

In line with our general inquiry, the question would now seem to be whether the goal of Black people in their involvement thus far in international legal process has been integration into the American mainstream or whether some different goal is being served. Where possible, international law has been invoked by Blacks and other petitioners as an adjunct of American constitutional guarantees, and thereby shares more or less the same goal as the previously discussed constitutional claims.[47] Also, the substantive content of human rights principles in international law is similar to U.S. constitutional guarantees, though taken as a body of law their ambit of protection (if they were conscientiously enforced) is somewhat wider (e.g., freedom of information versus freedom of speech; and the inclusion of additional principles such as freedom from hunger). Further, much of the juridical basis for international human rights principles being invoked in American legal process rests on Article VI Section 2 of the Constitution, stipulating treaties as the law of the land. This provision is a convenient legal vehicle to the extent that these international principles have been enshrined in treaties to which the United States can be construed a party. Additionally, the invocation of international legal principles of human rights similar or identical in content to U.S. Constitutional principles may possibly make an impact favorable to petitioners on judges hearing their cases, except for those blindly devoted to legal positivism and therefore unwilling to recognize the substantial debt owed by American jurisprudence to the natural law tradition. Finally, the inauguration of litigation inspired by international law in domestic courts against U.S. based multinational corporations will hopefully serve, among other things, as a source of leverage to pressure such defendants into making their benefits available on a more equitable basis to Black people, sometimes in areas other than those at the heart of the litigation. Seemingly, then, the introduction by Black people of causes of action invoking international law principles into American legal process shares the same general goal of Black integration.

But there is an equally important sense in which this goal is not primary. There are several reasons that the increasing invocation of international law in American legal process by Afro-Americans to help combat racism in Southern Africa cannot be descriptively confined to the goal of greater benefits for Afro-Americans. First, it must be noted that a number of white individuals and groups are contributing substantial

181

resources, including legal resources, to this particular effort. Second, taking the vigorous actions of Congressman Charles Diggs' House Sub-Committee on African Affairs as an example,[48] it is clear that the economic and political benefits to Black people from opposition to American involvement in Southern African racism are indirect at best. Diggs' subcommittee is taking action because (1) it is the right thing to do, even a moral obligation; and (2) the minimal resources now exist to do so. Afro-American involvement in the struggle against racism in Africa is not now and has never been, from the time of Padmore and Du Bois forward, subjected to the condition that the American struggle be substantially "won" before resources could be committed to transoceanic objectives. We must, however, qualify this by noting that the proportion of the latter category of resources has been small in comparison with those committed domestically; nevertheless, the principle remains valid and significant. We may ask why it is considered "right" to reach out to Africa internationally. It seems clear, in an existential sense, that the idea of Pan-Africanism has taken root in America to at least this minimal extent of producing quasi-normative standards for allocating Black resources in certain situations. Relative to the substantial numbers of whites involved, we may note in conjunction that one by-product, among many, of the technology and communications "revolution" is increased efficiency in internationalizing injustice from behind the barriers of national boundaries wherever it occurs.

There may be another reason why this particular use of legal process goes beyond the goal of more equitably slicing the pie. The pie (i.e., the benefits of the American political, economic, and social system as a whole) is territorially based. Its primary legal reference points remain those of the nation-state. The political boundaries of this country, in connection with the legal title of "citizen" on those deemed to belong and share rights and duties with those within, reflect the emergence of national states since the seventeenth century to be, as they remain, the primary participants in the international legal process. Accompanying this emergence was the presumption that if encapsulated peoples within states could not manage to speak internationally through, or with the approval of "their" governments (especially to voice grievances and demand redress), then, save in exceptional circumstances (including successful revolution), such peoples were presumed to have no just claim. Obviously, such total encapsulation has never been absolutely the case, but the presumption—an adjunct of the international law doctrine of sovereignty—remains bothersome and is heavily invoked by all states.

The use of international legal process for Pan-Africanist objectives by a Black minority in the world's richest and most powerful nation directly confronts this presumption by asserting a conflicting nonterritorially based loyalty, and by asserting the right to use domestic resources for that purpose—the right, in effect, of a people to choose its own friends and patterns of communication, and not to have them totally preselected by territorial delimitation. Presently this conflict is not an absolute one, but at the goal level, in that Pan-African aspirations to some degree have been incorporated into Afro-American norms, it surely exists. Here, the goal may be plausibly defined as the removal of the barriers of national boundaries in order to, in part, maintain an essential ingredient of Afro-American peoplehood.

And as such it relates to our previously posed historical question on the approach of the technocratic wasteland. Cultural and social diversity must be maintained to fight off stifling and destructive technological efficiency based standardization. To the extent that there are external reference points of peoplehood (e.g., Africa and the African connection) outside the wasteland, in connection with well-established (through legal process and otherwise) ways of invoking them, much more ammunition (figuratively) is on hand to defend cultural, political, and even economic diversity within the United States for Afro-Americans. Diverse objectives, bases of reasoning, and inspirations for strategies would be available to combat the flood of efficiency based rationales for the acceptance of programs and encroachments urged by the managers of American society. Material benefits would undoubtedly play their seductive part, but the managers could not so easily present them as a total universe of existence in the face of a confirmed internationally based sense of peoplehood. To this extent, then,

183

the invocation of international legal process by Afro-Americans serves a goal different from that of equitable benefits to Blacks from the American system.

To recapitulate our truncated discussion of Afro-American involvement in legal process, the goals of such involvement, where the interests of Blacks as a group can be identified, seem primarily to be integration of Blacks into the American mainstream. This emerges especially from our overview of litigation in American constitutional law, and to a lesser extent in labor law. In considering Black people and the criminal legal process, the goal recedes to that of survival. There seems to be no substantial body of Afro-Amercan interests yet identified in commercial law beyond those of Black capitalism, nor generally in the law of property except as it intersects with constitutional principles, though possibilities exist of making such identification in the future. The same is true in part for torts, except that here there is the chance of a different goal orientation if the claim for payment of reparations to Afro-Americans can be implemented successfully. And although the invocation of international law can be considered, in one sense, as aiding the more equitable distribution of economic and social benefits, in another sense a different goal of supporting Afro-American peoplehood, affecting the fundamental character of the American social process, is involved.

Can alternative goals for Afro-American participation in legal process be envisaged that show some promise of preventing the onset of the wasteland and also assuring Black economic development and cultural integrity? This issue invites a final few words.

IV CONCLUSION:
ALTERNATIVE GOALS OF LEGAL PROCESS

Both the possible implementation of tort constitutional law claims for Black reparations, and the bringing of domestic causes of action in aid of the Southern Africa liberation movement invite the formulation of alternative goals. By "alternative goals" are meant fundamentally basic reasons for Blacks to participate in legal process, where their interests as a people are involved, alternative to those of equitable access to the benefits of American society. Such alternatives seem to lie in the direction of either aiming to change the character of the society, or (simultaneously) directly affecting the criteria by which allocation of social benefits is now made. Our discussion so far indicates that some change in the nature of the society—not least in the character of its legal process—may be required to prevent social and cultural sterilization, deterioration of humanistic values and special destruction to Blacks by technocracy.

As noted earlier, the successful implementation of reparations would very likely require the federal government to explicitly recognize the peoplehood of Afro-Americans in order to effectively make payment, and in so doing to redefine the constitutional principle of equal protection of law toward some explicit incorporation of guarantees to Black people as a group as well as to them as individuals. By expanding the definition of a judicially perceptible "class" for class action suits, group recognition has been accomplished to some degree for specific situations, especially in the southern voting rights cases in the mid-1960s. But as indicated by recent decisions in stockholder derivative suits limiting the definition of a viable class, the handwriting may well be on the wall for the use of this strategy to vindicate interests of Afro-Americans as a people or a culture. Successful implementation of reparations, if it occurs, offers some hope of leaping over this barrier toward the direct judicial recognition of Black interests and hopefully their direct vindication. Such a leap relates in purpose back to our larger historical question about technology: to provide legal strategies to preserve diversity—cultural, social, and political. These strategies would hopefully be available to combat predicted increasing pressure from white society and government on Blacks to become increasingly standardized in all respects, in the name of a technocracy that theoretically promises to pay for its social efficiency in increased material benefits to its standardized citizens.

A word of caution must be added here. In considering alternative goals leading to direct judicial recognition of their interests, Blacks experience a conflict. First, there is the

185

promise of more direct recognition and fulfillment of Black interests than is currently possible via legal process. On the other hand, there is the potential threat of this direct juridical recogniton being applied as the other edge of the sword and used to justify in law apartheid-type restrictions and the forcible imposition of a kind of "homelands" confinement under the guise of protecting Black culture. The white South African legal experience must be studied carefully by Black lawyers, not only to aid in bringing that system down, but also for the lessons it can teach about recognizing the approach of, and preconditions for, the establishment of similar kinds of apartheid "legal" restrictions in the United States and elsewhere. Accordingly, great care must be taken here, and the requisite analysis must be wise, informed, and precise before the notion of a "color-blind" equal protection doctrine is given up in favor of an interpretation where Black interests are directly recognized in legislation and judicial orders. It may well be possible to accomplish more or less the same direct recognition of Afro-American interests under various extensions of current equal protection doctrines, preserving their safeguards against the double-edged sword while gaining the necessary latitude to preserve Black cultural and social diversity (e.g., a doctrine of equal latitude for group diversity as a protected right within the ambit of equal protection).[49]

The possibility of reparations also raises the prospect of alternative goals in tort law. To the extent that the legal personality of Afro-Americans as a people is confirmed, damage actions would theoretically be possible against those, especially governments and corporate officials, who intentionally or negligently harm Black interests. Such harm could conceivably be defined in terms of specific actions imposing technocratic standardization and shown to be real and injurious on that basis. This might include actions (e.g., the use by a school board of computers to order textbooks on a school-by-school basis, based, in turn, on computer-graded reading scores) where the entire process is discriminatory to Black students. "Legitimate interests" could include the maintenance of national, regional, and local diversity. However, substantial problems arise in implementing these causes of action. They include those of confronting the principle of sovereign immunity as a defense. Governmental acts perpetrating standardizing measures may fall mostly under the definition of "ministerial acts," for which most governments, including the federal government, have not yet consented to be sued, except on very narrow grounds. This barrier does not seem insuperable, however, since the clear trend is toward courts finding liability on the part of the government; the retention of immunity as a successful defense is increasingly the exception. And we noted earlier the potential of the *Bivins* case in this respect. There also will be major problems of finding whether Black people have legitimately consented to various technocratic policies, since such consent would be a strong defense to litigation challenging such policies.

We suggested earlier that the invocation of international law by Afro-Americans would tend to enhance the self-definition of peoplehood by giving normative content to the Pan-African tradition in the United States. More important is the challenge by Blacks to the *national* delimitation of that peoplehood. If the federal judiciary could be persuaded to recognize an inherent right, either under the Constitution or under international law as binding through the Constitution, of a group of citizens of the United States to communicate freely with other members of the same general group throughout the world irrespective of the approval of the U.S. government, the character of the society would be substantially changed. This impingement would be especially important relative to the traditional racist attitudes against nonwhite people immigrating to the United States. Such attitudes make realization of this goal a difficult proposition indeed. But current legal activities are presently laying a foundation which, if utilized by appropriate strategists, could serve as a decisive step in the right direction. However, the ultimate objective is fundamental change in the present nature of society and a reversal of the present anti-humanistic, oppressive tendencies concomitant to and more efficiently carried out through technocracy. The struggle promises to be as long and hard as it is crucial.

NOTES

I have benefited greatly from comments on an earlier draft of this essay by my colleagues Professors Alan Schwartz, Julius Getman, and Arghyrios Fatourus, and especially from those of Professor Barbara Brudno. Errors remain my responsibility.

1. Theodore Roszak, *Where the Wasteland Ends: Politics and Transcendence in Postindustrial Society* (Garden City, New York: Doubleday, 1972).

2. Ibid., pp. 32-33.

3. Ibid., pp. 34-35.

4. Ibid., p. 36.

5. Ibid., p. 42.

6. Ibid.

7. Ibid., p. 46.

8. Ibid., p. 55

9. Sidney M. Willhelm, *Who Needs the Negro?* (New York: Doubleday, 1971).

10. Samuel F. Yette, *The Choice* (New York: Putnam, 1971).

11. Charles V. Hamilton, *The Black Preacher In America* (New York: Morrow, 1970), especially p. 13.

12. Willhelm, see particularly the introduction.

13. See particularly articles by James A. Hefner and Thaddeus Spratlen in this volume. They discuss the high rates of Black unemployment.

14. Charles V. Hamilton, *The Black Political Experience In America* (New York: Putnam, 1973), p. xiff.

15. Derrick A. Bell, *Race, Racism and American Law* (Boston: Little, Brown and Co., 1973), p. 102f.

16. 60 U.S. (19 How.) 393 (1857): Bell, *Race, Racism and American Law,* pp. 2-45.

17. Bell, *Race, Racism and American Law,* pp. 52-56.

18. Ibid., pp. 86-87, 204-205.

19. See Hayward Burns argument in "Racism and Law," *Amistad II,* (New York: Random House, 1971).

20. See generally R. P. Anand, *New States and International Law* (Delhi: International Scholarly Book Service, 1973).

21. These three amendments were brought into force early in the post-Civil War Reconstruction period. The Thirteenth generally abolished slavery; the Fourteenth conferred citizenship on Black people and established the rights to due process and equal protection of the law of all people protected from violation by *state* action (as opposed to actions of private citizens—a distinction that remains today); the Fifteenth gave the

right to vote. All three amendments were in force by 1870. To them must be added the "radical" legislation of the Civil Rights Acts of 1866 and 1875, which guaranteed to Black people rights of public accommodation, due process, equal protection and other similar rights. Neither these amendments nor this legislation (soon to be vitiated by the Supreme Court) was sufficient to protect Afro-American political and civil rights. Southern resistance was stiff, and effective efforts at enforcement left much to be desired. Once they recovered from the initial staggering blow of Reconstruction legislation, the ex-Confederates set out to nullify it in every possible way. Bell, *Race, Racism and American Law,* pp. 198-199.

22. 347 U.S. 483, 74 S. Ct. 686, 98 L. Ed. 873 (1954).

23. Generally, since *Brown,* the right to an integrated education is the foundation on which all legal claims to full citizenship for Blacks have been built (Bell, *Race, Racism and American Law,* p. 431). Bell puts the case in perspective by discussing *Brown* and its predecessors, post-*Brown* southern school litigation, and the ramifications of *Brown* in nonschool segregation (principally housing and public accommodations). See pp. 431-573.

24. An excellent readable history of this judicial struggle is Loren Miller, *The Petitioners* (New York: Pantheon, 1966).

25. For an excellent current discussion of this area see Bell, *Race, Racism and American Law.*

26. See Bell, *Race, Racism and American Law,* pp. 713-856.

27. *Report of the National Advisory Commission on Civil Disorders* (New York: Bantam, 1968), pp. 268-269; Ramsey Clark, *Crime in America* (New York: Simon & Schuster, 1970), p. 35.

28. Bell, *Race, Racism and American Law,* p. 857.

29. For a disucssion of relevant cases, see ibid., pp. 857-883.

30. Clark, *Crime in America,* pp. 274-294.

31. Ample White House level paranoia about political dissidence has come to light through the Ervin Committee's Watergate hearings and the government's prosecution of Daniel Ellsberg; and general official paranoia through the continuing police harassment, imprisonment, and prosecution of the Black Panthers, the Black Muslims, the Republic of New Africa, and the Black Liberation Army. Bell, *Race, Racism and American Law,* pp. 116-117.

32. 2 Cal. 3d 493, 368 P. 2d 216 (1970).

33. Boris Bittker, *The Case for Black Reparations* (New York: Random House, 1973).

34. 403 U.S. 388, 91 S. Ct. 1999, 29 L. Ed. 2d 619 (1971).

35. See Bell, *Race, Racism and American Law,* p. 907.

36. See Boris Bittker, *The Case for Black Reparations* (New York: Random House, 1973), pp. 71-86.

37. *North Carolina State Board of Education* v. *Swann,* 402 U.S. 43, 45-46 (1971).

38. This concept covers both the possibility of successful Black judicial action to secure reparations, e.g., under 18 U.S.C. § 1983, or congressional action. These are alternative though not mutually exclusive strategies.

39. Bittker, *The Case for Black Reparations,* p. 86.

40. The sexism of the traditional formulation is obvious.

41. 408 U.S. 1 (1972).

42. *See* generally T. Olawale Elias, *Africa and the Development of International Law* (Dobbs Ferry, New York: Oceana, 1972), pp. 179-216.

43. *Diggs* v. *Schultz,* 470 F. 2d 461 (1972).

44. John Carey, *UN Protection of Civil and Political Rights* (Syracuse: New York: Syracuse University Press, 1970), pp. 91-92.

45. See *Sei Fujii* v. *State,* 242 P. 2d 617 (1952).

46. See, for example, Telford Taylor, *Nuremberg and Vietnam: An American Tragedy* (New York: Quadrangle, 1970).

47. *Sei Fujii* v. *State.*

48. Through this subcommittee, Congressman Diggs as Chairman has become a major spokesman for the closer conjunction of Afro-American and African interests. His open committee hearings on American involvement in Africa, especially Southern Africa, have produced a most useful series of reports.

49. Opinions differ as to the threat posed by this problem. Bittker takes it rather seriously, and I tend to agree on the basis of the South African example.

6

BLACK AND WHITE WEALTH: A COMPARATIVE ANALYSIS

Marcus Alexis

Marcus Alexis is Professor of Economics and Urban Affairs at Northwestern University. He is the author of numerous articles on urban economics.

INTRODUCTION

The relative economic status of Black Americans and the means by which their participation in the mainstream of American economic life can be accelerated is one of the liveliest areas of intellectual activity among economists. Data collected recently by the Office of Economic Opportunity bring new facts to the attention of those who are seriously interested in understanding the dimensions of the underrepresentation of Blacks in American economic life. Although asset data for Blacks have been collected in the past in the *Survey of Consumer Finances* by George Katona and his colleagues at the University of Michigan's Survey Research Center, the larger number of Blacks included in the 1967 Survey of Economic Opportunity (SEO) greatly improves our ability to make inferences about the wealth distribution in the Black community.

It should be clear to all that the current status of Blacks is in large measure attributable to limitations placed on them in the past. In this sense, no study that makes use of variables whose present values are dependent on past discrimination can isolate the effect of these variables and the process that gave rise to them. That is to say, current data on the distribution of income, occupations, and education reflect discrimination over time. Therefore, the effect of such variables on observed

193

outcomes is misleading. The measures do not mean the same thing for Blacks as they do for whites. Discrimination affects both the distribution of the income, occupation, and education variables and their effect on observed outcomes.

The likelihood that a Black person will complete a given number of years of schooling is less than it is for a white person. In addition, the quality of the schooling is likely to be poorer for the Black person. If education is a key variable in determining occupation and income, then the Black individual will also have a lower-status occupation and less income. Discrimination affects the observed outcomes in yet another way. Blacks with the same education, as measured by school years and achievement, do not receive as high returns on their investment in education as whites.[1] It has been argued that differences in employment security of Blacks and whites is partially due to differences in their distribution of job skills and partially to discrimination.[2] However, since the distribution of job skills is itself a function of discrimination, this argument understates the effect of discrimination on the economic status of Blacks.

The point of all this is that static analysis, such as we find in most published papers, cannot deal adequately with the interdependence of discrimination and its effects on variables affecting income and wealth. It can only tell us that given the distribution of the certain variables, differences in such variables as income and wealth are the result of *current* discrimination. This is a serious problem and must not be lost sight of, a possibility that is all too likely when attention is focused on the measures in an economic model and not on the more general questions, "How did the variables come to be distributed the way they are and why do the measures attached to them have their particular signs and values?"

ESTIMATING WEALTH

The definition of net wealth in the SEO data raises serious questions as to the completeness of the estimate of household wealth and the introduction of bias into the analysis due to the definition. Total wealth is defined as *the sum of bank*

194

accounts, stock, government bonds, housing equity, car and truck equity, farm equity, business equity and equity in other real estate. Consumer installment debt is conspicuously absent as an offset to the listed equities. Important forms of consumer installment debt that are more likely to be held by white than by Black households are: (1) retail credit, (2) bank installment loan credit, (3) installment loans from nonbank lenders, and (4) credit card credit. To the extent that these items loom larger in the portfolios of whites than Blacks, the estimates of differences in net wealth for Black and white households within the same income class are overstated.

Blacks have consistently less wealth even after adjustments for income are made. According to SEO data, even white families with incomes under $2,500 had (on the average) net wealth (from all sources) of $10,681. The figure for Blacks was $2,148. Whites had wealth eight times the midpoint of their income class; Blacks had twice the wealth of the midpoint. At this low-level income whites had four times the wealth of Blacks in the same income class. This is almost certainly due in part to the higher concentration of persons over 65 in the white sample who are retired but who have accumulated wealth during their working years (see Table 6.1).

Table 6.1. Total Net Wealth of White and Black Families, by Income Class (mean amounts in dollars)

Income Class	Net Wealth		Ratio of Black to White Wealth	Wealth-Income Ratio*	
	White	Black		White	Black
$ 0- 2,499	10,681	$ 2,148	20.1	7.51	1.61
2,500- 4,999	13,932	2,239	16.1	3.75	0.62
5,000- 7,499	13,954	4,240	30.4	2.25	0.69
7,500- 9,999	16,441	6,021	36.6	1.91	0.70
10,000-14,999	24,304	8,694	35.8	2.04	0.74
15,000-19,999	43,413	20,533	47.3	2.58	1.22
20,000 & over	101,009	30,195	29.9	3.37	1.26
All units	20,153	3,779	18.8	2.58	0.81

*Evaluated at mean income within each income class.
Source: Henry S. Terrell, "Wealth Accumulation of Black and White Families: The Empirical Evidence," *Journal of Finance,* 26 (May 1971), Table 1, p. 364.

Table 6.1 is interesting in another sense; the largest relative gain in the Black-white wealth ratio occurs as income increases from the $2,500-$4,999 income class to the $5,000-$7,499 class—14.3 percentage points. This is due to the negligible change in white wealth within these income classes compared to the almost doubling of the wealth of Blacks. This slowing of white wealth accumulation and relatively rapid advance for Blacks suggest that for whites wealth accumulation in the income range $2,599-$7,499 is not very sensitive to income. That is, what economists call the "income elasticity" (the relative change in wealth divided by the relative change in income)[3] for whites between the two classes is

$$\frac{22}{2,500} \times \frac{5,000}{13,943} = 3 \times 10^{-3} \text{ or } .003,$$

almost zero. For Blacks the corresponding elasticity is

$$\frac{2,001}{2,500} \times \frac{5,000}{3,240} = 1.24 \text{ or } 1,240 \times 10^{-3},$$

a considerable difference. An interesting unanswered question is, why the enormous difference in income elasticity of wealth accumulation for Blacks and whites at these two income levels?

One model that has been used to study differences in Black-white wealth/income ratios is the "Permanent Income Hypothesis" of University of Chicago economist Milton Friedman.[4] In his formulation, Professor Friedman argues that household income consists of two components, a permanent income based on such factors as age and labor-market skills (human capital) and a random (transitory) component. In the absence of discrimination, with Blacks and whites having the same (i.e., permanent) income, any observed differences from year to year would cancel out. But this as we know is not the case. How then do we explain differences in Black and white incomes and wealth?

Friedman is quite clear as to why Blacks have lower average incomes. Commenting on the situation in both the North and the South, he says,

The integration in the North means that Negroes tend to be specialized, their lower average incomes reflect very largely the fact they they engage in lower paid occupations; they depend on the white community, as it were, for the services of the most highly paid occupations. In the South, being less fully integrated in this sense in the society, Negroes may tend to depend more on their own community for these more highly paid occupations; their lower average income reflects not only their concentration in lower paid occupations but also, to a much greater extent than in the North, a lower return for each activity separately. The effects would presumably tend to be much more marked in large communities than in small cities or villages. A minor bit of evidence supporting this interpretation is that although the average income of nonrelief Negro familes is more than 20 percent lower in Atlanta than in Columbus (Ohio), a slightly higher percentage of all Negro families, 10.3 compared with 9.8 are classified as business or professional families, independent or salaried.[5]

What this quote illustrates is that the lower average income of Blacks is not an accident. In the North Blacks are more concentrated in lower paying jobs, and in the South, where the concentration of highly skilled, professional Blacks is greater, the compensation for their skill is less. This is why it is important to make clear the point that discrimination—past and present—is an integral part of any analysis of the economic status of Blacks. Indeed, this is important in understanding the activities into which Black capital flows and to see why the conclusion reached by Gary Becker is incorrect.[6] It is Becker's position that discrimination results in higher returns for Black capital. This is certainly not the case if one considers human capital as documented by the quote from Friedman.

The data in Table 6.2 are highly informative. The table distinguishes between wealth held in the form of nonliquid assets and that held in highly liquid assets such as common stock, bank deposits, and government bonds. The financial

Table 6.2. Net Wealth Accumulation, Distribution and Aggregates for Black and White Families*

Type of Asset	Mean Accumulation Per Family (Absolute Amount)			Distribution of Total Holdings (Percent)		Estimated Aggregate Holdings (Billions of Dollars)		Black Share of Total** (Percent)
	White	Black	Ratio	White	Black	White	Black	
Nonliquid Assets								
Equity in Home	$ 6,511	$2,125	32.6	32.3	56.2	$359.2	$12.7	3.4
Equity in Cars and Trucks	1,033	309	29.9	5.1	8.2	57.0	1.9	3.2
Equity in Other Real Estate	1,868	436	23.3	9.3	11.5	103.1	2.6	2.5
Farm Equity	2,769	309	11.2	13.7	8.2	152.8	1.9	1.2
Business Equity	1,904	216	11.3	9.4	5.7	105.1	1.3	1.2
Subtotal	$14,085	$3,395	24.1	69.8	89.8	$777.2	$20.4	2.6
Financial Assets								
Value of Stocks	2,631	39	1.5	13.1	1.0	145.2	0.2	0.13
Money in Banks	2,955	296	10.0	14.7	7.8	163.0	1.8	1.1
Government Bonds	482	49	10.2	2.4	1.3	26.6	0.3	1.1
Subtotal	$ 6,068	$ 384	6.3	30.1	10.1	$334.8	$ 2.3	0.7
Total, All Assets	$20,153	$3,779	18.8	100	100	$1,112.0	$22.7	2.0

*Evaluated at mean income within each income class.
**This is the Black share of the total for the entire Black and white population and does not include holdings of the less than 1 percent of the non-Black minority population.
Source: Henry S. Terrell, "Wealth Accumulation of Black and White Families: The Empirical Evidence," *Journal of Finance,* 26 (May 1971), Table 1, p. 364.

assets suffer from the possibility that they might be biased upward due to the underreporting or nonreporting of offsetting loans against the stocks and government bonds. That aside, the data are impressive in that they show that while the ratio of Black to white wealth as a whole is 18.8 percent, the ratio in the case of highly liquid financial assets out of which financial crises can be dealt with is even lower—a mere 6.3 percent.

From Table 6.2 we see that Black families hold, on the average, $39 in stocks. It would be useful to have the distribution of stock ownership of Black families by education and occupation with income held constant. This would tell us the responsiveness of stock ownership to changes in these variables. If stock ownership is affected by education and occupation in a positive way, then a policy implication that follows is that one means of increasing the participation of Blacks in the owning of corporate equities is to increase educational and occupational opportunities.

It should be noted that a larger fraction of the portfolios of Blacks is in assets assuring continued consumption services. This makes sense in terms of the greater economic instability of Blacks than that of whites.

One explanation of the observed differences in the holdings of stocks of Blacks and whites is that the relatively small and predominantly local markets fostered by a protective barrier of segregation, which characterize most Black businesses, are not large enough to support a securities market. The fact that most Black businesses are small would explain why the dominant form of business organization is the sole proprietorship or partnership, but not why Blacks do not choose to hold common stocks in their portfolios to a larger extent. The market for corporate securities is national in scope and Blacks with the requisite assets can acquire them as easily as whites by simply placing an order with their broker. In the South Blacks might be more reluctant to have their financial position known to whites, but here too, stocks can be purchased through an out-of-town broker.

DISTRIBUTION OF BLACK INCOME AND WEALTH

Data on Black incomes and wealth show that both are less equally distributed than those in the white population. This suggests that within the Black population there are wider disparities in income and wealth between the low and high ends of the respective distribution than there are in the case of whites. This is borne out in Table 6.3, which shows that for Blacks with 16 or more years of schooling (college degree) wealth is 2.9 times as great as it is for Blacks with some college, while for whites the corresponding factor is only 1.3. Clearly then, a college education for Blacks increases wealth accumulation propensity far more than it does for whites. A more telling way of putting it is that Blacks without college degrees are more seriously penalized than whites. The ratio of all wealth held by the relatively small number and percent of Blacks with college degrees is in excess of 70 percent of all wealth held by whites in the same educational class. The figure for all Blacks compared to all whites is 18.8 percent. Indeed, for Blacks 55-64 years of age the ratio is .71 at the $10,000 income level and .86 at the $25,000 level. We see here that not only are we becoming two nations, one Black and one white, but also that Blacks more than whites are becoming more separated in an economic sense depending on whether or not the family head does or does not have a college degee.

The policy implication to be derived from this is not that earning college degrees is the way for Blacks to achieve economic equality, but instead that immediate steps must be taken to equalize the opportunities of those Blacks without college degrees so that they may participate in the economy on the level of whites with the same education. It would be an extension of discriminatory thinking, indeed racism, to require Blacks to be college graduates in order to have chances of wealth accumulation more nearly equal to that of whites who are not graduates.

It is interesting to note that the distribution of equities in cars and trucks is less equally distributed among Blacks than whites. The reason for this is that income and wealth are highly correlated and the equities in cars are a function of income.

Table 6.3. Estimated Wealth Accumulation of Urban Black and White Families with an Employed Head, by Family Income, Age, and Education of Head*

Hypothetical Level of Family Income	Age of the Head of the Family											
	Head under 35			Head 35-54			Head 55-64			Head over 65		
	White	Black	Ratio	White	Black	Ratio	White	Black	Ratio	White	Black	Ratio
A. $5,000 Family Income												
0- 7 yrs. education	216	48	.22	588	108	.18	1,420	371	.26	2,680	625	.23
8-11 yrs. education	441	48	.11	1,200	108	.09	2,910	371	.13	5,480	625	.11
12 yrs. education	735	160	.22	2,000	247	.12	4,840	845	.17	9,130	1,430	.16
13-15 yrs. education	944	203	.22	2,570	458	.18	6,220	1,970	.32	11,600	2,200	.19
16 or more yrs. education	1,090	579	.53	2,980	1,310	.44	7,210	4,480	.62	13,600	7,580	.56
B. $10,000 Family Income												
0- 7 yrs. education	727	186	.25	1,979	417	.21	4,778	1,434	.30	9,018	2,416	.27
8-11 yrs. education	1,484	186	.13	4,038	417	.10	9,792	1,434	.15	18,440	2,416	.13
12 yrs. education	2,473	618	.25	6,730	955	.14	16,287	3,266	.20	30,722	5,527	.18
13-15 yrs. education	3,177	785	.25	8,648	1,777	.21	20,930	7,614	.36	39,034	8,503	.22
16 or more yrs. education	3,667	2,238	.63	10,028	5,063	.50	24,262	17,315	.71	45,764	29,297	.64
C. $25,000 Family Income												
0- 7 yrs. education	3,606	1,107	.31	9,816	2,481	.25	23,699	8,532	.36	44,729	14,375	.32
8-11 yrs. education	7,361	1,107	.15	20,078	2,481	.12	48,568	8,532	.18	91,462	14,375	.16
12 yrs. education	12,266	3,677	.30	33,381	5,682	.17	80,784	19,433	.24	152,381	32,886	.22
13-15 yrs. education	15,758	4,671	.30	42,894	10,573	.25	103,813	45,303	.44	193,609	50,593	.26
16 or more yrs. education	18,188	13,316	.73	49,739	30,125	.61	120,340	103,024	.86	226,989	174,317	.77

*Evaluated at mean income within each income class.
Source: Terrell, "Wealth Accumulation," Table 5, p. 376.

Therefore, if income is less equally distributed, so will be equities in cars.[7]

A measure of the inequality in the distribution of wealth is the Gini coefficient.[8] The Gini coefficient takes on values between 0 and 1.0, with a value of 1.0 representing the greatest possible inequality and a value of 0 representing complete equality in the distributed quantity. If all assets were held by a single individual, the Gini coefficient would be 1.0. On the other hand, if each individual held $1/n$ fraction of the wealth and there were n individuals the Gini coefficient would be 0. In Table 6.3 the assets in Table 6.2 and their Gini coefficients for Black, white, and combined groups are presented. It should be noted that in some cases the Gini coefficients exceed the upper limit of 1.0. This is due to the procedure used to compute the coefficients.[9]

Although there are difficulties with the estimates in Table 6.3 they do give a useful comparison of the relative inequalities in the distribution of different asset types. In only three cases is the distribution of wealth sufficiently diffuse to yield Gini coefficients considerably different from 1.0; this is true in the cases of equities in cars and trucks, equities in homes, and money in banks. Significantly, using either the "all families" or "families reporting accumulation" designations, Black wealth is more unequally distributed than white wealth for most asset types and for net wealth.

Inherited Wealth

Inherited wealth is one of the determinants of accumulated wealth. One should view with skepticism the findings of the *Survey of Financial Characteristics of Consumers* that the inheritances of only five percent of the units in its sample comprised a substantial portion of their total assets. This finding really begs the question: What fraction is substantial? In dollar terms, how much is substantial? Clearly, parents with equities in real estate, farms, and other assets pass most of it on to their heirs, and whites have more to pass on than Blacks. Therefore, inherited wealth plays a larger role in wealth accumulation of whites than of Blacks. This is true for Blacks and whites at all income levels and not only for whites reporting large amounts of accumulated wealth.

CONCLUSION

When all is said and done, some tentative conclusions can be drawn from the data that forms the basis of this paper. First, as we all know, Blacks have both less income and less wealth than whites. Second, even when adjustments are made for income differences, Black wealth is only a fraction of the wealth of whites with comparable incomes. Third, the income and wealth distributions of Blacks are more unequal than the same measures are for whites. Fourth, accumulated wealth of whites is influenced to a greater degree by intergeneration transfers in the form of inheritances than is true for Blacks. Fifth, education, which is supposed to be the great equalizer, does not operate to provide the same income or wealth benefits to Blacks that it bestows on whites Last, it is only the most educated Blacks—those with sixteen or more years of schooling—who are making any progress in closing the wealth/income ratio gap.

The unhappy message of all this is that Blacks are still a long way from achieving anything approaching economic parity. The culprit is continued, if more subtle, discrimination—or racism—against Blacks at all levels. Even Blacks with superior education and skills do not reap the full fruits of their labors or endowments. The effect is to discourage younger Blacks from acquiring the requisite education or skills in the numbers required to lift the entire income distribution of Blacks—and not merely that of what was formerly called "The Talented Tenth."

The remedy to the economic plight of Blacks is not to be found in economic activity alone. Until and unless Blacks achieve some degree of effective political power (i.e., command over institutions—public and private—that establish the rules of the game and determine the payoffs) they will continue to suffer from second-class economic citizenship. The purposes of this paper will have been served if Blacks view it as a challenge

203

to weld together politically potent structures to create an environment in which Black talent and aspirations might find opportunities for free expression and uninhibited success. Without such strucutres, the hope of Black economic development will continue to be just another dream of the Blacks—or worse, a cruel hoax perpetrated by a white society.

APPENDIX

Figure 6.1. Lorenz Curve and Gini Index of Concentration

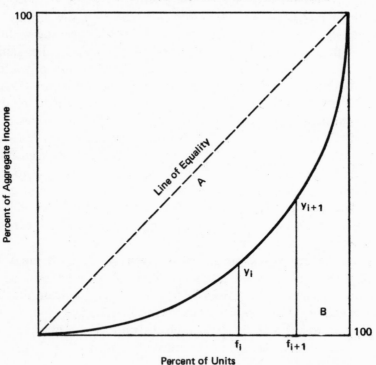

The Gini Index of Concentration is defined as the proportion of the total area under the diagonal that is between the diagonal and the Lorenz curve. This relationship can be expressed as follows using the notation in Figure 6.1 above:

$$(1) \quad G = \frac{A}{A+B} = \frac{\text{area between curve and diagonal}}{\text{area under diagonal}}$$

Substituting in the expression for G above yields the formula that is used in computing the Gini coefficient.

$$(3) \quad G = 1 - 2 \sum_{i=1}^{k} (f_{i+1} - f_i) \frac{(y_i + y_{i+1})}{2}$$

$$(3a) \quad G = 1 - \sum_{i=1}^{k} (f_{i+1} - f_i)(y_i + y_{i+1})^{10}$$

Since the cumulative percent on each axis adds to 100, the area in the entire square is unity and the area under the diagonal is 1/2. Therefore, the expression above can be rewritten as follows:

$$(1a) \quad G = 1 - \frac{\text{area under curve}}{1/2} = 1 - 2 \text{ (area under curve)}$$

If we assume that the curve between any two points is approximated by a straight line, the area for any segment of the curve can be expressed as follows:

$$(2) \quad (f_{i+1} - f_i) \frac{(y_i + y_{i+1})}{2}$$

When summed over all intervals, the area under the curve is

$$(2a) \quad \sum_{i=1}^{k} (f_{i+1} - f_i) \frac{(y_i + y_{i+1})}{2}$$

NOTES

1. Randall D. Weiss, "The Effect of Education on the Earnings of Blacks and Whites," *The Review of Economics and Statistics* 52, 2 (May 1970): 150-159.

2. Harry J. Gilman, "Economic Discrimination and Unemployment," *American Economic Review* 55, no. 4 (December 1965): 1077-1096.

3. Symbolically, this is $\frac{\Delta W}{W} \div \frac{\Delta I}{I} = \frac{\Delta W}{\Delta Y} \times \frac{I}{Y}$ where ΔW = change in wealth and ΔI = change in income; computed from the midpoints of the respective income and wealth categories where $\Delta W = W_2 - W_1, \Delta I = I_2 - I_1$, $I = (I_1 + I_2)/2, W = (W_1 + W_2)/2$. Thus income elasticity =

$$\frac{W_2 - W_1}{I_2 - I_1} \times \frac{(I_1 + I_2)/2}{(W_1 + W_2)/2}.$$

4. Milton Friedman, *A Theory of the Consumption Function* (Princeton, N.J.: Princeton University Press, 1957, pp. 20-26.

5. Ibid., pp. 84-85.

6. Gary S. Becker, *The Economics of Discrimination* (Chicago: University of Chicago Press, 1957).

7. For a detailed discussion of this, see Marcus Alexis, "Racial Differences in Consumption and Automobile Ownership," unpublished Ph.D. dissertation, Department of Economics, University of Minnesota, 1959, especially pp. 77-178.

8. See Appendix.

9. For a discussion of this point see Marcus Alexis, "Wealth Accumulation of Black and White Families: The Empirical Evidence: Comment," *The Journal of Finance* 26, 2 (May 1971): 461.

10. U.S. Department of Commerce, Bureau of the Census, *Income Distribution in the United States,* by Herman P. Miller (Washington, D.C.: U.S. Government Printing Office, 1966), pp. 220-221.

7

BLACKS IN THE AMERICAN ECONOMY: PROBLEMS, POLICIES, AND PROSPECTS FOR CHANGE

Thaddeus H. Spratlen

Thaddeus H. Spratlen is Associate Professor of Marketing, School of Business Administration, University of Washington. From 1969 to 1972 he taught at UCLA's Graduate School of Management. He received his Ph.D. in Business Organization from Ohio State University in 1962. He is the author of over twenty articles in professional journals and other publications on marketing, Black political economy, and related subjects. In addition, he has presented over thirty papers at professional meetings and conferences. He is a contributing author of *Modern Marketing* (Random House, 1974). His other professional activities include service as Secretary-Treasurer of the Caucus of Black Economists, the national professional association of Black economists, 1972-1974; Consultant to Minority Business Development Organizations in Los Angeles, Seattle, and other cities; and lecturer for the United Negro College Fund.

INTRODUCTION

In the American economy, Blacks have been and continue to be more restricted in gaining access to resources than whites and most other minority groups as well. Yet resources (i.e., income, wealth, and credit as well as specific means of participating in economic activities by using land, labor, capital, and entrepreneurial skills) are the primary determinants of economic status and well-being in an economic system. Hence, because of the many restrictions that Blacks encounter when they enter the marketplace, they are subject to distinct disadvantages in the production, distribution, and exchange of goods and services.

This chapter provides a description of some of the major factors that account for the restrictions experienced by Blacks in the economy. The approach that is used emphasizes the effects of discrimination, disparity, and deprivation on access to resources. These practices and conditions define the special forms of race-related barriers that place severe constraints on economic activities and relationships.

Whenever possible, comparisons are made of selected indicators of the relative position of Blacks and whites in social and economic terms. Extensive use is made of 1970 or more recent U.S. Census Bureau data.[1]

Because of time and space limitations, many topics must be only briefly reviewed. References are suggested for those readers who desire a more extended treatment of the subject.[2]

HISTORICAL BACKGROUND

The slavery experience of Blacks and its inherent racist foundations have defined the long-standing patterns of racial discrimination and segregation in the economy and society. For almost three centuries, the institution of slavery imposed legal, economic, cultural, and other forms of subjugation, which set the stage for the restrictions placed on Blacks since that time. It is essential that the impact of the restrictions in economic terms be understood. They have exerted cumulative and compound pressures. The economic consequences continue in the form of immobility, disparity, and other stifling conditions.

Immobility can be associated with the confining boundaries of the ghetto,[3] as well as with the oppressive captivity of slavery. It is a matter of the degree of subjugation and exploitation. Both situations restrict the movement of people and the flow of all forms of resources.

Disparity in the Black situation can be seen in the very large and persistent gap between the Black and white segments of the U.S. economy. This has always been a basic fact of American economic life. The gap is of sufficient magnitude and duration to be considered virtually permanent. It is also pervasive. Even when basic economic criteria (those proverbial "other things") such as education, income, occupation, and related means of economic power are similar, disparity between Blacks and whites persists. Blacks as a group have not been able to escape disparity.

Other stifling conditions in the Black experience include the many factors that perpetuate racial segregation and discrimination against Blacks. The widespread incidence of poverty, and extreme scarcity and lack of economic opportunity are familiar examples. Of special significance, too, is the lack of substantial business ownership and other forms of wealth in a system based on private enterprise and wealth-based economic and political power. Although many complex factors account for the latter condition, special importance must be attached to the circular and interdependent relationships of limited earnings and savings of Blacks; control of credit supplies of goods and other resources by whites; and exclusion of Blacks from social, political, and cultural connections that establish and sustain enterprise activities.[4]

As the discussion in other sections (and chapters) suggests, there are many direct and indirect effects of the race- and class-related experiences of Blacks in the American economy. It is important to keep in mind throughout the discussion that special importance should be attached to the historical patterns of Black-white relationships. Their impact is cumulative and exerts a strong influence on explanations of as well as solutions to the problems that they have helped to cause.

ECONOMIC STATUS AND PROBLEMS OF BLACKS

The economic status of Blacks is lower than that of whites on virtually every major indicator of position and participation in the U.S. economy. Of course, status differences between Blacks and whites reflect both cause and consequences of socio-economic relationships. They are analyzed here with reference to the major economic problems that Blacks encounter to a greater extent than whites in the general economy: persistently high levels of unemployment, lower-paying jobs, deprivation through low income and the lack of prosperity, more limited business opportunities, and generally lagging economic growth and development.[5]

Unemployment

The nonwhite unemployment rate has averaged over 1.9 times that for whites throughout the generation since the late 1940s. As shown in Table 7.1, the ratios of nonwhite to white unemployment rates can be compared as follows:

211

Table 7.1. White and Nonwhite Unemployment Rates, 1948-1972 United States, Annual Averages
(in percent)

Year	White (A)	Nonwhite (B)	Ratio of Nonwhite / White
1948	3.5	5.9	1.7
1949	5.6	8.9	1.6
1950	4.9	9.0	1.8
1951	3.1	5.3	1.7
1952	2.8	5.4	1.9
1953	2.7	4.5	1.7
1954	5.0	9.9	2.0
1955	3.9	8.7	2.2
1956	3.6	8.3	2.3
1957	3.8	7.9	2.1
1958	6.1	12.6	2.1
1959	4.8	10.7	2.2
1960	4.9	10.2	2.1
1961	6.0	12.4	2.1
1962	4.9	10.9	2.2
1963	5.0	10.8	2.2
1964	4.6	9.6	2.1
1965	4.1	8.1	2.0
1966	3.3	7.3	2.2
1967	3.4	7.4	2.2
1968	3.2	6.7	2.1
1969	3.1	6.4	2.1
1970	4.5	8.2	1.8
1971	5.4	9.9	1.8
1972	5.0	10.0	2.0

Source: U. S. Department of Commerce, *The Social and Economic Status of the Black Population in the United States,* 1972, p. 38. Data for 1959 and earlier years are from previous editions of the same publication.

2.0   time or more − 17 years
1.8-1.9 times   − 4 years
1.6-1.7 times   − 4 years

In the last quarter of a century, the nonwhite unemployment rate has not been less than 1.6 times that of whites. In a word, from recession to near-depression levels of unemployment have existed in the Black community.[6] Moreover, Blacks experience longer durations of unemployment, greater vulnerability to becoming unemployed, and, as indicated below, have lower labor force participation rates and a higher proportion of men who are not in the labor force than is true of whites.

Since jobs are the primary source of livelihood in the economy, to be without a job is to be without the means of individual participation, economic contribution, and income generation. Unemployment causes individuals and their families to rely upon transfer payments—receipts of money or money equivalents (such as food stamps) for which no current service is provided—as a means of economic survival. It carries with it a certain dependency status as part of the social welfare system.

Reducing the Black Unemployment Gap

A paradox of the Black unemployment gap is that even at full employment there would be a recession level of joblessness for nowhites. Currently, a 4.0-4.5 percent unemployment rate is being used in discussions of "full employment."[7] In accordance with historical patterns, this means a rate for nonwhites in the range of 8-9 percent. Clearly, then, something more than "full employment" is needed to reduce Black unemployment to levels comparable with those experienced by whites. After all, the rates for Blacks are higher than for other nonwhites generally. So at full employment in the general economy, Blacks in the Black economy would be experiencing unemployment at rates in excess of 10 percent.

The conventional prescriptions for reducing unemployment fall into five categories:

213

1. Improving productivity of workers so that they can become more employable, as through training, developing new skills, counseling, and the like

2. Increasing job information and the effectiveness of labor market operations in matching workers with jobs

3. Supplementing labor market operations through subsidies so that employers will have incentives to hire additional workers, especially when those hired may lack sufficient skills and work experience to be competitively productive

4. Public service employment in which the government takes on fiscal and manpower responsibilities for increasing jobs and decreasing the ranks of the unemployed

5. Implementing combinations of the foregoing in order to improve the interconnections between labor availability and labor utilization. (This might include a combination of training workers, giving employers a tax credit for employing them, and using special media programs to increase the flow of information about jobs.)

If the Black unemployment gap is to be reduced significantly, special efforts in each of the categories are required.

Lower-Paying Jobs

Employed Blacks tend to be concentrated in unskilled and semiskilled positions. There is task as well as occupational segregation in virtually all fields of employment. "White office work"; sales jobs; and managerial, technical, and professional employment comprise the most obvious areas of exclusion and discrimination. However, skilled trades generally represent another major area of traditional exclusion of Blacks. The representation of occupational groups in 1970 is summarized in Table 7.2.

214

Providing Higher-Paying Jobs

If the job and earnings position of Blacks is to improve materially, it means closing the substantial gap that exists in the craftsmen and foremen; clerical and sales; and professional, technical, and managerial occupations. (An effective policy that can help to bring this about is the widespread adoption of affirmative action programs for hiring and upgrading of Blacks.[8]) To be effective this must extend to the inclusion of policies equivalent to those identified with reducing the Black unemployment gap. Such action is essential for raising the level of personal income to a comparable proportion in relation to the representaion of nonwhites in the labor force and the economy in general. Such action needs to be compulsory, since on a voluntary basis compliance rests on the goodwill of individuals rather than lawful employment policies of both public and private sectors of the economy.

Policies are needed to correct the disproportionate representation in jobs that exists for nonwhites. For example, there are proportionately over 2.7 times as many white male professional, technical, and kindred workers as there are Blacks in these categories. In the case of nonfarm managers and administrators, there are proportionately over four times as many white males as there are Black males holding such higher-paying jobs. As shown in Table 7.2, a reverse pattern exists for the low-paying occupations, especially in the case of service workers and nonfarm laborers.

In terms of specific job categories, education and training of Blacks for the world of work will need to be geared more closely with the technological changes occurring in the economy. Employment growth in the 1970s will be concentrated in repair and maintenance services; computer sales, operations, and programming; banking and other fields of finance; and in urban, environmental, and health science engineering. Blacks entering the labor force would do well to adapt their education and training interests to these or related areas of employment growth.

Table 7.2. White and Nonwhite Occupational Distribution, United States, 1970

	Total		White		Negro	
	Male	Female	Male	Female	Male	Female
NUMBER (Thousands)						
Total employed, 14 years old and over	48,138,665	29,170,127	43,501,103	25,470,679	4,091,390	3,328,956
Professional, technical, and kindred workers	6,516,610	4,314,083	6,198,711	3,907,473	213,998	343,778
Managers and administrators, except farm	5,125,534	1,013,843	4,971,695	958,348	111,883	44,578
Sales workers	3,267,653	1,999,794	3,171,063	1,909,208	75,611	72,932
Clerical and kindred workers	3,452,251	9,582,440	3,116,427	8,863,413	293,472	613,464
Craftsmen, foremen, and kindred workers	9,501,588	494,871	8,879,325	446,174	540,484	42,758
Operatives, except transport	6,096,313	3,719,842	5,339,442	3,193,771	701,763	471,157
Transport equipment operatives	2,644,368	121,819	2,264,441	109,046	360,533	11,938
Laborers, except farm	2,944,649	268,505	2,345,373	220,450	556,814	44,689
Farmers and farm managers	1,281,160	61,934	1,243,494	58,621	29,667	2,218
Farm laborers and farm foremen	783,145	140,721	637,748	108,932	126,220	27,775
Service workers, except private household	3,640,487	4,424,030	3,008,142	3,612,472	563,613	749,881
Private household workers	39,685	1,053,092	22,248	533,246	16,121	508,729
Occupation not reported	2,845,222	1,975,153	2,302,994	1,549,525	501,211	395,059

	Total		White		Negro	
PERCENT	Male	Female	Male	Female	Male	Female
Total employed, 14 years old and over	100.0	100.0	100.0	100.0	100.0	100.0
Professional, technical, and kindred workers	13.5	14.8	14.2	15.3	5.2	10.3
Managers and administrators, except farm	10.6	3.5	11.4	3.8	2.7	1.3
Sales workers	6.8	6.9	7.3	7.5	1.8	2.2
Clerical and kindred workers	7.2	32.9	7.2	34.8	7.2	18.4
Craftsmen, foremen, and kindred workers	19.7	1.7	20.4	1.8	13.2	1.3
Operatives, except transport	12.7	12.8	12.3	12.5	17.2	14.2
Transport equipment operatives	5.5	0.4	5.2	0.4	8.8	0.4
Laborers, except farm	6.1	0.9	5.4	0.9	13.6	1.3
Farmers and farm managers	2.7	0.2	2.9	0.2	0.7	0.1
Farm laborers and farm foremen	1.6	0.5	1.5	0.4	3.1	0.8
Service workers, except private household	7.6	15.2	6.9	14.2	13.8	22.5
Private household workers	0.1	3.6	0.1	2.1	0.4	15.3
Occupation not reported	5.9	6.8	5.3	6.1	12.3	11.9

Source: U. S. Department of Commerce, Bureau of the Census, U. S. Population: General Social and Economic Characteristics, Table 81, United States Summary 1-375, 1972.

Low Income and Lack of Prosperity

Based on data for 1972, about 35 percent of all nonwhite families had incomes of less than $5,000. Approximately 14 percent of white families had such low incomes. The 35 percent figure also serves to indicate the approximate proportion of urban Black families that are poor, by criteria used for federal programs and defined by the Social Security Administration, U. S. Department of Agriculture, and the U. S. Department of Labor.[9] Since fewer than one-eighth of all white families are poor by such standards, the incidence of poverty is about three times as great proportionately for nonwhites as for whites. It should also be noted that the incidence of poverty is higher for Blacks than it is for other minority groups except American Indians.[10] For the Spanish-surnamed population, approximately one-quarter of the families are poor. For other nonwhites the proportion was 20.6 percent for 1969. The pattern of disparity is both widespread and persistent. Hence, as a categorical statement, Blacks in virtually all job categories are in lower income levels than their white peers. They earn, on the average, a disproportionately small share of total income, even in high-income situations. Black physicians earn less than white physicians; Black "star" entertainers receive less in salaries than white stars; Black athletes make less than white athletes, their greater athletic feats notwithstanding. For example, it was reported recently in the sports media that in 1973, Johnny Bench (star catcher for Cincinnati) made more money in advertising retainer fees and public appearances than all Black athletes in baseball combined!

But a broader and more representative basis for comparing the incomes of Blacks and whites is provided by the data in Table 7.3. The order of magnitude of relationships is indicated. Perspective on the data is provided by estimates for Blacks only: $38.7 billion and 6.4 percent of total income in 1969.[11] By 1972, this reached $51.8 billion or 6.7 percent of the total of $773 billion.[12]

The pattern of distribution of family income is shown in Table 7.4. Income is not only generally lower for nonwhites, it is also more unequally distributed among nonwhite families.

218

Table 7.3. Distribution of Familes by Income and Estimated Total Family Income, United States, 1969

Income Class	White Families			Nonwhite Families			Estimated Total Income (Billions of Dollars)	
	Number (Thousands)	Percent	Estimated Mean Income	Number (Thousands)	Percent	Estimated Mean Income	White Families	Nonwhite Families
Under $3,000	4,051	8.9	$ 2,600	1,220	22.7	$ 2,400	$ 10.53	$ 2.93
$ 3,000 to $ 4,999	4,185	9.1	4,000	917	17.0	4,200	16.74	3.85
$ 5,000 to $ 6,999	5,234	11.4	6,000	847	15.7	6,200	31.40	5.25
$ 7,000 to $ 9,999	9,539	20.9	8,000	1,011	18.6	8,200	76.31	8.29
$10,000 to $14,999	12,710	27.8	13,000	907	16.8	13,000	165.23	11.80
$15,000 to $24,999	7,753	16.9	21,500	424	7.9	20,000	166.69	8.48
$25,000 or more	2,299	5.0	37,500	72	1.3	34,000	86.21	2.45
Total	45,771	100.0	—	5,398	100.0	—	$553.11	$43.05

Source: U. S. Department of Commerce, Bureau of the Census, 1970 General Social and Economic Characteristics, Table 83, United States Summary 1-377, 1972.

Note: Estimates based on several statistical series. Elsewhere in the literature the proportion of income earned by Blacks for 1969 was reported to be $38.7 billion or 6.4 percent of total personal income. The above estimate of $43.0 for nonwhite families probably understates the total. Also the proportion of 7.8 percent is lower than estimates using total personal income.

Table 7.4. Percent Distribution of Number of Familes and Family Income, By Race, United States 1969

Income Class	White Families				Nonwhite Families			
	Number		Income		Number		Income	
	Percent	Cumulative Percent	Percent	Cumulative Percent	Percent	Cumulative Percent	Percent	Cumulative Percent
Under $3,000	8.9	8.9	1.9	1.9	22.7	22.7	6.8	6.8
$ 3,000 – $ 4,999	9.1	18.0	3.0	4.9	17.0	39.7	8.9	15.7
$ 5,000 – $ 6,999	11.4	29.4	5.7	10.6	15.7	55.4	12.2	27.9
$ 7,000 – $ 9,999	20.9	50.3	13.8	24.4	18.6	74.0	19.3	47.2
$10,000 – $14,999	27.8	78.1	29.9	54.3	16.8	90.8	27.4	74.6
$15,000 – $24,999	16.9	95.0	30.1	84.4	7.9	98.7	19.7	94.3
$25,000 or more	5.0	100.0	15.6	100.0	1.3	100.0	5.7	100.0
	100.0		100.0		100.0		100.0	

Source: Table 7.3.

Thus, there is substantial disparity of income between non-whites and whites as well as among nonwhites. The comparisons from Figure 7.1 can be read more precisely based on the percentages in Table 7.4.

Unfortunately, the relationships are distorted in the calculations for Figure 7.1. Grouping into percentiles should have been developed from original data. Apparently when this is done (at least in terms of quintiles) less disparity emerges. Thus, for 1969, the comparisons are shown in Table 7.5. The differences are slight, and slightly reversed. With the exception of the highest fifth, nonwhites at each quintile have, by a small margin, a larger share of aggregate income than whites. But emerging from all of the numbers is an unmistakable pattern of lower and maldistributed incomes for Blacks.

Figure 7.1. Cumulative Percent of Income and
Families by Race, United States, 1969

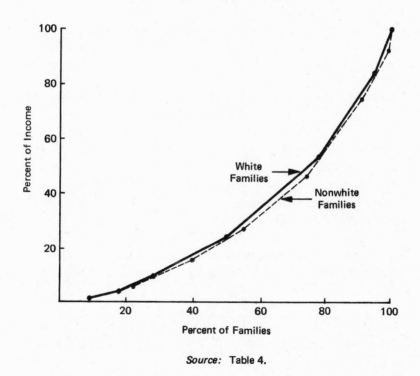

Source: Table 4.

221

Table 7.5. Percentage Share of Aggregate Income in 1969
Received by Each Fifth of Families Ranked by Income, by Race,
United States

Income Rank	White Families (in percent)	Nonwhite Families (in percent)
Lowest Fifth	3.3	3.5
Second Fifth	7.8	7.9
Third Fifth	13.9	14.4
Fourth Fifth	24.2	25.0
Highest Fifth	50.8	49.2
Total	100.0	100.0

Source: U. S. Department of Commerce, Consumer Income-Current Population Reports, Series P-60, No. 90, *Money Income in 1972 of Families and Persons in the United States* (Washington, D. C.: U. S. Government Printing Office, December 1973), p. 46.

The limited means implied by low income reflects the absence of prosperity—exclusion from sharing in economic growth, high levels of consumption, and otherwise receiving few of the benefits generally provided for whites in the American economy. Besides the data already presented on the point, it should be kept in mind that as a group Blacks are substantially less prosperous than whites just based on median income. Black median income remains at about 60 percent that of whites—a 40 percent income gap. Corrective measures need to be focused on increasing income and prosperity among Blacks.

Raising Black Incomes and Extending Prosperity

Income must generally be (1) earned through the employment of capital (knowledge or human capital) in the case of the individual worker; or (2) granted through some form of subsidy or transfer payment. If Black incomes are to be raised and greater prosperity realized in the Black economy, policies and programs must be implemented that will increase Black worker earnings, increase the amounts received as subsidies, or some combination of the two. Thus, the basic options are:[13]

1. Remove barriers to employment in job access and availability (examples: ending discrimination in hiring and rewarding Blacks; creating jobs in or accessible to central cities; providing housing, transportation, and other services and infrastructure[14] to bring jobs to Blacks or Blacks to jobs).
2. Remove barriers to employment in worker preparation and availability (examples: manpower and motivational training programs; upgrading and improving productivity through on-the-job training).
3. Supplement income earned or provide minimum guaranteed income levels (examples: various income maintenance schemes).

Another area in which disparity prevails is in business enterprise—all aspects of the ownership and management of organizations engaged in producing and distributing goods and services. This is presented in the following section.

More Limited Business Opportunities

The role of Blacks in business enterprise has been perhaps the most restricted aspect of participation in the economy. The walls of segregation have been highest for many reasons. Business ownership requires some minimum accumulation of wealth as equity capital, as collateral for loan capital, or as skill and technology for the acceptance of risks by other investors, as well as the development of some good or service for sale or leasing. Blacks have been severely restricted in their access to the accumulation of all forms of capital.

This situation has absolutely devastating consequences from the standpoint of survival and success in a capitalist system. As a further explanation of the character of the Black experience with respect to enterprise, special attention is focused on the major constraints on Blacks in corporate management and the ownership of businesses.

223

As a further reflection of disparity and restricted opportunity, Blacks are concentrated in the lower ranks of management. Moreover, they are likely to be confined there because of their assignments outside of the main functional areas of business that lead to middle and top management positions—through marketing, finance, and accounting. Blacks are more typically found in such staff areas as community affairs, personnel (especially minority recruitment), and special markets. In the corporate world, such assignments rarely lead to the upper echelons of management.

Black-owned businesses are constrained even further in serving essentially a residual market demand. Purchases from Black businesses are made mostly by Blacks. But even so, such purchases are made primarily because of restrictions of choice in the general marketplace. Blacks, for the most part, buy from Black businesses what they cannot readily buy elsewhere. The dual aspect stems from the characteristics of the Black consumer market in comparison with the general market. The Black business structure is dominated by small-scale firms rather than by large chains and other forms of corporate enterprise. Black business serves a population with a higher incidence of low income than is generally the case. The setting of Black business tends to be surrounded by stagnation and decline rather than growth and prosperity.

An example of magnitudes is suggested by the estimated $38.7 billion in personal income earned by Blacks as of 1969. Total business receipts of all Black businesses (not just retail firms) was about $4.5 billion in the same period. So Black firms do not capture much in excess of 10 percent of the consumption expenditures made by Blacks. (This recognizes that about 7-8 percent of Black income is saved.)[15]

Developing Business Opportunities for Blacks

At the corporate level, special recruitment, training, and management development programs are needed. This means that firms must establish and maintain contact with the business schools that have the largest enrollment of prospective Black candidates. Harvard, Wharton, UCLA, and Columbia especially appear to have established themselves affirmatively on the side of admitting and providing financial support for Black MBAs. But once recruited, Blacks must be encouraged to pursue assignments in the main line of corporate activity, sales, investments, information systems, and other technical-managerial fields. Blacks should recognize that special assignments in minority problems and projects tend to be blind alleys rather than pathways to advancement.[16]

Black business development encompasses a broad category of activities designed to increase the viability of Black enterprise. But the challenges and problems are enormous.

Structural change alone could easily absorb the resources available for the task. That is, there is a need to alter both size and type of businesses in which Blacks are concentrated.

Single proprietorships predominate when it is the corporation that has led to innovation and domination of markets.

As to type of business, retailing and personal services establishments make up the two major categories (about 30 percent in each). Other services amount to about 12 percent; construction 10 percent; manufacturing 3 percent; and all other kinds of business 14 percent. A further reflection of small size is indicated in the approximately one-third of minority-owned businesses run by family members and without paid employees (as compared with about one-quarter of white-owned firms). Only about 5 percent of minority-owned firms have 10 or more paid employees. Almost 20 percent of white-owned firms provide employment for 10 or more workers.

From the comparisons presented, it is clear that Black-owned enterprise adds very little to the economy in terms of jobs and income—the foundation elements for a sustained economic base. Only large-scale efforts at ownership transfers and programs for minimum income guarantees offer prospects for significantly altering the situation for Blacks.

Beyond the aspects of structural change, technical assistance in a variety of forms is needed to provide support for minority businesses. This includes such wide-ranging efforts as set-aside contracts,[17] information and research on business opportunities, formation of trade associations, and special equity funding as well as widely used forms of loan packaging and management training for minority business.

Lagging Economic Growth and Development

Economic growth generally refers to increases in the capacity to produce and consume in an economy. Typically it is measured by real,[18] per capita income, output and consumption expenditures. Such measures are not readily available for the Black community. But in light of the comments made earlier on family income, and the lack of prosperity, it is appropriate to infer that there is lagging economic growth in the Black community.

Development, on the other hand, refers to a process of qualitative as well as quantitative change in an economy. It may be defined as a process through which the economic conditions and effectiveness of institutions serving the economic well-being of a community, region, or nation are improved. Improvement, of course, has numerous dimensions and measurement criteria generally defined as important economic goals. Development, then, would include all forms of positive and beneficial change (including growth) that result in a greater capability to carry out the complex activities of building and sustaining the modern economy. The following activities are illustrative for the Black community.

1. establishing ghetto-owned business or other instruments of capital accumulation
2. increasing employment and income levels of Black families
3. enlarging the scale and specialization of Black-owned enterprises
4. alleviating the higher incidence of poverty in the Black community
5. redistributing equitably wealth and power in the economy
6. achieving socioeconomic power and parity for Blacks in the economy

226

7. increasing the variety of goods, services, and amenities consumed bv Blacks in the economy

The combination of factors that restrict growth and development are summarized in Figure 7.2. Because the factors interact, special efforts must be directed towards their combined impact. Otherwise there will not be sufficient counterforce to offset their stifling effects on growth and development.

Figure 7.2. Barriers to Growth and Development in the Black Economy
The Cycle of Cumulative Causation

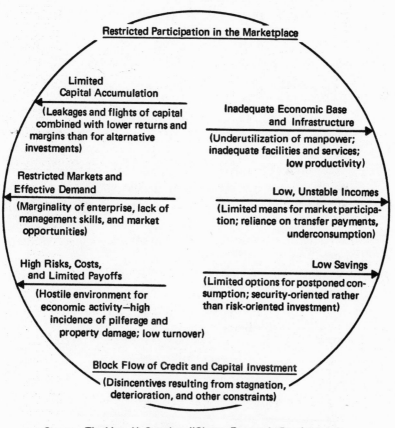

Restricted Participation in the Marketplace

Limited
Capital Accumulation

(Leakages and flights of capital combined with lower returns and margins than for alternative investments)

Inadequate Economic Base
and Infrastructure

(Underutilization of manpower; inadequate facilities and services; low productivity)

Restricted Markets and
Effective Demand

(Marginality of enterprise, lack of management skills, and market opportunities)

Low, Unstable Incomes

(Limited means for market participation; reliance on transfer payments, underconsumption)

High Risks, Costs,
and Limited Payoffs

(Hostile environment for economic activity—high incidence of pilferage and property damage; low turnover)

Low Savings

(Limited options for postponed consumption; security-oriented rather than risk-oriented investment)

Block Flow of Credit and Capital Investment
(Disincentives resulting from stagnation, deterioration, and other constraints)

Source: Thaddeus H. Spratlen, "Ghetto Economic Development: Content and Character of the Literature," *The Review of Black Political Economy* 1, (Summer 1971): 52.

Stimulating Black Economic Growth and Development

Policies that are likely to be effective in stimulating economic growth and development in the Black community include the guidelines listed below. They reflect a broad range of requirements for overcoming the barriers identified in Chart 7.2. Priority should be given to:

1. Channeling substantially greater quantities and qualities of resources and investments into the Black community
2. Expanding programs of technical training and skills combined with actual placement in the labor force as well as meaningful opportunities for career advancement and personal growth
3. Increasing significantly the income, savings, and capital ownership of Blacks
4. Making the benefits of innovation and increased productivity more widely available to Blacks
5. Planning and coordinating development programs for the more effective utilization of the scarce resources available for Black economic development
6. Reducing the outflow of consumption expenditures and investments from the Black economy through more efficient production of marketable values and the creation of wealth by Blacks
7. Making the Black community less risky and more profitable as an investment alternative in comparison with other regions of the larger economy, but for the benefit of the Black community
8. Providing management training and administrative experience for use by Blacks in their own businesses as well as in major corporations
9. Expanding business opportunities in the Black community
10. Assigning greater weight to social benefits and externalities associated with development activities in the Black community

Expanded Role of Government

With reference to an overall strategy of resource use for Black economic development a wide latitude of government involvement seems inescapable. Its role will be as a positive, propulsive agent and not just as a catalyst or passive participant. Whether the mechanism or requirement is saving, stimulating the entrepreneurial role, training for management or other skills, government should play a larger role in the development process in the Black community than it has in the larger regional and national economy. The task is a more complex and difficult one. There are numerous factors that suggest that neither the guidance of the entrepreneur nor the free play of market forces is adequate to the task. Further, the potential gains in economic, social, and simply human terms, and the urgency of making significant short-term progress all warrant greater government involvement. Likewise, the risks and compensatory programs associated with removing the barriers to advancing economic development lend support to greater government involvement. Furthermore, the high social costs of postponed development justify it.

The Community Focus of Activities

It also seems likely that activities supportive of Black economic development will become more group- and community-focused than has been true of the traditionally personal and selfishly focused entrepreneurial effort. The basic justification of activities on the grounds of social externalities rather than individual profit or gain helps to explain this much needed shift. The more compressed time dimension for bringing about change also causes a shift away from reliance on the classic style of the entrepreneur. The special case of needing to build a community that has lacked the group focus of pride, solidarity, and other qualities of a social and political nature also suggests a community focus of development activities. A prime objective is to make enterprise and ownership indigenous to the Black community. Accompanying such a

229

goal will be community control of resources, which in turn should lead to greater satisfaction of community needs and wants.

PROSPECTS FOR IMPROVING BLACK ECONOMIC STATUS

Having outlined what needs to be done, it seems appropriate to summarize the judgments expressed regarding what can be expected in terms of contributions to the improvement of Black economic status. Any realistic outlook realizes the improbability of ending the disparity between Blacks and whites in the economy. Such a viewpoint is supported by even a brief look at the technological, economic, political, and social realities of the times.

In the broadest social terms it is by no means clear what values and sentiments will prevail regarding our national goals and priorities.[19] Such uncertainty is compounded by the continuing restrictions of institutional racism.[20] As one example, the increasingly Black cities are imperiled by short-sighted policies of public resource allocation. In political terms there seems to be more rhetoric than commitment regarding Black economic development. From local community leadership to the highest level of the federal government, action and resources continue to lag considerably behind the problems and needs of the Black community. Economically and technologically, conditions would not seem to favor a reversal of the stagnation and decline that is so prevalent in the inner city. The gap between the larger regional or national economy and the inner city has not been significantly narrowed during a decade of unprecedented prosperity. Actually there are some areas in which the gap has widened. Two prime examples include (1) the absolute dollar gap between white and Black income, and (2) the proportion of nonwhites who are poor relative to whites who are poor.[21] But in several other areas such as unemployment, housing, and wealth, improvement for Blacks has been very slight indeed, considering that the 1960s was a decade of unprecedented national prosperity. Further, there

230

appears to be little evidence on which to base an expectation of a significant redirection of effort in behalf of improving the economic status of Blacks.

In sum, underdevelopment, at least throughout the 1970s and 1980s, seems destined to be the common status of the masses of nonwhites in America's cities. Opportunity, vitality, mobility, and other qualities desired as measures of their improved well-being will be little changed from their present circumstances unless a dramatic reversal of policies and practices occurs. Some of the changes that should form part of such a reversal have been indicated in this discussion. If commitments and investments equal to the task are made, policies and programs can be implemented that will greatly improve the quality of life for Blacks in the American economy.

The needs and resources exist for bringing about such improvement. Whether it occurs will be determined ultimately by the political and economic changes that can be effected in and on behalf of the Black community. As noted here and in other chapters, the outlook is at best uncertain. But struggle against great odds has been characteristic of the Black experience in America. This is one characteristic that will remain with us through the 1970s and beyond.

NOTES

1. The most extensively used single source of data is: U. S. Department of Commerce, Bureau of the Census, *The Social and Economic Status of the Black Population in the United States, 1972* (Washington, DC: U. S. Government Printing Office, July 1973).

2. One of the most comprehensive and condensed surveys of the Black experience in economic terms is the one by Andrew F. Brimmer, "The Negro in the National Economy," in John P. Davis, ed., *The American Negro Reference Book* (Englewood Cliffs, N.J.: Prentice-Hall, 1966), pp. 251-336.
See also Harry A. Ploski and Ernest Kaiser, eds., *The Negro Almanac* (New York: The Bellweather Company, 1972), sections 11 and 12, especially.
For summaries of more recent experiences, the following articles provide data and background comments: Andrew F. Brimmer, "Economic Developments in the Black Community," *The Public Interest*, no. 34 (Winter

1974): 146-163; and Thaddeus H. Spratlen, "The Record and Rhetoric of Black Economic Progress," *The Review of Black Political Economy* 4, (Spring 1974): 1-27.

3. Economists have made little effort to date to define the ghetto for purposes of economic analysis. The concept adopted for this discussion identifies its major attributes as the combined effects of (1) involuntary segregation, (2) ethnic composition of the population (3) racial or ethnic discrimination, and (4) cumulative immobility. The ghetto, then, is defined as an enclave inhabited by people who, as a group, are subjected to the combined effects of involuntary segregation, racial discrimination and cumulative immobility in social, economic, and political processes. (See the chapter by Hefner for a further discussion.)

4. A sociologically based explanation has been well developed by Ivan H. Light, *Ethnic Enterprise in America—Business and Welfare Among Chinese, Japanese, and Blacks* (Berkeley: University of California Press, 1972).

It should be noted that the extensive literature on "Black Capitalism" (some of which is referred to by Light) also covers many aspects of historical and current experience regarding Blacks and the American enterprise system.

5. Omitted from consideration are differences in education, housing, health care, and related restrictions on services and amenities in the economy. Coverage of these broader aspects of social and economic life would have made the chapter considerably longer than was considered desirable. Also it would have overlapped topics and ideas covered in other chapters in the book.

6. There are several meanings of "Black community." In its broadest sense it refers to the physical and social space occupied by the settlements or concentrations of Black people in both urban and rural America. But it carries with it common characteristics and conditions associated with segregation, discrimination, and related forms of restricted participation of Blacks in the larger economy and society. The term identifies the totality of Black households, businesses, and other institutions that make up the Black socioeconomic, cultural, and political substructure in America. More limited terms that convey some of the same meanings are "ghetto" and "inner city."

7. See Stephen K. McNees, "The Path to Full Employment," *Monthly Review of the Federal Reserve Bank of Boston* (May-June 1972): 11-19; and Robert A. McMillan, "A Re-examination of the 'Full Employment' Goal," *Economic Review,* Federal Reserve Bank of Cleveland (March-April 1973): 3-17.

Although specific target rates of unemployment consistent with a "full employment" economy vary, there are some basic criteria that are taken into account in the definition. In general the concept of full employment refers to the capacity utilization of the labor force at levels that provide a desired combination of (1) people who are available for and seeking work, (2) jobs that require workers, and (3) a sustainable level of economic activity in terms of output, productivity, the work-week, and inflation.

Blacks are subject to doubly high unemployment rates because of what are described as "structural" barriers, in addition to the social, locational, and other factors that determine the supply and demand for labor. In structural terms this means that Blacks may be put out of work as a result of technological changes; declines in demand for particular goods and services (medium-sized automobiles serve as a good current example); and regional losses from plant closings, loss of government contracts, and the like. Blacks tend to be more adversely affected than whites by such changes because of lesser mobility, skills, seniority, and other job-retention factors. A barrier of increasing importance is that of exclusion by credentials—"the use of educational credentials as a quick and allegedly inexpensive device for screening out socially undesirable individuals." (Bennett Harrison, *Education, Training, and the Urban Ghetto* (Baltimore: Johns Hopkins Press, 1972, p. 30.)

As one further technical point, the notion of an "unemployment-inflation" trade-off should be recognized. Although in some considerable dispute among economists, it is the proposition that, roughly, the general price level is affected by policy measures to reduce the level of unemployment. Students may wish to pursue this in gaining an understanding of the "Phillips curve" controversy.

From a Black perspective, especially, some qualifications are in order. The basic relationship assumes a given amount of frictional and structural unemployment. Blacks experience relatively little of the former, but very much of the latter. The policies used to lower unemployment (in any form) may vary, and combinations of policy measures certainly affect the price level in different ways. Hence, we should be wary of justifying or "explaining" doubly high levels of Black unemployment in the context of the unemployment-inflation trade-off. The economic welfare interests of Blacks demand a more straightforward confrontation of priorities and policies that address the need for jobs. If appropriate manpower or human resource investments are made, Black unemployment can be brought into line with the standards generally accepted in the affluent U.S. growth economy.

8. The concept of setting goals and specific timetables to hire and upgrade minority workers and women. In terms of federal government policy, it is associated with Executive Order 11246, "Nondiscrimination Under Federal Contracts," as amended. Originally, it was issued by President Johnson on September 24, 1965. Portions have been superseded by Executive Order 11478, signed by President Nixon on August 8, 1969. The underlying principle is that an employer must do more than simply ensure employment neutrality with regard to race, color, religion, sex, and national origin. Specific, positive steps must be taken if the action is at all "affirmative."

233

9. Typically based on the minimum income needs of an urban family of four to provide for basic requirements of food, clothing, housing, and related services. It was reported in early 1973 that such a family was considered "poor" if its income were under $4,200 a year. For a farm family the level was set at $3,575. (*Christian Science Monitor*, January 26, 1973, p. 10.)

10. Since published tabulations of income for American Indians were not obtained, no data on the extent of their poverty are presented.

11. Andrew F. Brimmer, "Economic Development in the Black Community," *The Public Interest* no. 34 (Winter 1974): 148.

12. Ibid.

13. Two comprehensive discussions that review the relevant issues are: Charles Sackrey, *The Political Economy of Urban Poverty* (New York: Norton, 1973), chapter 4—"Liberal Remedies for Urban Poverty;" and James Tobin, "Raising the Incomes of the Poor," in Kermit Gorden, ed., *Agenda for the Nation* (Garden City, N.Y.: Doubleday, 1968).

14. A term used to include supporting structural and institutional arrangements and processes in a community, region, or other level in an economic system. Besides the examples given, education and training, public transportation, and health services form part of the infrastructure needed to create and sustain prosperity in the Black community.

15. Data on Black businesses are taken from U. S. Department of Commerce, *Minority-Owned Businesses: 1969* (Washington, D. C.: U. S. Government Printing Office, August 1971).

16. The magazine *Black Enterprise* contains some excellent material on the whole question of business opportunities for minorities. See especially, the following issues:

June 1973, "The Nation's 100 Top Black Businesses."

March 1973, "Corporate Mobility" and several other articles relating to corporate opportunities and involvement.

March 1972, "Opportunities 1972" and several articles on occupations and job opportunities for Blacks.

January 1972, "The Black Executive and the Corporation—A Difficult Fit" (by Stuart A. Taylor, a Black faculty member at the Harvard Business School) and articles by several other outstanding Blacks in higher education, consulting, and public service.

August 1971, "A Profile of Black America."

February 1971, "Blacks in Business."

April-May 1970, "Black Management 1970."

April-May 1969, "The Search for Black Management."

17. Provisions in contracts in which a specified amount or proportion is made available to minority businesses or small businesses. It is in reality a plan based on the notion of quotas. This represents affirmative action in the purchasing side of the business.

234

18. Income adjusted for price-level changes so that actual purchasing power or physical volume of goods and services is indicated.

19. Indeed at the time of this writing, Watergate is occupying the national attention along with the state of the economy. As further evidence of problems that lie ahead, the 1973 resignation statement of Rev. Ralph Abernathy as head of the Southern Christian Leadership Conference signaled a low point in concern of the plight of Blacks, especially among the very middle class of Blacks who benefited most from the gains won through the civil rights struggle of the 1960s. Viable coalitions are no closer to being a reality today among minority groups in America than they were before the assassination of Martin Luther King, Jr. The Nixon-appointed membership on the Supreme Court is regressing to a position of nonsupport of civil rights under the guise of a "strict constructionist" (i.e., conservative) interpretation of the Constitution. Benign neglect, initially a policy of lowering the priority of government as an active ally of minorities, has turned into a policy of absolute disregard for the plight of minorities. Efforts to dismantle the Office of Economic Opportunity, impoundment of funds for urban schools, the freeze imposed on housing subsidies and programs in 1973, and elimination of certain model cities grants are just a few examples of policies that reflect the national mood of this period of the 1970s.

An opposing viewpoint on the current economic status of Blacks and the outlook is presented by Ben J. Wattenberg and Richard M. Scammon, "Black Progress and Liberal Rhetoric," *Commentary* (April 1973): 35-44. These authors develop a theme of "a conspiracy of silence regarding Black progress." They present the case for great strides in reducing Black-white disparity. Particular emphasis is given to gross changes without regard for qualifications. As an example, they note the increase in the ratio of Black-white median family income from 53 percent in 1961 to 63 percent in 1971. But, even Census figures show the ratio to be only 60 percent for Blacks and 63 for nonwhites (Negro and other races). Moreover, they do not recognize the importance of the *increased* absolute dollar gap in nonwhite and white family income—from $3,428 in 1960 to $3,720 in 1970. And the gap would be larger if data were reported for Black families only.

For an instructive critique of the Wattenberg-Scammon article see Karl Gregory, "Brief Report on the State of the Black Economy, 1973" *The Review of Black Political Economy* 4, (Spring 1973): 13-16. The "record vs. rhetoric" controversy is reviewed in Spratlen, "Record and Rhetoric of Economic Progress."

20. Racially biased practices and policies that are inherent in the operating procedures and policies of schools, colleges, business firms, the news media, and other dominant or white economic, social, cultural, and political institutions. More specifically, this would include the stereotypes and slurs of racial minorities in television and films, the evaluation criteria

of admission and performance in educational institutions that favor middle-class whites, and the credentials required for employment that categorically exclude Blacks and other minorities.

21. The median income "dollar gap" was $2,602 in 1960. It was $4,443 in 1972. In 1960 nonwhites made up to 29.0 percent of those below the low income level. By 1972 this increased to 33.9 percent. (*Social and Economic Status of the Black Population,* pp. 37, 28.)

8

PUBLIC POLICY AND SOME POLITICAL CONSEQUENCES

Charles V. Hamilton

Charles V. Hamilton received his MA and PhD degrees in political science from the University of Chicago, after receiving his law degree from Loyola University in Chicago. He is presently a professor of political science and Wallace S. Sayre Professor of Government at Columbia University. He is the author of *The Black Preacher in America* and *The Bench and the Ballot: Southern Federal Judges and the Right to Vote* and has co-authored, with Stokely Carmichael, *Black Power: The Politics of Liberation in America.* He is the Editor of *The Black Experience in American Politics.* Professor Hamilton has worked with several civil rights organizations in the North and South and is a former vice-president of the American Political Science Association, a former visiting scholar at the Russell Sage Foundation, and was appointed a Phi Beta Kappa Visiting Scholar for 1973-74. Since 1975 he has been President of the Metropolitan Applied Research Center (MARC).

INTRODUCTION

For more than a decade the country has witnessed the birth and development of an array of federal programs aimed, ostensibly, at alleviating deteriorating socioeconomic conditions in local areas. In many instances, these policies were enacted in response to the crises generated during the decade of the 1960s. The purpose of this paper is to begin to assess the political impact of these programs on the various communities—especially Black communities—where they have been implemented.

"Citizen participation" became an important rallying cry for some political proponents in the 1960s, and, indeed, the Economic Opportunity Act of 1964, which set up Community Action Programs, contained the mandate (in title II) that there be "maximum feasible participation" on the part of residents in the area to be served. The brief history of that experience has been well documented in a numer of publications.[1]

Generally, however, as a new, post-1969 national administration has begun to dismantle much of the structure of the "Great Society Programs," supporters of the Kennedy-Johnson policies have come forth to defend the overall thrust, direction and tentative results of those earlier policies. One of the most frequently heard arguments is that the various community action agencies not only provided greatly needed services but

239

they also provided the vehicle whereby relatively large numbers of poor people were able to acquire valuable political skills. One Black commentator made the following observation:

> New programs were developed out of community action. Among them: Headstart, Legal Services, innovative manpower efforts and new health-delivery programs. But the main development was that groups of hitherto powerless people had, for the first time, the opportunity to handle sufficient amounts of money to generate for themselves the beginnings of some power. They also developed government skills and new community service opportunities for people who needed jobs. . . . The principal legacy is that the poor are a little stronger, considerably more self-aware and somewhat more self-sufficient. In many instances, their vision of their own potential has been enlarged. There is around the country a network of poor people and their advocates who know something about manipulating the system in order to alleviate poverty. That network did not exist in 1964.[2]

This assessment is popular, but it is by no means universal. Another Black writer has a different view:

> Some of my best friends are middle class, or upper middle class Black folks.
> But I'd be less than honest if I didn't say that the greatest rip-off that has occurred in this country in the last ten years has been not a rip-off of whites against Blacks, but a rip-off of poor Blacks by upper middle class Blacks.
> That rip-off came when Lyndon Baines Johnson began pouring Federal money into the hands of upper class Blacks in the hope that the money would be funneled down by them into the hands of poor Blacks. He called it the war against poverty.
> . . . The rip-off of the poor Blacks by the middle income Blacks makes it relatively easy for Nixon to say "Lets kill the whole thing." And the encouragement he is getting from other ethnic groups, who think that all Black people got all that money makes

his job a damn sight easier than relatively easy (sic).

Who got the Money?

... The middle class Blacks know where the money went. And so do the poor Blacks. If the poor Blacks don't know where it went—they do know one thing— they know they didn't get it.

... The same old formula was repeated too often by the middle class Blacks. You know the formula:

The Man said to a middle class Black: "Here is $150,000 to start a program to teach young Blacks how to read and write. Take it and do your best for those poor kids."

Well, you know what happened. The middle class Black took the money and said: "I'll need an executive director of this program at $25,000 a year—and that will be me. Then I'll get me a deputy director for $20,000 and that will be my boon coon buddy (who was always middle class).

"Now I'll get myself an administrative secretary (middle class) at $15,000, a program director at $12,000 and two secretaries for me and my deputy, at $9,000 each. Then I'll start looking for an office suitable to people making salaries like that."

By the time he got through spending $60,000 for office furniture, rent, travel, telephone, seminars, and consultants, there was no money left to even hire teachers!

So what did he do. He ran right back to Big Daddy, LBJ, and asked for more money! He didn't tell Johnson that the poor folks had not yet received any of the money. But LBJ loved Black poor folks— so he gave out with more money.

Not so with Nixon. Nixon doesn't love poor Black folks, or rich Black folks either! And being the businessman that he is, if Blacks go running to him with their tails and elbows and unbalanced ledger sheet like they did to LBJ, he will have only one answer for them.

He is going to say like Aretha Franklin: "Ain't No Way!"

And all of us are going to understand exactly what he means.[3]

There is probably more than a modicum of accuracy in both accounts of the operation and impact of the programs. Like other vast, complicated and important periods and policy programs (e.g., Jeffersonianism, Jacksonianism, Reconstruction, the Progressive Era, the New Deal), there will be volumes produced, analyzing the mood, method, and meaning of the "Great Society." This paper intends to discuss five rather important political consequences developing in some places as a result of public policy response over the last several years.

These developments will have quite profound consequences for the way Blacks proceed politically in their various communities. The concepts articulated here are put forth for purposes of further analysis as much as for purposes of stating hard and fast conclusions. These are, in other words, theories to be examined and tested.

PUBLIC-SECTOR COMMUNITIES

It is quite clear that we are seeing the development in many urban areas of what I choose to call low-income, public-sector communities. There are many census tracts where close to two-thirds of the residents are, in some form or other, connected with the public sector: public assistance and welfare; public housing; low-cost, federally financed housing; food stamps; supplemental security income; or public service employment. Even in tracts where the income and educational levels are higher than in some other sections of the city, one finds that a substantial portion (as much as 25 to 30 percent) of these people are employed in the public sector: teachers, social caseworkers, postal employees, poverty program officials.

The public-sector character of Blacks is particularly manifest. The 1970 national statistics show that of all professionals in 1970, 42 percent were employed by the government; for Blacks, the figure was an overwhelming 62 percent. Of managers and administrators, 16 percent overall were government workers, but 35 percent of Black administrators were public employees. Many of these people are employed in "soft money" situations. There were, for instance, in 1974, three major sources of funds coming into Harlem, that is, three major budgets providing jobs and services: the poverty program (Haryou-Act); Model Cities, and the local community school board. The first two are operating on soft money. Thus, when, as in the spring of 1974, there is a possibility that funds would be cut back or cut off, what one finds is a reversion to a politics of protest on the part of community groups. Employees and recipients of services are mobilized to march on City Hall (which is not normally the correct target for federal funding protest) and/or the nearest federal building.

Low-income, public-sector communities are at best hardly stable, viable economic entities. They exist on grants (usually from either the federal government or foundations), and what one finds is the development, very frequently, of an organizational style and operational mentality that focus on obtaining control of funded programs. Relatively little attention is paid to mobilization of forces for the capture of positions of institutional power. If a local leadership group can consolidate its control over a public-sector, soft-money budget, it seems to do little else toward transferring that political capacity to making an impact on local offices of institutional power (i.e., positions that determine capital and expense budgets that regulate on-going municipal services). The people who ran the earlier political machines in the urban areas did not make this mistake. They understood the relationship between local political action and continuing administration. They knew that the city would always provide some essential services, and that those who controlled the allocation of resources for the dispensation of those services (e.g., sanitation, housing code enforcement, law enforcement, health delivery services, education, recreation) also controlled "hard money," not "soft money," budgets. Granted, the size of the budget might increase or decrease from time to time (due to the shrinking tax base in some cities, for example), but there *will* be a budget, there *will* be resources (revenue-sharing funds, for example) over which to exericse authority. The cities themselves are becoming more oriented toward the federal government, but this developing relationship is not based solely on ephemeral programs.

Low-income, public-sector communities that pursue a

243

politics essentially aimed at capturing control of soft-money programs are not laying a base for a protected (and meaningful) political struggle aimed at capturing positions of institutional power.

There is another political consequence of a growing public-sector community. Its relation to electoral behavior. Substantial literature indicates that the higher the Socio-Economic Status (S.E.S.) the more likely the person is to vote to the right, or to move to the Republic party—in other words, to make more conservative electoral choices.[4]

However, some rather interesting electoral behavioral patterns are observed among higher S.E.S. Blacks in public-sector communities. Such people do *not* move to the right. In fact, tentative data in three cities (New York, Atlanta and Detroit) show that they tend to move further toward the liberal progressive pole.[5] They tend to vote *less* for the perceived conservative candidate than do lower S.E.S. Blacks. They tend to make more leftist electoral choices on matters involving governmental aid for economically poorer areas.

This suggests that a Black public-sector middle-status voter has different interests vis-à-vis public policy than does a white private-sector middle-status voter. This does not imply that there are not status differences in the Black community—there clearly are, and the middle-status Blacks frequently behave *socially* much like their white counterparts: yachts, summer homes, Caribbean cruises, cotillions. But the *status* differences do not manifest themselves *politically* in the same way as they do among whites. The middle-status Black is based in the public sector. Such a person could well see his or her econmic interest tied to greater positive governmental intervention in the economy. (This is so no matter which of the two descriptions of the poverty programs described above one accepts.)

The long-term implications of this are as yet uncertain, but it is possible at this point to suggest that there need not be (what some have hypothesized or anticipated) a political schism developing along "class lines" in the Black community. The phenomena of race and an economic interest base operate to make status differences among Blacks politically irrelevant.[6]

VERTICAL STRUCTURES OF
FRAGMENTED INFLUENCE

One result of government-funded and foundation-supported programs has been to create what I call "vertical structures of fragmented influence." A number of community-based groups have developed since the mid-1960s, each offering services to a certain prescribed constituency, and each developing its own lines of contact and communication with extracommunity funding sources—public and private. Many of the leaders of these local groups have been involved over the years in civic action in their communities, and their ogranizational and representational skills are extensive. They have a constituency that is community based. But one notes that frequently they negotiate their own organizational support, establishing and maintaining good contacts with federal agencies, private corporate sources, and philanthropic foundations. In 1973, in Harlem, there were at least 212 such organizations, and at least 80 percent operated this way.

This facilitates building relationships and ties vertically, (up and out) not horizontally, throughout the community—and, thus, the fragmentation. They see no need to come together for collective, communitywide action, because they are able to maintain their own organization and operation by maintaining their own individualized contacts with their external "angels."

More frequently than not, these various groups (and their leaders) are not involved in the electoral party organizational process in their communities and the city at large. This means, as pointed out earlier, that they are effectively outside the continuous struggle for control of positions of institutional power. Notwithstanding the fact that these groups, in some places, have effectively replaced the local party clubhouse as the locus for dispensing services, they do not perform the *political* function their role offers, although they have the "patronage," because they get the funds to provide the services: day-care centers, senior citizen's programs, emergency housing, emergency clothing, new low-cost housing, and an array of other day-to-day needs of poor people.

245

But these groups remain fragmented, jealously guarding their relationship to their external contacts, and for the most part, they exist on economies based on soft-money grants. Unless they become involved in something such as a low-cost housing venture where they end up owning the apartment building (financed through arrangements with the city housing authority, HUD and a local bank that puts up the initial capital and realizes a decent profit, as in New York City with the Bowery Savings Bank and several Harlem community organizations), they have no sustained economic base beyond the periodic grants to operate their programs.

FROM PATRON-CLIENT TO
PATRON-RECIPIENT RELATIONSHIPS

It is out of these kinds of structures, along with the growth of power of the municipal bureaucracies, that we get what we hear so much about, namely the displacement of the traditional party machine. These soft-money, vertical structures of fragmented influence receive a grant to perform certain services, and in the process, they create a patron-recipient relationship, which replaces the older, traditional patron-client relationship built up by the political party machine. In the latter situation, the party delivered benefits (divisible and indivisible) and got back loyalty and support (i.e., votes) in return. The relationship was one of reciprocity, quid pro quo, and with all its merits and demerits, it operated *politically* to capture local positions of institutional power (not just funded programs), for whatever benefits could be derived from such positions.

But what is happening in a number of places is that the community groups ask not for support from their constituencies in efforts aimed at capturing positions of institutional power, but only that they be available to be serviced. In fact, in many instances, the groups are stopped from engaging overtly in partisan activity by law. Thus, there must still be strenuous, episodic voter registration drives conducted by still other groups, who have, it should be noted, much less "pulling power" in the way of ability to offer material incentives to people. The newer community agencies do not, in other words, mobilize for the sustained process of a politics of governance, but they mobilize only intermittently for the sporadic process of a politics of protest. And even then, the goal is a renewed soft-money grant, more often than not.

In this sense, one might conclude that the present impact of the government programs has been to depoliticize the community. Occasionally, as in Harlem, we will see political activists (councilmen, state legislators, borough president, congressmen, local party officials) who also control the governing apparatus of the poverty program, but this overlap is not transferred into political mobilization for purposes of impacting on citywide struggles for power. Rather, these strategic positions are utilized to consolidate hegemony *within* the circumscribed community.

FUNCTIONAL ANONYMITY

As stated earlier, a substantial number of people who live in central city areas have considerable contact with public-sector authorities. These people live under guidelines and rules that have an impact on and regulate their daily lives in ways that private-sector people do not experience. For example, there are extensive regulatory rules for getting into and then remaining in a public housing project. In the early 1960s a regulation of the New York City Housing Authority listed thirty-eight social behavioral rules that served as guidelines to determine if a family should be allowed occupancy in a public housing apartment.[7] Violation of any of these could be cause for application rejection or subsequent eviction. One is reminded of the case of *Thorpe* v. *City of Durham.*[8] A tenant in a public housing project became active in the local tenants' council and one month later, in August 1965, she was given an eviction notice with no prior notification and no reason stipulated. She took her case to the U. S. Supreme Court where, four years later, the issue was finally resolved—in her favor. One wonders, however, how many such residents are prepared to sustain the aggravation of a four-year court battle.

There are innumerable instances of persons on welfare who

are suspected of not reporting small sums of earned income. The rules are sometimes applied stringently, other times not, but the potential for controlling behavior is always present. As a result, many low-income, public-sector people want to maintain a low political profile. They do not choose to become politically active; they do not engage in or support politically controversial matters. In other words, they opt for "functional anonymity."

This is not precisely the same as Anthony Downs' notion of "rational obstention," but it has elements of it. Neither is it properly to be considered apathy. I hypothesize that in a low-income, public-sector community, especially, there are those persons who will not act politically precisely because they feel that to do so will put them in jeopardy with the public authorities who administer rules over their daily lives. They are, for varying reasons, most vulnerable to the immediate decisions made by others over whom they have no control. They opt, therefore, for functional anonymity—maintenance of a low political profile.

Whether political organizations on the local, community level (welfare rights groups, tenants' councils, block associations, etc.) can deal effectively with this is important to know, and I suspect that it is a fairly important matter.

CONDUIT COLONIALISM

It is fashionable (and at times accurate) to talk about the lack of funds available for social service needs in the urban areas. Observers point to the shrinking tax bases of the cities, to the fact that high ratable industries are relocating job-producing plants outside the cities, and to the fact that middle-income tax payers (mostly white) are constantly moving out of the cities. It is known, for example, that three-quarters of union members under age 40 live in the suburbs.[9] For a number of economic reasons, the public sector (at all levels) is required to do more than before for the recent, low-income, unskilled residents in the central cities. One source concluded:

Today's unskilled migrants encounter frustrations unknown to their predecessors. The urban economy used to have lots of room for unskilled workers. Factories and construction were more dependent upon hand labor than they are today, and the municipal government employed large numbers of menial laborers. There are still many such opportunities, but their proportion of the urban economy has diminished markedly. Literacy is increasingly required for even the lowest-paid and least permanent jobs. The spread of the labor movement and union control of apprenticeship programs mean that today's ethnic newcomers suffer from institutionalized discrimination by fellow workers as well as by prospective employers.[10]

There is no questioning the accuracy of descriptions that define many urban areas as in economically dire straits. But there is another fact that should be taken into account. It is clear that more than a small amount of funds already comes into the cities ostensibly for purposes of caring for the needs of poor people. One major program, of course, is public welfare. In a recent fiscal year, the annual welfare budget for New York City alone was $700 million. One half of this money comes from the federal government, one fourth from the state, and one fourth from the local government. Of this amount, $329 million was spent for housing allowances alone. That is, the Department of Social Services paid out to landlords in rental monies well over a quarter of a billion dollars.

The important point is that the people on welfare receive this money and immediately transfer it into the hands of, for the most part, absentee slumlords. The welfare people, then, serve as *conduits* in a public-sector to private-sector economy. The housing allowance comes into the welfare community (24.5 percent of the people in central Harlem are on welfare) as *subsistence* allowance, and it is paid right out to and becomes *venture* capital for landlords. This is a form of conduit colonialism, with the poor serving as *conductors* of resources from one segment of the economy to another. If the welfare family is to be identified as a "welfare recipient," then it is quite proper to

249

identify the landlords, merchants, and loan sharks as "welfare beneficiaries."

In addition, a vast bureaucratic apparatus is needed to manage this conduit-colonial policy program. One newspaper item described the situation:

> "Like managers everywhere, the new men at the department of Social Services talk of productivity, time studies, utilization rates and cost-benefit ratios. ...
>
> "Welfare is just a fantastic area, a fantastic opportunity," exults Arthur H. Spiegel, who became the department's executive director last August at the age of 32, four years after graduating from the Harvard Business School.
>
> With that approach and a budget authorization of $3 million for 200 new administrative positions in the department, Mr. Spiegel has hired 70 managers, data-processing specialists and industrial engineers since October—mostly from private industry at salaries competitive with what they earned there.[11]

These new "managers of the urban colonies," are former employees in the private sector. But that sector is rapidly finding that it does not need the human resources previously hired in order to maximize profits. This was stipulated in a *Wall Street Journal* article in 1972:

> The realization that companies can operate effectively with far fewer employees than they dreamed possible back in 1969 may be comforting to top corporate brass and shareholders. But it's not particularly good news for job-hunting graduates, former middle-management executives technicians and other salaried employees. Nor is it very happy news for factory hands.[12]

The fact is that vast sums of public-sector dollars already come into the Black communities, but they go right out. This money serves interests other than those of the immediate residents, who need it most. In addition to the fact that the cities are strapped for funds, there is also the clear fact that vested economic interests are exploiting the use of what monies already are expended.

There are strategies that can deal with this exploitation in a way that *can* provide at least a modicum of benefit to the indigenous residents.[13]

OBSERVATIONS

Many urban areas have been politicized around a politics of protest, and this has seen the development of certain kinds of oratorical and mobilization skills. Spokesmen—frequently self-appointed or arising out of the ranks of the dissatisfied— have developed around specific issues, and they have, under- standably, used the weapons of disruption or threat of disruption. But the important point is that they have been focusing their attention on specific public policy outputs, and not on capturing positions of institutional power.

This means, of necessity, that their political protest activity will be episodic and ephemeral. We have not seen in too many places the building of *sustained* structures of political leverage, largely because this has not been the main organizational goal. Protest politics might yield certain kinds of indivisible benefits, but these benefits come from soft-money policies and programs. When the protest action that brought them about is over, there is the possibility (or even the likelihood) that these policies and programs will be the most vulnerable to being cut off (or cut back) at a later time. And the political action that brought them about is not available to protect their continuations. Thus, the protesters must gear up again, almost starting anew.

Therefore, out of the unrest of the 1960s, when a relatively large number of people were activated and politicized periodi- cally, we still do not see, in very many places, new community- based leadership cadres prepared to function on a sustained basis, especially in electoral politics. I suspect this to be less true in the South than in the North, but the southern activism had its genesis in' the civil rights protest movement, while a great deal of northern urban activism was nurtured by the Great

251

Society programs. However, I suspect that one will still find a stronger political protest mentality in the northern urban areas than elsewhere. And as the inner cities continue to be subject to the uncertainties of federal and local policies, there will continue to be the likelihood of protest activity with potentially violent consequences.

There are sound reasons for emphasizing an organizational strategy oriented toward electoral politics. Anything less, of necessity, must be primarily crisis oriented, and it is most difficult to build and sustain viable organizations around periodic crises. I am not optimistic that organizational emphasis on the franchise is a panacea in itself. Rather, I suggest that it is important in three ways:

1. it develops a habit of organization and a consciousness of ability to act
2. it is easier to transfer electoral activity to other arenas of political action, namely, protest politics
3. it provides an ongoing mechanism for civic education, namely, how to articulate demands and hold decision makers accountable on a range of issues, not just a single or few issues

A crisis-oriented strategy relies on starts and stops, jerks in the political system, and it does not mobilize enough people for the protracted political struggle. It is most vulnerable to a waxing and waning of political interest. And by this I mean that at a particular low point of political interest, the crisis-oriented organization is quite apt to die or go into a critical stage of limbo from which it might not recover. Dr. Martin Luther King, Jr. noted some of the weaknesses of his own episodic mass mobilization strategies when he made the following observation:

> Many civil rights organizations were born as specialists in agitation and dramatic projects; they attracted massive sympathy and support; but they did not assemble and unify the support for new stages of struggle. The effect on their allies reflected their basic practices. Support waxed and waned, and people

252

became conditioned to action in crises but inaction from day to day. We unconsciously patterned a crisis policy and program, and summoned support not for daily commitment but for explosive events alone.[14]

This is less a problem with a franchise-oriented organization. It is reinvigorated automatically and periodically. Its focus is on power, not solely programs. It contains an ongoing constituency that is not required to maintain a constantly high level of civic enthusiasm. It is more readily able to effect transference of political styles (from electoral politics to protest politics), precisely because it has a sustained base. It has an intact leadership cadre that does not have to be recruited and reactivated anew with each developing new issue. It does not rely on the requirement of a particularly high level of civic enthusiasm; it can, in other words, withstand inevitable periods of subdued political energy and activism. It also provides the vehicle for an ongoing, albeit modest, supportive treasury, precisely because it is able to cultivate the habit of dues among its own indigenous members, mitigating the need to rely almost exclusively on external sources for the minimum financial necessities.

Anything less than this will mean that we will continue to experience sporadic, protest politics—sometimes expressive violence, sometimes instrumental violence—which might be good for the soul, but does little for the solution.

NOTES

1. See John H. Strange, "Citizen Participation in Community Action and Model Cities Programs," *Public Administration Review* 32, special issue (October 1972): 655-669. This is an especially useful source for further bibliographic materials.

2. Roger Wilkins, *The New York Times,* June 4, 1974, p. 37.

3. James L. Hicks, *New York Amsterdam News,* January 27, 1973, p. A4.

4. See Heinz Eulau, "Perceptions of Class and Party in Voting Behavior: 1952," *American Political Science Review* 49, (1955): 364-384; and Angus Campbell, Philip E. Converse, Warren E. Miller, and Donald E. Stokes, *The American Voter* (New York: Wiley, 1960).

5. These data are taken from my research (in progress) on *"Political Benfits,* A study of who gets what, when and how in urban minority politics."

6. This conclusion is in stark contrast to a statement made by C. Vann Woodward. In writing a Preface to Bayard Rustin's book, *Down The Line,* Woodward wrote: "But more profound, and of special significance to Rustin's analysis, are differences of class. 'It is utterly unrealistic,' he writes, 'to expect the Negro middle class to behave on the basis of color alone. They will behave, first of all, as middle-class people.' " Woodward's quote from Rustin is not precisely accurate, unfortunately, although he probably did not distort Rustin's basic meaning too much. Rustin stated in an article entitled "The Role of the Negro Middle Class," (reprinted from the *Crisis,* June-July, 1969): "Some ... are asking the Negro to behave as if class were totally unimportant. By ignoring the class factor, they arrive at a sentimental notion of Black solidarity if they are apologists for middle-class Negroes; and if they are their critics, they condemn them for deserting their poor Black brothers. Both the apologists and the critics in this case fail to understand that there are serious class divisions in the Negro community which must be recognized for what they are. The apologist is blind to these divisions, the critic thinks that they should not exist, and both are bound by the feeling that race—and not class—is the force that motivates group behavior. Therefore they are caught by surprise when the Negro middle-class acts in a typically middle-class way, and their response is either to close their eyes to this phenomenon or to become enraged about it."

Both Rustin and Woodward should be more careful (especially since both call themselves scholars) how they discuss the class phenomenon among Blacks. Their empirical (as opposed to impressionistic) data base should be examined.

7. In November 1961, the New York City Housing Authority adopted a long list of eligibility requirements called Desirability Standards for Admission of Tenants. The list was revised in April, 1964. It contains two categories: (1) Clear and Present Dangers (e.g., grossly unacceptable housekeeping; record of unreasonable disturbance of neighbors or destruction of property; past or present engagement in illegal occupation); and (2) Conditions Indicative of Potential Problems (e.g., alcoholism; record of anti-social behavior; frequent separations of husband and wife; husband or wife under 18 years of age; placement of children; common-law relationship where there is no impediment to marriage; poor housekeeping standards, including lack of furniture; presence of one or more children who are not the offspring of the applicant).

8. 393 U.S. 288 (1969).

9. Robert L. Lineberry and Ira Sharkansky, *Urban Politics and Public Policy* (New York: Harper & Row, 1971), p. 28.

10. Ibid., p. 36.

11. "City's New View of Welfare: A Job for Businessmen," *The New York Times,* February 1, 1972.

12. *Wall Street Journal,* March 8, 1972.

13. See Charles V. Hamilton, "Urban Economics, Conduit-Colonialism and Public Policy," *Black World* 21, no. 12 (October 1972): 40-46.

14. Martin Luther King, Jr., *Where Do We Go From Here: Chaos or Community?* (New York: Harper & Row, 1967), pp. 158-159.

CONCLUSION: THE ILLUSION OF INCLUSION

James A. Hefner

The purpose of this conclusion is not to present a systematic summary of other chapters, as was done in the introduction, but to integrate the tools of economics and political science for the purpose of understanding the nature of the American Black dilemma. This dilemma is primarily political and economic. Within this scope are symbolic powers that are meaningless in nature; and absolute economic progress when viewed correctly is an optical illusion. To pinpoint the true nature and extent of power within the American Black community, we will discuss the role of symbols and the difference between symbolic and real power. On the economic side, we will examine the absolute and relative economic progress of Blacks, and how this translates into power.

THE ROLE OF SYMBOLS

People who rely on symbolic representation do so in relation to identification with a select group. This, according to Leon Festinger and associates, is done to gain and maintain support for the specific interpretation that the symbol represents.[1] The Festinger study also notes that where there has been high prior commitment to what the symbol represents, such commitment will be maintained by the group in the face of contrary factual information. Moreover, not only will the contrary information be disregarded, but it will serve to reinforce commitment to the symbol and thereby cause even greater detachment from the *actual issue* in an effort to maintain the "quiescence" provided by the symbol.[2]

Murray Edelman has characterized groups with a symbol dependency as having (1) the presence of economic or social problems that threaten the group as a whole, and (2) a lack of organization through which their desires and interest might find expression.[3] Such groups are therefore confronted with a threatening situation without the available means for relieving it and hence rely on, or seek the ambiguity inherent in symbols as a method of both quieting their fears and allowing them the comfort of the assumption that they are able to control their situations to a degree. To be sure, the reliance on symbols is important to groups that lack the necessary organization or ability to "sift" through various complexities with which they find themselves confronted, but such a reliance is foolhardy when it turns to the ambiguity of symbols as a means of satisfying both their lack of comprehension and their need to feel that they are in control of the factors affecting their lives. The following sections of the chapter will elucidate on this particular point.

SYMBOLIC VS. REAL POWER

Consistent with the explanation of symbols presented above, we will define "symbolic power" as a "familiar image" that a select group has chosen to associate with its limited conception of power in the absence of any other satisfactory understanding, and within those confines they seek expression and alleviation from some common problem. It is the representative of the more ambiguous, less understood "image," which is reasoned to be actual power, and to which therefore one attaches his hopes and aspirations, comfortable in the belief that they will be fulfilled, notwithstanding the lack of a clear delineation between fact and fantasy.[4] Within this definition, it is easy to see that symbolic power is a mere distortion, brought about through the maze of simplifications that permits personal or group resolution in the absence of definite understanding. As it seeks to soothe and satisfy, much of the reality may be forfeited and the result can be the application of such misdefined power to situations outside its ability to satisfy, as well as attaining results that are inconsistent with desires or that fail to materialize altogether.[5] Therefore, it can be called what Professor Mack Jones has cited as a "source of nourishment" under which the "symbol reliant" group may find substance and the important stimulant that enables them to acquire some measure of importance.[6]

However, if a group seeks to rely on symbolic power as a means of attaining goals, the ambiguity of symbols would restrict their identifying its specific sources and dimensions and hence would inhibit the effective organization and implementation of such power. This is a demonstrable fact in the case of the general American public as a select group and its reliance on the eagle as the symbol of American world power. Though this symbol is in fact representative of power, the inability of the American public to mobilize such power, or to even fully understand where this power originates, attests to the inefficiency of reliance on symbols and the lack of ability to identify its specific sources and dimensions. On the other hand, were the general American public accustomed to dealing with the specific tools that go into making America a world power, we could anticipate very little difficulty in its being able to utilize such tools to accomplish a specific task.

Without the ability to specifically characterize power, there is no means of accurately tracing and tying it to any particular observed event. Therefore, attributing results to such power is highly subject to speculation and leaves the group subject to deception. Hence, we can conclude that symbolic power does not lend itself to specific cause/effect analysis, and therefore cannot be viewed as reliable means of achiving an end. It does provide strength where the mere existence of appearances is sufficient to satisfy particular needs, and as such, should be viewed within this limited context only.

In contrast, real power is identified as having a specific source, organized to provide specific goals; it is measurable and easily identified as producing specific goals. It is based on tangible resources and is hence substantive enough to be effective and reliable enough to be used by well-organized groups whose goals are less satisfied by reliance on the ambiguity inherent in symbols.[7] Organizations such as the American Medical Association are examples of groups that have real power due to their ability to organize along distinct lines in a manner that insures their visibility and thereby maintains needed public interest and political sanction. Hence, real or substantive power is the primary means by which goals are attained and the only way in which we can gage the ability of a select group to mobilize society in their behalf.

In recent years, the Black American has come to realize that only by possession and exertion of power will he ever be sufficiently "visible" enough to inspire changes that will ultimately result in the betterment of his life. This was the lesson taught by Malcolm X and Stokely Carmichael through their concept of "doing for self," and the importance of projecting a powerful image has long been regarded as the basis of the teachings of Marx and Lenin, two brilliant power technicians. It was the recognition of this fact, among other factors not necessarily unimportant,[8] that prompted much of the activity of the sixties, in which state laws on discrimination were passed, the American labor council was organized, Black caucuses were formed, Blacks were elected to political offices, and reparations demanded[9] for the historical sufferings of all Black Americans.

In spite of such gains, however, close examination of Black progress reveals that it is drastically lagging, and more important, there seems to have been only negligible gains in acquiring power, except where we credit power in numbers. Examination of some concrete economic areas indicates the dimensions of the problem.

ECONOMIC REALITIES AND ILLUSIONS

Poverty

Traditionally, poverty has poignantly exemplified the net results of all economic, social, and political forces that have victimized Blacks since their arrival in America as slaves. More specifically, poverty is commonly viewed as the lack of "sufficient" income. However, a more correct view of poverty is "the lack of freedom and the absence of choice," which is not mere low income, but degradation and dependence. This dependence and dehumanization are perpetuated by a vicious circle of social, economic, political, psychological, and educational forces[10] —forces that have a dynamic and causal interrelationship that impact directly and heavily on the ghetto. Moreover, they have manifested themselves in such a way that the "permanent-ghetto hypothesis"[11] has been engendered in the minds of many Blacks.

The permanent-ghetto hypothesis is based on the fact that the ghetto is very similar to a neo-colony, which is totally dependent upon and dominated by outside forces. Further, it can be clearly seen that the resources of the Black economy, whose boundaries virtually coincide with those of the physical boundaries of the ghetto, are limited. The most abundant resource is unskilled labor, the demand for which is far less than the supply, in an ever-increasing technological economy. Income as a resource is limited and virtually insignificant. With Black unemployment at least twice that of the national average, and with the limited access of Blacks to higher paying jobs, a significant level of income entering the Black economy is through subsistence wages and public assistance payments. The result is meager saving and investment.

Few Blacks own businesses that contribute significantly to the Black economy as employers or investors. Factors of production—land, labor, capital, and entrepreneurship—are held primarily by whites. The profits, wages, and salaries of white-owned businesses and employees seldom if ever remain in the Black economy. That portion of consumption that is done outside of the community generates no return to the Black community; hence, the flow of capital for the Black economy is mainly outward.

While the Black economy can be termed an "exporting" economy, its exports, mainly surplus unskilled labor, do not generate the kind of return that would lead to "domestic" wealth and capital accumulation and thus independence. Such sustained poverty and powerlessness keep the masses of Blacks confined, walled-in, subjugated, and isolated.

Income

Income has always been the focal point at which economic progress and growth are measured and evaluated for Blacks as well as for whites. To be sure the income differential between Blacks and whites is one of the first measures examined by those espousing the "significant" progress of Blacks. Richard Scammon and Ben Wattenberg have asserted that the majority of Blacks have now reached middle-class status[12] based on the rise in income of Blacks over the past decade or so. While it cannot be denied that Blacks made very noticeable gains in the 1960s in terms of income and employment, these gains must be analyzed very thoroughly and placed in their proper perspective.

The median family income for Blacks relative to whites rose from 54 percent in 1964 to 60 percent in 1972, which showed that Blacks did make some headway in closing the gap between themselves and whites. But such income gains have not manifested into any real power. In 1971, only 30 percent of Black families had incomes over $10,000, while 59 percent of white families enjoyed incomes over the same amount. At all educational levels, the earnings of Black male workers 25 to 34, and 35 to 54 years of age, were substantially below that of the same group of whites.

In 1969, growth of Black incomes outpaced that of whites— 12 percent for Blacks and 9.6 percent for whites. However, the Black family median income of $5,899 remained well below that of white families of $8,794. In 1972, the median income of Black families was $6,900 compared to $11,500 for white families. Note that the Black median family income of $6,900 in 1972 was 59 percent that of whites, a clear decline from the 60 percent a year earlier, and 61 percent in 1969. Note further that the absolute dollar gap between Black and white median family incomes widened from $2,895 in 1969 to $4,600 in 1972. In short, Blacks lost ground in attempting to achieve income parity.

The number of low-income Black families did not change from 1967 to 1972. However, during the same period, the decline was substantial for low-income white families. In 1971, 25 percent of Black families received public assistance income, of that about 61 percent were below the low-income level; five percent of white families received income from public assistance, and of these 45 percent were below the low-income level.

Employment

During the decade of the 1960s, Black employment in the nation as a whole showed marked improvement. A substantial growth in full-time employment, coupled with a shift into more skilled and higher paying jobs, brought about significant improvement in the income level of Black workers. Total employment of Black workers rose by 1.3 million between 1961 and 1968, or about 20 percent, whereas employment of white workers increased by 15 percent. Between 1960 and 1968, there was an increase of about 42 percent in the employment of Black teenagers. Nevertheless, the increase in the 16- to 19-year-old labor force had actually exceeded its job gains, producing an unfortunate rise in joblessness. Indeed in 1972, 33.5 percent of Black teenagers were jobless. This compared to only 14.2 percent for white teenagers.

Despite the gains achieved by Blacks by 1968, there were about 3.6 million, or 44 percent, who were still employed in the low-skilled, low-status and farm jobs. On the national level, the occupational upgrading of Black workers occurred from 1957 onward. During the 1957 to 1967 period, much expansion occurred with respect to the employment of Blacks in those industries considered to offer the best jobs in terms of pay, advancement, and security. Employment of Blacks grew especially rapidly, by one third or more, in the fields of education, public administration, and durable goods manufacturing. The number of Black workers in these fields rose from 1.3 million in 1962 to 2.1 million in 1967, an increase of almost 60 percent, whereas for whites the increase was 25 percent.

263

Have Black workers made progress exclusively? The above figures show Black progress in an overpowering way, but more recent Department of Commerce statistics show that during the period 1967-1972, employment of Blacks grew at a slower pace than that for white workers: 8 percent for Blacks and 10 percent for whites. In 1972, Black employment rose 2 percent as compared to 3 percent for whites, while the jobless rate for Blacks remained at the 1971 level of 10 percent, and the white unemployment rate declined from 5.4 to 5 percent. More important, perhaps, is the fact that despite the significant gains in Blacks being employed during the sixties, the jobless rate for Blacks over the entire decade, indeed since 1953, has remained roughly twice that of whites.

In the 1960s, the number of Blacks in clerical jobs doubled and Blacks in professional and technical occupations increased 131 percent. But the percentage increase clouds the real issue of Blacks attaining real power. To be more explicit, Black workers constituted 10 percent of the employed in 1971, but only 2 percent of the engineers, 2 percent of the physicians, 3 percent of the managers and administrators, 5 percent of the professionals, and 6 percent of the craftsmen, as contrasted to 17 percent of the service workers, 20 percent of the laborers, and 50 percent of the household workers.

From 1967 to 1972, while Black white-collar employment increased, most of the entries were sales and clerical workers, not managers or administrators, who participate in decision making and policy formation. (It is worth noting, too, that the unemployment rate in sales was about 3 to 1 for Blacks to whites.)

While looking at the status of Black workers, one should not forget Black women, the most oppressed workers in the labor market. In 1971, about 44 percent of all Black women workers were in domestic services. Also, in 1971, 13 percent of Black women workers were in the professional, technical, and managerial occupations, which was about the same for Black males.

In 1969, the median income for Black women working 50 weeks or more was $4,126, about 80 percent of the $5,182 for white women working the same length of time. On the

264

average, Black women earn less money than Black men. Then, too, unemployment of Black women age 20 and over declined less dramatically than that of Black males, due to the increase in female labor force participation in 1969 and 1970.

The above statistics show quite readily that Blacks are still seriously underrepresented in higher paying and more prestigious jobs as managers and adminsitrators. Some of this underrepresentation has been due to low education attainment levels and lack of skills. But noneconomic factors such as poor information about job opportunities, and discrimination have also severely curtailed Blacks' access to higher paying occupations. Moreover, "if at each level of education Blacks had the same opportunities for jobs as whites, the proportion of Black craftsmen would double and the percentage of managers and proprietors would triple."[13]

Black workers are disproportionately affected by part-time employment. About 500,000 nonwhites worked part-time in 1968, which represented 25 percent of all involuntary part-time workers. The high concentration of nonwhite workers in this category is partly a reflection of their entrapment in lower skill occupations.

Housing

It has been noted that poverty reflects not merely the lack of income, but also the lack of freedom, and the lack of choice. Housing for the millions of Blacks in America is certainly one area that gives stark testimony to such a condemnation.

Poor housing has always plagued Blacks for many reasons, not the least of which is segregation. Indeed the existence of segregation is one of the most obvious facts of American society.[14] And while low incomes, which determine what can be afforded, are commonly used as the basis for systematic racial residential division, "discriminatory treatment in housing has remained as an institutional barrier to Blacks finding adequate housing."[15] Discriminatory practices in pricing, financing, selection of houses, and the selection of neighborhoods characterize entire metropolitan areas. Such practices are the

265

product of formal and informal allegiances between government agencies and the private sector. According to Franklin and Resnik:

> Behind price discrimination is the institutional wall of segregation determined by larger forces operating through the whole metropolitan area. This institutional wall, made up of governmental policies, consumers, real estate brokers, landlords, banks, insurance companies, savings and loan associations, and other financial intermediaries, prohibits Blacks from acquiring, at sufficiently rapid rates, the older stock of dwellings in the grey areas of the central cities, even though many Blacks could afford to rent or buy such dwellings.[16]

Federal agencies such as the Federal Housing Administration (FHA) and the Veterans Administration prior to 1967, explicitly aided and abetted the segregationist practices of the financial institutions and local governmental entities. Governmental agencies made policy that would insure the perpetuation of such tactics as blockbusting, racial covenants, and racial zoning, to avoid the wrath of powerful private and financial institutions. The collusion between these public and private entities is seen to be necessary and vital for the survival of the profit motive in housing in general and slum housing in particular.

While low income has historically been used to exlude Blacks from good housing, history reveals that given the gains in income, and the general rise in the socioeconomic status of Blacks, segregation has either remained at a high level or increased still further. In 1960, only 12 percent of whites with income above the poverty level lived in poverty areas, while this was true for 67 percent of Blacks.

In 1970, the median gross rent for Black renters was $89 compared to $112 for white renters, but Blacks paid a larger proportion of their income for rent than did whites. About 43 percent of Black households expended at least 25 percent of their income for rent compared to only 35 percent for whites. In mortgaged home ownership, 30 percent of Black households paid at least 25 percent of their income for housing cost, as compared to 18 percent of whites paying 25 percent or more. Such differences in the rent-income ratio between Blacks and whites show quite clearly that all income classes of Blacks pay more of their income for housing than do whites.

Furthermore, about 59 percent of Black-owned homes were built before 1950 compared to 45 percent of white homes. With the supply of old and new homes strictly controlled by white exclusionary interests, and the choice or availability of good, soundly structured houses limited for Blacks, the purchasing power of the dollar spent by Blacks is less than the purchasing power of the dollar spent by whites.

Urban renewal and public housing programs have been dismal failures. Masses of Blacks have been forced out of their homes, dislocated and subjected to inconvenience and placed all too often in public housing, most of which is sterile and devoid of homelike amenities so essential to decent living.

Finally, while there have been acclaim and lofty praise by some for the "significant" progress made by Blacks, it is still true that over 70 percent of Blacks live in the ghetto, contained, restricted, and confined. Most Black Americans in 1976 are still denied entry to those houses that would indicate that symbols of power are being changed into realities of power.

GETTING AWAY FROM SYMBOLS

To expose the symbolic trappings of power as mere illusions and not real power we have elucidated the structural dimensions of Black externality and analyzed the political and economic components of the Black crisis. Certainly one crucial aspect of that crisis is the low economic status of Black Americans. We would be wise to remember that employment and income differentials, and housing availability between Blacks and whites are only symptoms of a larger and more deadly disease, which must be eradicated—the failure of our system to reward Blacks for their role in the making of America. Indeed, there is a failure of our system to provide decent housing and adequate employment for all those who desperately seek it and are qualified to produce the goods and services we badly need.

The symbols of power have thus far been discussed in terms of concrete economic examples. But inextricably linked to economic progress are the political realities that directly affect economic issues. Politics and holding elected offices have always been at the heart of attaining power, or so it is thought. But the mere holding of an elected office does not guarantee economic parity for Blacks. From the period of 1969 to 1972, Black elected officials increased 61 percent, while at the same time the percentage of Black income to white income decreased from 61 percent to 59 percent. Such evidence reflects that the realities of power have increased only in numbers, not in real policy-making power. Only large increases in Black voter registration and voting can be given credit for such corresponding increases in Black elected officials. The fact remains that the policy-making and decision-making positions have still escaped Blacks. Once elected, Black officials are still outside of the inner sanctum of ultimate policy formation, which is still influenced by those who are producers, wealth owners, and capital generators. But it is this very image, or reliance on the symbolic trappings of power, that seems to be satisfying the Black American's dream (and as such is blinding him to the true issues and conditions), though his dreams are frequented with nightmares of unfulfilled promises, and having to make unwarranted concessions. True to the groups that depend on symbolic power to fulfill their dreams, Black Americans will continue to be misdirected and misinformed until they are able to specifically identify the sources and dimensions of real power in America. But until then they will continue to be at the mercy of "every fast talking, double dealing charlatan, both Black and white, who hits the streets."[17]

Therefore, the progress of Blacks in America rests on their ability to specifically locate real power sources.[18] Symbolic power, as with symbols themselves, is far too unclear and intangible to effectively attain Black American goals, and therefore attention must be turned from fantasy to the serious, systematic acquisition of real power. Such power *must* be truly representative of and responsible to the people. It is the obligation of Black people in positions and seeking positions meant to serve the Black community at large, to fully face the multiplicity of burdens before them, and not to fall prey to symbolic trappings or to the illusion of inclusion.

NOTES

1. Leon Festinger, Henry Riecker, and Stanley Schachter, *When Prophecy Fails* (Minneapolis: University of Minnesota Press, 1956); see also T. W. Adorno and others, *The Authoritarian Personality* (New York: Free Press, 1950).

2. Festinger, Riecker, and Schacter, *Prophecy,* p. 35.

3. Murray Edelman, *The Symbolic Uses of Politics* (Urbana: University of Illinois Press, 1964), p. 31.

4. Ira Progoff, *The Symbolic and the Real* (New York: Julian, 1963), pp. 82-87. But in spite of the imagery, Edelman states that such image association is sufficient to reassure and "quiese" (See Edelman, *Symbolic Uses of Politics*, p. 32).

5. Mack Jones, "Black Politics: Symbolism and Reality," (Mimeo paper prepared for delivery at the Second Annual Political Science Seminar at South Carolina State College, March 15, 1972). Also see Edelman, *Symbolic Uses of Politics*, pp. 23-25.

6. Jones, "Black Politics," p. 1.

7. Edelman, *Symbolic Uses of Politics*, p. 22.

8. For example, sit-ins, boycotts, and the written works of the late Dr. Martin Luther King, Jr.

9. For a comprehensive discussion of reparation, see Robert S. Browne, "The Economic Basis for Reparation in America," *The Review of Black Political Economy* 2 (Winter 1972): 67-81.

10. For an in-depth discussion of these forces, see William K. Tabb, *The Political Economy of the Black Ghetto* (New York: Norton, 1970), chapters 1-2; Lee Rainwater, *Behind Ghetto Walls* (Chicago: Aldine, 1970); Robert E. Forman, *Black Ghettos, White Ghettos, and Slums* (Englewood Cliffs, N.J.: Prentice-Hall, 1971), chapter 1; Gerald D. Suttles, *The Social Order of the Slum* (Chicago: University of Chicago Press, 1968), parts 1-2; and Raymond S. Franklin and Solomon Resnik, *The Political Economy of Racism* (New York: Holt, Rinehart and Winston, 1973).

11. Tabb, *Political Economy of the Ghetto,* chapter 2.

12. See chapter 2 of this book.

13. Tabb, *Political Economy of the Ghetto,* p. 201.

14. See the chapters in this book by Spratlen, Alexis, Barnett, and Hefner; additional sources are Tabb, *Political Economy of the Ghetto*, chapters 1-2; and Franklin and Resnik, *Political Economy of Racism*, chapters 1-2.

15. Tabb, *Political Economy of the Ghetto*, p. 12.

16. Franklin and Resnik, *Political Economy of Racism*, p. 16.

17. Jones, "Black Politics," p. 13.

18. For an excellent discussion of "power sources," see Matthew Holden, "Black Politicians in the Time of the 'New' Urban Politics," *The Review of Black Political Economy* 1 (Fall 1971): 56-72.